Australia's Security in China's Shadow

Euan Graham

D1088236

'This is a contemporary and concise book. It analyses what has happened on the ground, and how things will likely move in the foreseeable future regarding Australia and China but also involving ASEAN and South Pacific states in the wake of the contestation for influence and power by Beijing and Washington. The key takeaway is that foreign policy begins at home, and no quick fix is possible.'

– Ambassador Ong Keng Yong, Executive Deputy Chairman of the S. Rajaratnam School of International Studies (RSIS) at the Nanyang Technological University, Singapore; Ambassador-at-Large, Singapore Ministry of Foreign Affairs; former Secretary-General of ASEAN

Australia's Security in China's Shadow

Euan Graham

IISS The International Institute for Strategic Studies

The International Institute for Strategic Studies

Arundel House | 6 Temple Place | London | WC2R 2PG | UK

First published March 2023 by **Routledge**
4 Park Square, Milton Park, Abingdon, Oxon, OX14 4RN

for **The International Institute for Strategic Studies**
Arundel House, 6 Temple Place, London, WC2R 2PG, UK
www.iiss.org

Simultaneously published in the USA and Canada by **Routledge**
52 Vanderbilt Avenue, New York, NY 10017

Routledge is an imprint of Taylor & Francis, an Informa Business

DIRECTOR-GENERAL AND CHIEF EXECUTIVE Dr John Chipman
SERIES EDITOR Dr Benjamin Rhode
ASSOCIATE EDITORS Alice Aveson, Daniel Edwards
EDITORIAL Gregory Brooks, Christopher Harder, Jill Lally, Michael Marsden, Laura Priest,
Dr Liat Radcliffe Ross
GRAPHICS COORDINATOR Jana Phillips
PRODUCTION Alessandra Beluffi, Ravi Gopar, Jade Panganiban, James Parker, Kelly Verity
COVER ARTWORK James Parker

The International Institute for Strategic Studies is an independent centre for research, information and debate on the problems of conflict, however caused, that have, or potentially have, an important military content. The Council and Staff of the Institute are international and its membership is drawn from almost 100 countries. The Institute is independent and it alone decides what activities to conduct. It owes no allegiance to any government, any group of governments or any political or other organisation. The IISS stresses rigorous research with a forward-looking policy orientation and places particular emphasis on bringing new perspectives to the strategic debate.

The Institute's publications are designed to meet the needs of a wider audience than its own membership and are available on subscription, by mail order and in good bookshops. Further details at www.iiss.org.

British Library Cataloguing in Publication Data
A catalogue record for this book is available from the British Library

Library of Congress Cataloging in Publication Data

ADELPHI series
ISSN 1944-5571

ADELPHI AP490–492
ISBN 978-1-032-54660-5

Contents

AUTHOR

Euan Graham is the Shangri-La Dialogue Senior Fellow for Indo-Pacific Defence and Strategy at the IISS in Singapore. His expertise lies in Australia's strategic policy, maritime strategy and security in the Asia-Pacific region. Euan has lived and worked in Japan, Singapore and Australia, where he was executive director of La Trobe Asia, in Melbourne, and director of the Lowy Institute's International Security Program. Before that, he served with the UK government as a research analyst in the Foreign and Commonwealth Office, covering both Northeast and Southeast Asia. He has written and commented widely for international media on a range of regional security issues.

GLOSSARY

ADF	Australian Defence Force
ADMM–Plus	ASEAN Defence Ministers' Meeting–Plus
AIFFP	Australian Infrastructure Financing Facility for the Pacific
AIIB	Asian Infrastructure Investment Bank
ALP	Australian Labor Party
ANU	Australian National University
ANZUS	Australia, New Zealand, United States Security Treaty
APEC	Asia-Pacific Economic Cooperation
ASD	Australian Signals Directorate
ASEAN	Association of Southeast Asian Nations
ASPI	Australian Strategic Policy Institute
ASW	anti-submarine warfare
AUKUS	Australia–United Kingdom–United States security partnership
BRI	Belt and Road Initiative
CCP	Chinese Communist Party
ChAFTA	China–Australia Free Trade Agreement
CHEC	China Harbour Engineering Company
CPTPP	Comprehensive and Progressive Agreement for Trans-Pacific Partnership
CSIRO	Commonwealth Scientific and Industrial Research Organisation
DCP	Defence Cooperation Program
DFAT	Department of Foreign Affairs and Trade
DHA	Department of Home Affairs
DSU	Defence Strategic Update
DWP	Defence White Paper
EAS	East Asia Summit
EEZ	exclusive economic zone
FIRB	Foreign Investment Review Board

FITS	Foreign Influence Transparency Scheme
FONOPs	freedom-of-navigation operations
FPDA	Five Power Defence Arrangements
FPWP	Foreign Policy White Paper
FTA	free-trade agreement
HADR	humanitarian assistance and disaster relief
HIMARS	High Mobility Artillery Rocket System
HMAS	His Majesty's Australian Ship
IA–CEPA	Indonesia–Australia Comprehensive Economic Partnership Agreement
IADS	Integrated Area Defence System
LHD	landing helicopter dock
LNG	liquefied natural gas
LRASM	Long-Range Anti-Ship Missile
MoU	memorandum of understanding
MP	member of parliament
PAP	People's Armed Police
PIF	Pacific Islands Forum
PLA	People's Liberation Army
PLAN	People's Liberation Army Navy
PMSP	Pacific Maritime Security Program
PNG	Papua New Guinea
PNGDF	Papua New Guinea Defence Force
PRC	People's Republic of China
RAAF	Royal Australian Air Force
RAN	Royal Australian Navy
RCEP	Regional Comprehensive Economic Partnership
SOE	state-owned enterprise
SSBN	ballistic-missile submarine
SSN	nuclear-powered attack submarine
TLAM	*Tomahawk* land-attack missile
UAV	uninhabited aerial vehicle
UFWD	United Front Work Department
UNCLOS	United Nations Convention on the Law of the Sea

UNSW   University of New South Wales

USAF   United States Air Force

USFPI   United States Force Posture Initiatives

USMC   United States Marine Corps

USN   United States Navy

WTO   World Trade Organization

Note on Australian dollars: According to data from the IMF October 2022 World Economic Outlook, the average exchange rate in 2022 was 1 Australian dollar = 0.71 US dollars.

Map: **Australia and its surrounding region**

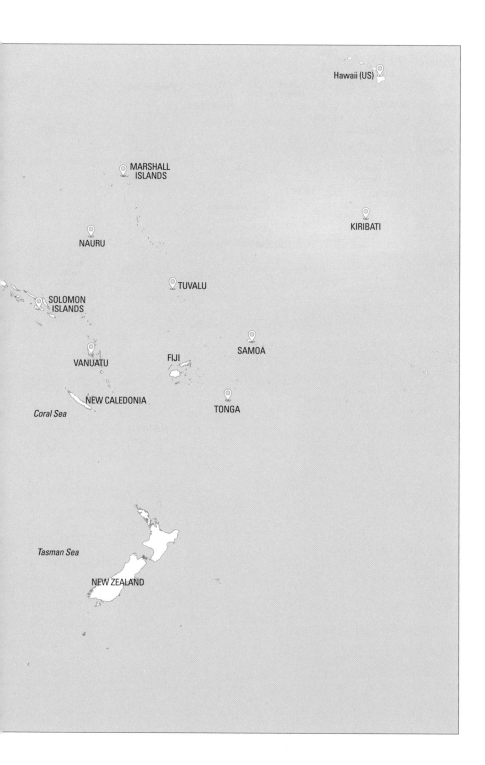

CHAPTER ONE

The end of the affair

This book proceeds in six chapters, each analysing a different aspect of the multifarious challenges that China poses to Australia's security and assessing the efficacy of Canberra's policy responses. The focus is primarily on Australia as it faces its most important strategic challenge since the Second World War, one that manifests itself domestically as well as externally.

This introductory chapter situates the Australia–China bilateral dynamic in wider historical, strategic and political contexts. It is followed by an analysis, in Chapter Two, which charts the Chinese Communist Party's (CCP) efforts to influence and interfere in Australia's domestic affairs, highlighting the Australian government's subsequent 'pushback' and introduction of counter-interference measures across vertical and horizontal layers of government. Chapter Three examines economic relations, for so long a stabilising foundation for the bilateral relationship until China began its punitive trade campaign against Australia in 2020. Australia's ability to withstand and adapt to China's economic punishment can offer a strong example at the international level. Chapter Four focuses on recent changes and enhancements to Australia's defence capability, alliance policy and deterrent posture, driven by intensifying threat perceptions related to China's military build-up, strategic intentions and 'grey-zone' operations, which are carried out below the threshold of armed conflict. The final two chapters consider China as an integrated external-security policy challenge for Australia's regional statecraft, centred on the nearby sub-regions of maritime Southeast Asia[1] and the Southwest Pacific,[2] where Australia's interests and influence are concentrated. The concluding chapter also draws together these various threads and identifies the most important lessons that other countries can deduce from Australia's recent experiences with China.

* * *

Australia was considered, until recently, to be a prisoner of its geography: an underpopulated anglophone outpost consigned to an alien region, far from the succour of its maritime allies and economic partners, originally the United Kingdom and later the United States. For most of Australia's history since European settlement, Asia was perceived as a vector of instability and a potential threat, though Australia's trading connections to China have long roots.[3] Conversely, geography has also provided a substantial measure of security for Australia; it is rich in resources and located well away from geopolitical fault lines and flashpoints, with great strategic depth. Australia has neither territorial nor maritime boundary disputes of significance. Its involvement in armed conflicts has been largely expeditionary and coalition-based. Australians have almost always fought elsewhere and never alone.

From the 1970s, Australia started to pivot away from the prisoner-of-geography paradigm, embracing Asia and the newer construct of the Indo-Pacific region as a vector of economic opportunity, immigration and, more controversially, identity.[4] Australians' evolving conceptions of geography and their place in the surrounding region touch on loftier questions, such as whether the country is to remain part of the 'Anglosphere' or develop a new identity more in tune with the surrounding region and the country's contemporary demographic diversity.[5] Australia includes a large community of people claiming Chinese heritage, numbering more than a million out of a total population of 26m, though this community has diverse origins, including from Southeast Asia and Hong Kong, as well as China. Considerations of national identity are mostly outside the scope of this analysis. But Australia's conception of China, and Asia more broadly, is closely related to the question of how the country defines itself. Australia's perception of China is also refracted through the prism of its relationships with the US and, to a declining extent, the UK. China is sometimes a proxy for other important points of contention in Australia's national debates, including the proposition that Australia should become more integrated into Asia, or that the alliance with Washington has prevented Canberra from exercising an independent foreign policy.

In this fluid, sometimes vigorously contested context, China looms expansively and ambiguously on Australia's horizons. The dichotomy of China as a threat and opportunity is now felt in many countries, but it is perceived particularly keenly in Australia. For its first two decades, Communist China was predominantly perceived in Australia as a threat, and Canberra did not officially recognise the People's Republic of China (PRC) until December 1972.[6] The story of the last three decades, by contrast, has centred on China's economic rise and the vesting of Australia's future prosperity in the assumption that this trend would be open-ended and without downsides attached. During this time, China moved into pole position among Australia's trade partners; in 2020–21, two-way trade was valued at A$267 billion[7] and China was the destination for close to 39% of Australia's exports. China's demand for iron ore, above all, helped to drive a global commodities 'super-cycle' following its accession to the World Trade Organization (WTO) in 2001. That cycle had run its macroeconomic course by 2020, if not before, and is sustained only by Beijing's policy of stimulus spending. But for more than a quarter century, from 1992 to 2020, Australia enjoyed continuous economic growth, a unique feat among developed economies and one fuelled largely by China's demand for Australian products. China is the leading trading partner of many countries in the Indo-Pacific, but Australia's level of dependence on China as an importer of its goods and services is exceptional.

Despite the two countries' political dissimilarity, such intense economic complementarity between Australia and China inevitably colours how Australians have approached the bilateral relationship. The fatalistic belief that Australia's dependence on China as a market constitutes a permanent and irreplaceable fact of international relations became an *idée fixe* in Australia's China-watching circles. According to this view, Australia has no alternative but to forge a pragmatic partnership with China's ruling party on the best terms available. Even in the throes of an openly adversarial political dynamic, wholesale economic decoupling from China remains anathema within the Australian debate.

Over the past decade, and especially in the last five years, the political relationship between Australia and China has been increasingly characterised by tensions. Relations took a pronounced turn for the worse in 2020, as Beijing launched a wave of de facto economic sanctions against Australia, ostensibly in retaliation for Canberra's call for an inquiry into the origins and spread of the coronavirus outbreak. This was accompanied by a full-throated propaganda campaign, in which Australia found itself the target of extreme invective from China's state media. In April 2020, Hu Xijin, the former editor of *Global Times*, compared Australia to 'a piece of chewed up gum stuck under China's shoe'.[8] In November 2020, China's Ministry of Foreign Affairs spokesperson Zhao Lijian tweeted a doctored picture of an Australian soldier holding a bloody knife to the throat of an Afghan child, in an apparent attempt to capitalise on international sentiment in the wake of the Brereton inquiry into the alleged unlawful killing of 39 Afghan civilians by Australian special-forces soldiers. In the same month, a list of 14 grievances, detailing alleged Australian hostile behaviour towards the PRC, was leaked by a Chinese embassy represen- tative to an Australian journalist.[9]

Between 2018 and June 2022, China effectively froze high-level contact with Australia: no visits by politicians or senior officials from either country took place. Canberra's efforts to rekindle high-level communication with Beijing were rebuffed until a new, Labor government was formed follow- ing the May 2022 general election. However, the change in Australia's government is likely to have only a marginal influ- ence on the basic settings of the bilateral relationship. Two years earlier, in May 2020, Richard Maude, a former senior Australian diplomat, warned of a 'permanently adversarial relationship, with bilateral and multilateral cooperation severely limited and parts of the economic relationship regularly at risk'.[10]

* * *

Since the end of the Cold War, Australian governments from both the left and the right of the political spectrum have main- tained a shared commitment to strengthen the partnership with China, making this a defining feature of Australia's diplomacy and international trade. The most important exception occurred in the wake of the Tiananmen Square massacre in June 1989, when high-level contacts were suspended for one year. Bob Hawke, prime minister from 1983 to 1991, made an emotional speech to parliament in which he extended an impromptu amnesty to thousands of Chinese students studying in Australia. After this brief hiatus, however, Hawke's successor, Paul Keating (prime minister from 1991 to 1996), reinforced Australia's engagement with China, in the belief that this would not only help to integrate Australia into Asia, but also incorporate China into a post-ideological, globalising economy.[11] The Liberal Party-led conservative coalition government of then-prime minister John Howard, who replaced Keating in 1996 and was prime minister until 2007, adopted a congruently non-ideological stance based on setting aside 'differences' with China and pursuing 'common interests'. Canberra would not 'hector and lecture and moralise', Howard told a press conference during an April 1997 visit to Beijing.[12] Notwithstanding Howard's close identification with the US alliance in the aftermath of the 11 September 2001 terrorist attacks, as prime minister he visited China more than any other country. Australia's exports to China expanded more than sixfold during the decade that Howard's government was in power, which straddled China's accession to the WTO. Howard's foreign minister, Alexander Downer, raised American eyebrows in 2004 by stating publicly that Australia was not treaty-bound to join the United States in a military conflict with China over Taiwan. This was no more than a statement of fact based on the provisions of the 1951 Australia, New Zealand and United States Security Treaty (ANZUS), but it signalled a conscious shift towards a diplomatically hedged position between China and the US, even as Canberra found itself tagged by the international media as a 'deputy sheriff' during the US-led global war against terrorism.

Australia's pursuit of a closer political partnership with China has always been more than just pragmatically maximising the economic benefits of China's rise, important though the commercial motivation is. It is difficult to overstate the extent to which Australia's political and foreign-policy establishment collectively invested in relations with China as a grand project of Australian foreign policy.[13] This pursuit was inextricably bound up with the ambition of developing a bridging role for Australia between China (and Asia generally) and the West – a grand design that runs back to former prime minister Gough Whitlam's (1972–75) embrace of diplomatic normalisation with the People's Republic. The desire to position Australia as a bridge-builder between the US and China was a defining foreign-policy theme of Kevin Rudd's first term as prime minister from 2007 to 2010. Rudd brought intensity to the China relationship. Fluent in Mandarin and with diplomatic experience in China, he pursued an ambitious 'creative middle power diplomacy' role for Australia as a broker between Washington and Beijing.[14] The long-term objective of integrating Australia into Asia was further encoded in the 'Australia in the Asian Century' White Paper, issued in 2012 under Rudd's successor, Julia Gillard (2010–13), whom he served as foreign minister.

Acknowledging the collapse of the bridge-building dream, at least the version that is centred on China, is important to understanding the ideational baggage that still freights Australia's relationship with China, even as ties have deteriorated to a low point not experienced since the 1960s. Australia's China 'dream' was in tune with a prevailing neo-liberal aspiration that undergirded much of the West's engagement with China around the turn of the century. But Australia has long believed that it has a special role to play, as a Western country that is physically located alongside Asia. According to Australian academic Mark Harrison, it has been possible 'for key sections of Australian public, political and corporate institutions to embrace China but simultaneously ignore the complex realities of the party-state because the policy rhetoric is not about China as a real place. Instead, it has always been about how Australia should understand itself and its national future.'[15]

Australia's ties with the People's Republic have experienced previous downturns since relations were normalised. Barring episodic disruptions, however, Australia's elite has been committed to the open-ended pursuit of closer relations with Beijing. Australia and China designated each other as 'comprehensive strategic partners' in 2014. In that year, President Xi Jinping became the third Chinese leader to visit Australia, following in the footsteps of Jiang Zemin and Hu Jintao, becoming only the second to address its parliament. The 'historic' high point arrived the following December, in the form of the China–Australia Free Trade Agreement, several years in the making.[16] The bilateral relationship reached this official zenith under a conservative government, rather than a Labor one, despite the latter's reputation for sympathising with Beijing more so than the Liberal Party.

Yet Canberra's concerns about China's strategic intentions in the East China and South China seas began to multiply from around 2009. Beijing reacted angrily to the language used to describe China in Australia's Defence White Paper released the same year, though Canberra's wording was relatively guarded.[17] Also in 2009, an Australian Rio Tinto executive, Stern Hu, was arrested on bribery charges and imprisoned for nine years by the Chinese authorities, following the collapse of iron-ore price negotiations.[18] In retrospect, this case was a harbinger of coercive behaviour by the Chinese state affecting commercial relations. China's proclivity towards more assertive, harder-line positions, both domestically and externally, predates Xi's ascendance as paramount leader in late 2012, but it has intensified under his rule.[19]

From 2013 to 2022, each of Australia's three prime ministers under the Liberal–National coalition government underwent his own learning curve on China, including several attempts to 'reset' relations with Beijing, only to be led to a similarly constraining set of conclusions about China's strategic course: Tony Abbott (2013–15), Malcolm Turnbull (2015–18) and Scott Morrison (2018–22). Abbott pithily summarised the most important influences on Australia's relationship with China as a mixture of 'fear and greed'.[20] There is an elegant simplicity and a ring of truth to Abbott's reduction, but also more to it.

Australia's current policy settings on China date from 2017, the midpoint of Turnbull's tenure as prime minister. From around 1990 until then, economics was the dominant factor framing the Australia–China relationship. Since then, however, geopolitics has re-emerged as the prevailing paradigm. Thus the pendulum has swung away from viewing China through the lens of economic opportunity back towards strategic threat, as Beijing's rhetoric and behaviour towards Australia have taken on coercive and punitive hues.

Turnbull began his term in office under suspicion from domestic critics that he would bow to Beijing,[21] especially given his business background. In office, he initially sympathised with China's desire for a bilateral extradition treaty, a move that was only aborted in the face of political opposition – a rare break in Australia's prevailing bipartisanship on China. Turnbull's administration subsequently set about developing a suite of policy responses designed to 'push back' against Beijing's increasing assertiveness, both in the region and inside Australia. Turnbull was vocal on the South China Sea and other regional issues where he identified China's behaviour as expansionist and coercive. He dubbed China a 'frenemy'.[22] Yet the pushback was carefully calibrated in order to avoid major strategic risk. For example, Australia opted not to participate in freedom-of-navigation operations in the South China Sea, despite encouragement from the United States, because Turnbull judged it to be too dangerous.[23] As evidence accumulated of hostile activities within Australia conducted at the behest of China's party-state, Turnbull's advisers instead focused initially on enhancing measures against CCP interference and influence.[24] Australia's security officials had become increasingly concerned about the scale and intensity of Chinese influence and attempts at political interference inside Australia, at federal, state and local levels.[25] Not all of this was clandestine; indeed, much of it was occurring in plain view. However, such concerns were not yet mirrored in Australia's media or parliamentary discourse.

There were multiple reasons for Australia's adoption of a more robust stance towards Chinese interference and influence. But a crucial trigger was allegations of CCP-led political interference, which raised broader questions about Beijing's intentions and the trajectory of Australia–China relations. The role of the media in bringing these allegations to light, and thus creating pressure for policy change, was vital.

Turnbull's best-remembered speech about China, in December 2017, called for the Australian people to 'stand up'. This phrase, delivered in Mandarin as a pointed and unmistakable signal to the CCP of Australia's intention to defend its sovereignty against external interference, was chosen as a conscious echo of a revolutionary slogan widely attributed to chairman Mao Zedong.[26] Promoting greater transparency in Australia–China relations became the basic principle of the Turnbull government's pushback policy. The Foreign Influence Transparency Scheme was its lead legislative element.[27] The new law, which entered into force in late 2018 after Turnbull left office, made it a requirement for those lobbying on behalf of a foreign power at the federal level to declare themselves on an official register. The Turnbull government's terminal act, in August 2018, was to exclude Chinese firms from bidding for Australia's future 5G communications network.[28] Australia thus became the first among the Five Eyes intelligence partners to exclude Chinese telecommunications firms Huawei and ZTE from participation in 5G, based on the advice of the Australian intelligence community that these companies posed an unacceptable security risk to national critical infrastructure. This decision was announced by then-treasurer Scott Morrison, one day before he replaced Turnbull as prime minister. Also of rising concern to Canberra was the scale of espionage against Australian targets by China's intelligence agencies, though this was rarely attributed to China in public. In his memoirs, Turnbull was more candid, revealing that China was the source of cyber espionage against Australia on an 'industrial' scale: 'Their appetite for information seemed limitless, ranging from businesses, to universities to government departments and much else besides.'[29]

The reference points for the Australia–China strategic dynamic are not only binary; the bilateral relationship also forms part of a strategic triangle with the United States. Canberra's alliance with the US and its membership in Five Eyes intelligence-sharing and the Australia–United Kingdom–United States (AUKUS) strategic-technology partnership arrangements increase Australia's significance for China. Beijing's investment in alternately wooing and punishing Australia derives ultimately from China's interest, as a rising revisionist power, in weakening the regional US-led alliance system. Australia is a conspicuous target in this regard, given its self-identification as a stalwart US ally. Australia's desire to extract economic benefits from China and its ambitions to play a bridging role between the West and Asia have combined to give Beijing the impression that it is a potentially pliable country.

The United States plays an outsized role in Australia's strategic debates on China. Some Australian critics of a hardline policy towards China have expressed concern that it could be intended to imitate a hardening US line or even to obtain credit in Washington.[30] This critique, though long present, became more frequently voiced during Donald Trump's presidency, which introduced a tougher US line on China.[31] China is sometimes treated in Australian debates as if it is a vehicle for a foreign policy that is less reliant on the US alliance.[32] US–China competition is also sometimes misconceived, including at the highest levels of government, as if Australia has no direct interest in the outcome of this competition.[33] Fears of entrapment and abandonment have always been part of the dynamics of Australia's alliance with the US. But these anxieties have intensified as China's power rises and that of the United States continues its relative decline. America's domestic political divisions and distractions have little to do with China, but they understandably weigh on Australian decision-makers' minds, casting doubt on the credibility of the US as a security guarantor and raising the prospect that Canberra may have to deal with China without dependable support from Washington. Somewhat paradoxically, while Australia's alliance with the US is continually strengthening and becoming steadily more integrated in terms of military capability, it has moved onto shakier ground politically because of deepening fractures within the American polity.

* * *

Given its worrisome trajectory, the Australia–China dynamic prompts a number of questions. The most important of these relate to the nature of Beijing's strategic intentions towards Australia and the extent to which Australia matters to China, other than as a supplier of minerals, foodstuffs, tourism and education services. In the economic domain, the question of Australia's vulnerability to coercion by China has recently been tested. In addition, intensified US–China rivalry is likely to have strategic implications for Australia. In the military arena, China's growing capabilities pose serious questions about Australia's future defence posture and its ability to deter military adventurism and grey-zone operations in Australia's vicinity. Australia's need to form ad hoc coalitions of like-minded countries to balance China will test its ability to shape its external security environment. Outside Australian policy circles, international observers should consider the lessons that can be drawn from the strategic dynamic between Australia and China: what is it that makes Canberra's turbulent ties with Beijing worthy of wider attention, and does Australia live up to its frequent description as 'a canary in the coal mine' with regard to China?[34]

Australian commentary often places the onus for the deterioration of bilateral relations on the proximate triggers of China's anger, notably Canberra's April 2020 call for an inquiry into the causes of the coronavirus pandemic. However, the substantive issues that divide Australia and China are symptomatic of fundamentally divergent national interests, which have been accentuated by Beijing's steady tilt towards hardline positions across the policy spectrum. Points of tension include Australia's concerns about China's interference inside Australia, its military build-up, its expansionist behaviour and its grey-zone operations, especially in the maritime domain. Canberra has also been concerned about China's increasing influence in, and long-term intentions towards, the Southwest Pacific and maritime Southeast Asia. These challenges touch on Australia's fundamental security interests, not just the ephemera of diplomatic 'ups and downs'. Australia and China have also occasionally clashed over Beijing's anti-democracy crackdowns in Hong Kong and the mass incarceration of Uyghur Muslims in Xinjiang. These concerns do not impinge on Australia's vital defence and security interests, but they reflect frictions that flow from basic differences in regime type: between Australia, as a liberal democracy, and China, as a one-party state and authoritarian regime.

Australia's relationship with China arguably presents a cautionary tale: a warning of what lies in store when Western democracies pursue open-ended economic engagement with an authoritarian Marxist–Leninist party-state, heedless to the negative ramifications of dependency and fundamental political difference.

CHAPTER TWO

China policy begins at home

Much of the recent heat and noise in Australia–China relations has been generated within Australia's own borders. It is on the home front that Canberra's 'pushback' has been concentrated in policy terms and where international interest in Australia's responses has been centred.

China's malign behaviour in other countries includes espionage, intimidation, misinformation, disinformation and political interference. These extraterritorial activities are conducted with varying degrees of openness and legality, but are sometimes obscured more by the language barrier than by the veil of secrecy. Covert activity, by its nature, is difficult to detect, let alone to prove. Yet former prime minister Malcolm Turnbull's candid assessment, made after he left the post, was that 'China represented by far the bulk' of espionage activity against Australia that was detected during his period in office, especially in the cyber domain.[1] Separating covert and illegal activity from legitimate and lawful forms of influencing is difficult, posing dilemmas for liberal democracies, like Australia, which must navigate between protecting themselves against internal interference by authoritarian states and preserving pluralistic freedoms at home. Defining foreign interference and differentiating it from lawful lobbying and influencing activities is critical to the efficacy of governmental responses in liberal democracies, which have enshrined principles of free speech and fair competition. Thus, while sometimes legitimate, foreign influence activities and behaviour, as Turnbull noted, may also be 'covert, coercive or corrupt'.[2]

Australia's Department of Home Affairs (DHA) attempts to differentiate foreign influence from interference by describing the former as open and transparent efforts by governments to influence discussions on issues of importance, while defining the latter as going beyond routine diplomatic influence to encompass activities that are 'coercive, corrupting, deceptive and clandestine' and 'contrary to Australia's sovereignty, values and national interests'.[3] The DHA further contends that foreign actors, including foreign intelligence services, 'are creating and pursuing opportunities to interfere with Australian decision makers at all levels of government and across a range of sectors[,] including: democratic institutions[;] education and research[;] media and communications[;] culturally and linguistically diverse communities[; and] critical infrastructure'. The Chinese Communist Party (CCP) is regarded as the dominant threat in this regard in Australia, because of the scale of its activities and its deliberate blurring of interference and influence.[4] However, the Australian government has adopted country-agnostic language in its definitions to avoid singling out China, while at the same time recognising that other authoritarian regimes, such as Russia, may also pose threats.

It is important to acknowledge that influence is a two-way street. Outright coercion aside, influence requires a certain receptivity among the target population to the arguments or positions proposed. For many decades, a diverse assortment of people in Australia, consciously or unconsciously, have in various ways echoed or simply agreed with aspects of the CCP's international narrative.

A home-grown constituency

The existence of a constituency within Australia that has been ready to promote closer Sino-Australian relations is not new. The journalist Donald Horne, writing in 1964 (eight years before Canberra gave diplomatic recognition to Beijing), observed that 'there are Australians of many kinds, on the Right as well as the Left, who – like people all over Asia – are fascinated by Communist China, held in the grip of what they see as destiny, and anxious to accommodate themselves to the "facts"'.[5]

Currently there exists a diverse, largely home-grown group within Australia who argue that Canberra's interests are best served by closer engagement with Beijing. Their motivations are disparate. They include business leaders who are attracted to China's economic power for commercial reasons and who believe that China is bound to represent an important element in Australia's economic future. Others, impressed by the scale and pace of China's recent economic and military development, see an accommodation of China by the United States and its allies as preferable to the risks of adversarial competition and, in the worst case, war. According to this latter view, Australia should steer clear of entrapment in a Sino-American contest over regional primacy and avoid clashing with Beijing on issues that do not directly concern Australian interests. Others have endorsed open-ended engagement with China because they associate this with the fulfilment of an 'independent' foreign policy more attuned to Australia's regional environment and less reliant on the US. Some simply believe that history is on China's side and it is better to 'go with the strength'.

The goal of integration with Asia has emerged as an increasingly important grand project of Australian foreign policy over the past half-century, albeit one that, at different times, has variously centred on Indonesia, Japan or the Association of Southeast Asian Nations (ASEAN) as a whole. The idea has deep roots as a modern counterpoint to older fears that, as a European outpost on Asia's periphery, Australia was destined to be a 'prisoner of geography'. However, it acquired greater momentum with the surge in bilateral trade that followed China's accession to the World Trade Organization in 2001. Gradually, as exponential trade growth with China began to crowd out more established partnerships, such as that with Japan, 'engaging Asia' became equated with 'engaging China' for many in Australia. This has become evident, during the past 15 years, in the almost exclusive weighting towards China in Australian state governments' economic-engagement strategies and a myopic focus from Australian universities and export industries on the Chinese market. A bias towards engaging more closely with China also appears in the 2012 'Australia in the Asian Century' White Paper, in spite of its diplomatically finessed attempt at demonstrating balance within Australia's regional engagement. At the start of the century, Australia's foreign-policy establishment developed a consensual belief that an approach ruled by pragmatism was a viable basis for bilateral relations with China. Tensions that might arise from the difference in regime types between Australia and China were thought to be manageable. Across Australia's elite, it became axiomatic that a China-centred regional economic order, in which Australia would position itself to commercial advantage, could be decoupled from the less desirable 'Sino-centric' political vision emanating from Beijing. Influence, to the extent it was a concern, was assumed to flow towards rather than from China.

China has both real and symbolic value as an alternative power centre in Australia's foreign-policy debate: it sometimes plays the role of the 'anti-United States'. Growing distrust of US leadership in Australia, especially following the 2003 invasion of Iraq and more recently during the Trump presidency, benefitted China in the sense that Australians became more sceptical of their country's international orientation – notwithstanding the fact that popular support for the US alliance has endured.[6] Even some former prime ministers have strongly criticised Australia's alliance with the United States: the late Malcolm Fraser, from the conservative Liberal Party, wrote – well into his retirement – that 'China does not represent a threat to the integrity of an independent Australia', averring that the US and Japan pose greater challenges to Australia's security.[7] Another former prime minister, Paul Keating, from the Australian Labor Party (ALP), has urged Australia to de-emphasise its military alliance with the United States and has reacted sceptically to claims that China poses a threat to the region.[8]

A surprising number of Australian politicians and former officials have been prepared to make statements that appear sympathetic to China. References to China's success in pulling so many citizens out of poverty and criticisms of Australia's alleged 'megaphone diplomacy' and 'Cold War mindset' have permeated mainstream discourse.[9] While such terminology sometimes parallels Beijing's own rhetoric, it would be incorrect to ascribe all arguments for closer ties to Beijing to bad faith or malign activity.

In order to better understand this phenomenon in its Australian context, three important matters are central: first, the motivations for and modus operandi of the CCP's influence operations abroad in general; second, how these operations have materialised within Australia, including the question of interference in its domestic affairs; and third, how the Australian federal government has responded.

Political influence

China's desire for greater international influence is a function of its rising power and ambition to stake out a more confident and active role on the world stage. Related to this, under President Xi Jinping, China has aimed to export the CCP's governance model as an alternative to the Western liberal paradigm; this has involved 'democratising' the prevailing international order on the party's own terms.[10] In the geo-economic domain, Xi has closely associated himself with such flagship programmes as the Belt and Road Initiative (BRI) – which he himself announced in 2013 – and 'Made in China 2025', which aim to place China at the apex of technological development and to ensure Chinese dominance of value and supply chains on an inter-regional if not global scale. Xi has also promoted the more nebulous 'China Dream', based on national rejuvenation, abroad as well as at home.[11] He has placed significant emphasis on boosting Beijing's soft power and fostering favourable narratives about China internationally, using such means as influencing foreign journalists so that they 'tell China's story well'.[12]

Central to the CCP's role in promoting Xi's vision internationally is the notion that China's rise is both inexorable and inherently peaceful. 'Win–win' benefits will accrue to those countries, companies and individuals that are receptive to China's economic embrace, as long as they are willing to accommodate Beijing's interests. Beijing's front-line effort to forge overseas links is usually, by design, economic. Fostering a psychology of economic dependence among China's trading partners is considered a prerequisite for gaining political influence. To China's leaders, the commercial-value proposition that the People's Republic of China (PRC) presents to other countries is a means to gain support for the CCP's core political interests. Receiving economic benefits from China entails corresponding trade-offs. This proposition can be viewed as an extension of the CCP's de facto compact with the Chinese people, whereby the party delivers economic growth and in return maintains a monopoly over political power. The Chinese people have no choice in this forfeiture of their personal freedoms, but the party links this political arrangement to the delivery of material benefits as an explicit benefit and feature of its governance. To succeed overseas, where the party's remit is weaker, requires a mix of commercial inducement, persuasion and coercion.

Beijing has not abandoned the goal of winning hearts and minds internationally through persuasion, but it relies increasingly on China's economic pull to attract other countries into its orbit and hold them there. As China's power has grown, the incentives that Beijing can offer and the costs that it can impose combine to enable more aggressive and coercive behaviour. The CCP's pursuit of influence, licit and illicit, in Australia and other democracies is best understood as chiefly an exercise in hard power, posited on economic and commercial leverage. According to Turnbull, China's biggest weapons aren't 'fleets and armies' but 'RMB [renminbi] and dollars'.[13]

Presented with a binary choice, very few people in liberal democracies would likely choose the PRC's authoritarian governance model over their own. The CCP's ability to command the loyalty of converts, especially at an ideological level, has never been great beyond China's borders. Now it is diminishing further as the party's ethno-nationalist policies (in particular, the subjugation of the Uyghur population in Xinjiang) and 'wolf warrior' diplomacy (involving the use of combative and uncompromising language to denounce perceived criticism of the Chinese government and its policies) alienate potential international sympathisers. As indicated by a Pew survey of international public opinion in June 2021, unfavourable views of China 'are at or near historic highs' among democracies, including Australia, South Korea and Sweden.[14]

Therefore, the claim attributed to former director general of security at the Australian Security Intelligence Organisation (ASIO) Duncan Lewis that foreign interference poses an 'existential' threat to Australia appears overblown.[15] The risk is more subtle. According to the independent researcher Jichang Lulu, 'efforts to coopt foreign elites and shape discourse abroad are as important to the CCP's foreign policy as state-to-state diplomacy and other modes of international engagement familiar in non-Communist polities'.[16] A rich authoritarian power of China's dimensions can do a lot to subvert a liberal democracy without trying to overthrow it. Broadly, the party aims to encourage compliant behaviour over the long term by linking deference to its interests with a set of inducements and punishments. Engendering self-censorship, out of commercial self-interest linked to fear of offending China, is a more sophisticated and attainable aim than promoting revolution in parliamentary democracies. Self-censorship has become common on subjects deemed sensitive to Beijing, notably Taiwan, Tibet and Xinjiang. According to the Australian historian and China expert John Fitzgerald, from Beijing's perspective, the 'preservation of limited national sovereignty is predicated on ritual displays of respect for the regime in Beijing that sets and polices the rules'. Governments are expected 'to refrain from commentary or conduct that could possibly offend the party leadership in Beijing'.[17] China's respect for other countries' sovereignty is conditional on such self-censorship.

The CCP has a specific interest in securing support from the Chinese diaspora. Almost since its formation, the party has designated ethnic-Chinese communities outside China as a priority for influence and control. From the CCP's perspective, 'overseas Chinese' (a loaded term in itself) are perceived through the twin lenses of opportunity and suspicion. The instrumentalisation of the Chinese diaspora in China's foreign policy has waxed and waned since the PRC was established. But it has been revived as a priority under Xi Jinping, who views the diaspora as a force multiplier, both as a source of capital and technology to boost China's development, and as a strategic asset to help realise the CCP's objectives overseas.[18] At the same time, the party has long feared the Chinese overseas diaspora could serve as a breeding ground for separatism in China, with the potential to subvert party rule.[19]

The CCP's chief vehicle for engaging the Chinese diaspora and ensuring that relevant diaspora groups and leaders are organised and aligned with party interests is the United Front Work Department (UFWD), which operates under the Central Committee with support from more than two dozen party agencies.[20] The UFWD has undergone a major reorganisation under Xi since 2016, giving it a more centralised role in China's overseas influence operations. It has subsequently operated internationally with greater depth and granularity, by individually identifying people of influence in many countries of interest to the CCP.[21] One cardinal objective is to establish a monopoly for the CCP as the sole legitimate representative of China among ethnic-Chinese communities outside mainland China, supplanting locally organised grassroots organisations and rival Taiwan-affiliated bodies. The UFWD is also responsible for countering and delegitimising the CCP's opponents abroad, whom Beijing has classified as advocates of one of the 'three evil forces' of ethnic separatism, religious extremism and terrorism, as well as proponents of democracy on the mainland.[22] Discrediting pro-independence sentiment and promoting 'reunification' with Taiwan on Beijing's terms is a particular preoccupation. National-reunification bodies feature prominently among the UFWD's sub-organisations overseas.

The party's dominance of Chinese-language media internationally, particularly in the West, gives it an advantage in terms of influence. At the same time, though, there are limits to the receptivity of Chinese diaspora communities in Western countries to CCP propaganda, notably among younger and second-generation migrants and those who fled China for political reasons. Related to its interest in the diaspora, the CCP has stepped up efforts via the UFWD and other organs to monitor Chinese students studying overseas. Other activities have included disrupting the CCP's potential opponents on university campuses overseas, including Hong Kong pro-democracy activists and pro-Tibet advocates.[23]

China's state-security apparatus has subjected members of the Australian-Chinese and Australian-Uyghur communities and PRC citizens in Australia to intimidation, and has sometimes resorted to harassment and threats against family members in China.[24] The CCP is interested in monitoring not only PRC nationals abroad and the wider ethnic-Chinese community, but also others deemed hostile to the party. For example, the family of Mack Horton, an Australian Olympic swimming champion who publicly accused a member of China's Olympic swimming team of using a banned substance, was harassed and intimidated.[25] The Australian-Chinese community is at significantly greater risk in China itself. Two Australian-Chinese dual citizens, the writer Yang Hengjun and broadcaster Cheng Lei, have been imprisoned at length in China on espionage charges, which they and their supporters claim to be spurious.[26] Australia's ambassador in Beijing, Graham Fletcher, and former foreign minister Marise Payne both declared Yang's case to involve 'arbitrary detention'.[27] Cheng underwent a closed trial in March 2022, but has not been informed of the outcome or allowed to contact her children since her arrest in August 2020.[28]

Why Australia?

Australia is not as peripheral in China's world view as is sometimes assumed in Australian domestic debates. Before Beijing called a halt to high-level diplomatic contacts in 2018, senior Chinese officials visited regularly to promote closer Australia–China ties across the breadth of the Comprehensive Strategic Partnership inaugurated in 2014. Xi has conspicuously visited all of Australia's states and territories. Bilateral municipal and state-to-province ties have proliferated since the mid-1990s, underscoring the CCP's emphasis on engagement at various levels of government. Beijing's evident commitment to engaging with Australia before 2018 occurred despite the obvious differences between the two countries' political systems. Yet it is precisely Australia's openness as a liberal democracy that makes it such a tempting target for China to try and influence, belying Beijing's public depiction of bilateral relations as characterised by mutual non-interference and economic cooperation.

The concerted attention China has shown towards Australia during Xi's tenure in office suggests that, in the CCP's calculation, the country's value extends well beyond being a stable supplier of natural resources, and a suitable location to educate its youth and entertain its tourists. Australia is a significant US ally and Five Eyes intelligence partner, whose loyalties have been judged worthy of contestation. According to Turnbull, his government's baseline assumption was that China intended to 'supplant the United States as the leading power in the region' and, under Xi, had become confident enough to 'demand compliance' from other regional states, including Australia.[29] If that assumption appears unrealistic in light of the subsequent deterioration in ties, it nevertheless chimes with the thinking of former US assistant secretary of state for East Asian and Pacific Affairs during the Obama administration Kurt Campbell, who once said that Washington regarded Australia as 'one of the countries most likely to shift away from the US in favour of a closer relationship with Beijing'.[30]

The pursuit of 'people-to-people' links, encouraged as part of the Comprehensive Strategic Partnership, provided the CCP with opportunities to cultivate connections with a wide range of influential individuals within Australia's establishment. Until China's interactions with Australia became openly confrontational, engagement with China received fairly widespread support among Australia's elites. However, China's heavy-handed treatment of Australia from around 2018 and more open coercion since 2020 have precipitated a reversal of previously favourable sentiment towards China. According to the annual Lowy Institute poll for 2021, 63% of Australians perceived China as 'more of a security threat to Australia' than 'an economic partner', a 22-point jump year-on-year.[31]

As Beijing has stepped up the rhetoric against Canberra, the CCP's prospects for extending its influence in Australia have narrowed in scope, though not disappeared. Beijing now sees the punishment of Australia as a demonstration to regional and global audiences that defiance of Chinese demands may incur economic and political costs. In November 2021, the Chinese embassy in Canberra informally released to the Australian media a list of 14 grievances against Australia about its perceived behaviour towards China:

1. blocking Chinese investment projects based on 'opaque national security grounds'
2. banning Huawei and ZTE from the Australian 5G network, and 'doing the bidding of the US by lobbying other countries'
3. adopting foreign-interference legislation 'viewed as targeting China'
4. encouraging the 'politicization and stigmatization of the normal exchanges and cooperation between China

and Australia … including the revok[ing] of visas for Chinese scholars'

5. calling for an international independent inquiry into the origins of the coronavirus pandemic

6. pursuing 'incessant wanton interference' in Xinjiang, Hong Kong and Taiwan

7. being the 'first non[-]littoral country to make a statement on the South China Sea to the United Nations'

8. 'siding with US' anti-China campaign and spreading disinformation' on China's efforts to contain COVID-19

9. introducing 'legislation to scrutinize agreements with a foreign government targeting towards [sic] China' and Victoria's participation in the Belt and Road Initiative

10. funding an 'anti-China think tank' and 'manipulating public opinion against China'

11. authorising the 'early dawn search and reckless seizure of Chinese journalists' homes and properties without any charges and giving any explanations'

12. making 'thinly veiled allegations against China on cyber attacks'

13. voicing of condemnation of the CCP by Australian members of parliament (MP) and 'racist attacks against Chinese or Asian people'

14. allowing the publication of 'unfriendly or antagonistic' media reports on China.[32]

These 14 points illustrate not simply the decline in Australia's official relations with China, but also the deterioration in China's diplomatic conduct – to a low point not witnessed since the Cultural Revolution, in the 1960s and 1970s. This type of polemic has little realistic prospect of influencing the Australian government to yield to Chinese pressure. More plausibly, Beijing was highlighting its anger for consumption by countries in Australia's surrounding region, as well as for its domestic audience in China.

Political interference

It is likely that many instances of Chinese interference in Australian politics have gone unreported. According to Turnbull, 'a number of prominent Chinese businessmen were working closely with the UFWD and their agenda included coopting Australian politicians and opinion leaders'.[33] In April 2017, there was a clear attempt to interfere in Australia's federal politics when Meng Jianzhu, who was then secretary of the CCP's Central Political and Legal Affairs Commission, thus overseeing the Ministry of State Security, met in Sydney with then-opposition ALP foreign and defence frontbenchers Penny Wong and Richard Marles, respectively. Meng is reported to have told them that 'it would be a shame if Chinese government representatives had to tell the Chinese community in Australia that Labor did not support the relationship between Australia and China'.[34] This meeting occurred shortly after the Turnbull government withdrew its planned bilateral extradition treaty with China, in the face of human-rights concerns expressed by both Labor MPs and some Liberal Party backbenchers.[35] Earlier, in March, when Labor leaders met China's then-ambassador to Australia, Cheng Jingye, to discuss support for the planned extradition treaty, a similar 'veiled threat' was allegedly made by Chinese officials with regard to the Australian-Chinese community.[36] Despite such alleged pressure tactics by Chinese officials, the ALP maintained its opposition to the draft treaty, forcing its cancellation by the government, with the cooperation of a number of Liberal Party senators. The incident is notable as a rare breach in Australia's generally bipartisan approach towards policy on China.

Federal fault lines

Federal systems, with their duplicative layers of governance, generate exploitable vulnerabilities for foreign actors
seeking to bypass central authority and develop relations
at the subnational level. These vulnerabilities can be exacer-
bated by local ignorance about the threat of interference and a
tendency to view external engagement in commercial terms.[37]
While Australia's federal government is solely responsible
for defence and most foreign-policy functions, as per Section
51 of Australia's constitution, the states maintain significant
autonomy, including authority to conduct their own activities
for international trade promotion and cultural diplomacy.[38]
This autonomy has created opportunities for foreign interference, especially where such activities intersect with domestic
political and jurisdictional fault lines. As has been highlighted
by the coronavirus pandemic since 2020, Australia is a surprisingly fissiparous federation, given the powers wielded by state
premiers and their often fractious relations with Canberra and
with each other.[39] As a Leninist organisation, the CCP relies on
the exploitation of political and social cleavages as a general
tactic informing its external modus operandi. The ability to
deal directly and form relationships with state governments
and municipal authorities, via provincial administrations or
other organs of the Chinese state, allows the CCP to bypass
scrutiny from Canberra and fan internal divisions in Australia.
Australia's federal structure is vulnerable to economic
approaches by the Chinese state because the states have been
able, effectively, to conduct semi-autonomous foreign relations
for the purpose of promoting trade and investment.

The most significant instance of tensions regarding China
between state and federal administrations stemmed from the
decision of the state of Victoria's ALP government to conclude a
memorandum of understanding (MoU) with China's National

Development and Reform Commission (NDRC) on participation in the BRI. China was already the centrepiece of Victoria's international trade and investment strategy. State Premier Daniel Andrews attended the inaugural Belt and Road summit in Beijing in May 2016 – the only Australian state leader to do so – with then-federal minister for trade, tourism and investment Steven Ciobo.[40] As premier, Andrews visited China six times and insisted that each of his cabinet ministers went there at least once.[41] Andrews signed an MoU with the Chinese government on 8 October 2018. This was followed by a framework agreement just over a year later, in October 2019.

As an exercise in 'divide and conquer' tactics, Victoria's BRI MoU is compelling. The late federal senator Kimberley Kitching described it as part of the CCP's strategy of bypassing Canberra to create an internal 'wedge'.[42] The Victoria state government has been criticised for not consulting the Department of Foreign Affairs and Trade (DFAT) in sufficient depth regarding its decision to officially engage China on the BRI.[43] In response to criticisms of his government's Belt and Road agreement by federal politicians, Andrews pointed out that the federal government had itself concluded an earlier, preliminary agreement on the BRI in Beijing.[44]

Senator Kitching argued that 'the CCP used the Victorian deals as a propaganda tool to spruik [promote] the BRI to our neighbours' – a reference to nearby countries in Southeast Asia and the Southwest Pacific.[45] While China's motivations for concluding the state-level MoU are a matter for conjecture, a significant pay-off was that the episode fanned tensions between state and federal governments, prompting Victoria's state premier and his cabinet colleagues publicly to criticise Canberra's China 'pushback' policies.[46] The MoU worked to Beijing's advantage, netting political returns in the form of domestic discord over Canberra's tougher China policy settings, without any binding commitments to new investments in Victoria. Ultimately, the federal government stepped in with new legislation that effectively trumped Victoria's BRI agreements: the Foreign Relations (State and Territory Arrangements) Act of 2020 gives the federal government heightened powers of oversight and a veto over partnership agreements with foreign entities across a wide range of sectors, including trade cooperation, infrastructure, tourism, science, health and education.[47] Two older Victorian state agreements, with Syria and Iran, were expunged simultaneously.[48]

At the municipal level, there has been a total of 87 'sister' and 'friendship' (China's preferred term) agreements between cities in Australia and China. Fifty-seven of these predate the Xi Jinping era, but more than half of such agreements in South Australia, Western Australia and Tasmania were concluded after 2013, suggesting an intensified effort under Xi to build influence and contacts in Australia beyond the major conurbations of Sydney and Melbourne.[49] Urban centres where the Australian-Chinese population is concentrated remain a priority for the UFWD. One demonstration of how poorly the risks of foreign influence and interference are sometimes understood at the local level in Australia occurred in October 2019, in the Melbourne suburb of Box Hill, when the neighbourhood police station agreed to fly China's flag from its roof, ostensibly in honour of a Chinese-community festival to mark the 70th anniversary of the PRC's founding and the beginning of the Whitehorse Chinese New Year Festival. While the incident may appear trivial, the Box Hill police station episode may suggest the lengths to which the Chinese state is motivated to go to establish the PRC's legitimacy and to assert Beijing's monopoly over representing the Chinese diaspora, especially in areas with large ethnic-Chinese populations.[50]

As a result of these experiences and others, Australia has made efforts to narrow some of the country's subnational vulnerabilities to foreign interference. Somewhat heavy-handed legislation eventually had to be enacted to counter Beijing's divide-and-rule tactics. That there has subsequently been no repeat of Victoria's BRI experience in other states, despite a clear appetite to attract infrastructure and other investment from China, suggests that awareness of the risks has increased. However, some Australian state premiers have continued to criticise Canberra's policies towards China, even while Beijing has been inflicting economic punishment on Australia.[51]

China and Australian academia

Universities are a tempting, multifaceted target for influence operations and interference from the Chinese state. The CCP considers it important to monitor the Chinese and Hong Kong student population, and Chinese student associations – many of which report directly to China's embassies and consulates – are used for this purpose.[52]

Universities also offer tempting targets for Chinese intelligence agencies and the People's Liberation Army (PLA). Their defences against cyber intrusion and intellectual-property theft are often considered weak. The Australian National University, for example, has suffered repeated cyber attacks, one of which was directly attributed by Australia's former minister for home affairs, Karen Andrews, to China's Ministry of State Security.[53] Illicit data acquisition serves commercial and strategic purposes, and could also be used to construct targeting profiles of university staff and students for intelligence purposes.

Australia's academic sector attracts people with specialist knowledge and skills whom China has been interested in recruiting to support its strategic research and development (R&D) effort. The main vehicle for recruitment in support of China's defence-science and R&D sector is the 'Thousand Talents Plan', which is directed at identifying and attracting foreign researchers in areas of strategic interest, either to work in China or to remain overseas and work on China's behalf.[54] Alex Joske has identified 325 individuals reportedly recruited from Australian universities under this plan.[55] Joske has also meticulously catalogued the extent of PLA involvement in Chinese universities, highlighting the associated risks of partnership agreements between Australian and Chinese universities that are sometimes entered into without sufficient due diligence.[56] The Commonwealth Scientific and Industrial Research Organisation (CSIRO), the federal government's statutory body for scientific research, has also come under scrutiny in Australia for some of its collaboration with Chinese institutions and because of alleged links between CSIRO research personnel and China's talent programmes.[57]

Beijing has long specialised in sourcing strategic technologies illicitly and indirectly to evade post-1989 arms embargoes.[58] Nonetheless, the distinction between civilian and military/internal-security applications of advanced technology has become increasingly blurred. Overall, Australia's technology and defence-industry base is considerably less advanced than those of the US or the UK, but its R&D effort is disproportionately concentrated in the university sector. No evidence has yet surfaced to prove that illicit technology transfer from an Australian university to China's defence sector has occurred. But universities are obvious potential targets of interest for hostile intelligence organisations, such as China's. For example, the University of Queensland, which has close links to China, has hosted sensitive hypersonics research and joint projects involving Australia's Defence Science and Technology Group and the United States Air Force Research Laboratory.[59]

Rising concern about the end-user applications of research collaboration with Chinese institutions has prompted Canberra to intervene. In December 2020, then-education minister

Dan Tehan rejected five applications for government grants for collaborative projects with China, reportedly on security grounds.[60] Australian media have reported particular concerns about research projects related to the 'internet of things', autonomous vehicles, lasers, wireless power transmission, and radar and satellite technologies.[61]

Universities also offer political-influence opportunities for the CCP, including through Confucius Institutes and think tanks hosted on Australian campuses. Confucius Institutes have attracted controversy in Australia, as elsewhere, for their demonstrated links to the CCP through their parent organisation, the Chinese Ministry of Education Centre for Language Education and Cooperation, formerly known as Hanban.[62] While university-based Confucius Institutes have been mostly excluded from the academic curriculum, many offer Mandarin-language classes to local schools, giving them access to the wider community. The Confucius Institute hosted by the University of Queensland has attracted attention because, unusually, it has a science and technology brief and had funded academic courses at the university.[63] The Royal Melbourne Institute for Technology announced that the Chinese Medicine Confucius Institute that it hosts would cease operations in 2021 due to budgetary pressures resulting from the coronavirus pandemic.[64] However, it has not followed through on this plan and, as of mid-2022, all 13 university-based Confucius Institutes in Australia remained in operation, despite growing unease about their existence within the federal government.

The university sector has become increasingly financially dependent on China. Before the coronavirus pandemic began, in 2020, Chinese students comprised around 40% of the total overseas-student cohort, or 10% of the total number of students.[65] In some major universities, the figure has been closer to two-thirds of fee-paying international students.[66] A prolonged boom in student recruitment from China in the first decade of the century funded a breakneck expansion of the higher-education sector, even as central-government funding declined. Moreover, in 2018–19, Australia exported A$12.1 billion of education services to China, accounting for one-third of overall education export earnings.[67] Some Australian universities may have found it difficult to contemplate being cut off from research collaboration with Chinese universities given how important these are for their academic rankings and for student recruitment from China.[68]

Curtailments of freedom of speech in China have been paralleled on some Australian campuses where matters sensitive to China are raised. Self-censorship on China and Taiwan is reportedly rife among Australian academics.[69] References to the 1989 Tiananmen Square massacre have been removed from some course materials. Chinese students who have criticised the PRC government or engaged in activities to which the CCP objects, including attending pro-Hong Kong democracy demonstrations, have been physically intimidated in Australia or have reported that their family members in China have been visited by police.[70] In August 2020, Chinese students at the University of New South Wales (UNSW) protested against an online article and social-media posts on the university website that featured quotes about Beijing's crackdown against pro-democracy supporters in Hong Kong from Human Rights Watch's then-Australia director and UNSW adjunct lecturer in law Elaine Pearson. They also reportedly contacted the Chinese embassy in Canberra to request its assistance in pressuring the university to remove the material. The university issued an apology, including a disclaimer that 'opinions expressed by UNSW academics do not always represent the views of the University', adding 'we have a long & valued relationship with Greater China going back 60 years'.[71] UNSW attracted further controversy when it was discovered that the Mandarin version of its letter of apology included no reference to freedom of speech or academic freedom, unlike the English version.[72]

Another case that gained global media attention was that of Drew Pavlou, a University of Queensland undergraduate who was physically assaulted while leading a peaceful pro-Hong Kong democracy demonstration on campus in July 2019.[73] Pavlou drew particular attention to the involvement of the University of Queensland's Confucius Institute in teaching and course development.[74] The university was also criticised for appointing China's consul-general in Brisbane to an honorary adjunct professorship.[75] In 2020, Pavlou was initially suspended from the university for two years, following misconduct proceedings.[76] This was later reduced on appeal to one semester.[77]

Australian academics and think-tank researchers continue to publish research in areas that China deems sensitive, such as Tibet and Xinjiang. But online retaliation and harassment against institutions and individuals publishing research that is critical of China is increasingly common. Chinese state media and foreign-ministry officials have repeatedly attacked the credibility of the Australian Strategic Policy Institute (ASPI) following its publication of high-profile reports into human-rights abuses in Xinjiang and links between Chinese universities and the PLA.[78] ASPI may be the supposed 'anti-China think tank' referred to in the tenth of China's 14 grievances against Australia.

Responses

Before 2017, concern about the scale and intensity of activities undertaken on behalf of, or directed by, China's party-state to influence, coerce and corrupt Australia from within was present within the Australian intelligence community but was not the majority view. It took a highly influential classified report on China's influence operations and persistent media exposés to jolt the federal government and parliament into a more concerted and comprehensive policy response, including new counter-interference legislation. The internal government report, authored by the former journalist and China correspondent John Garnaut, who was brought into the Turnbull administration as an adviser, was a catalyst for a cross-government response and Turnbull's commitment to adopting a set of 'pushback' policy responses. As a result, greater transparency has been imposed on Australia's wide-ranging engagement with China, exposing some of the more potentially exploitable cracks and crevices within Australia's governmental and party-political structures.

The CCP does not pose a set of compartmentalised challenges that falls neatly within the departmental remit of defence, or foreign or home affairs. What sets the CCP apart, other than sheer size, is its ability and willingness to apply linkages and conditionalities that span policy 'silos'. China's ability to integrate strategic-policy objectives across the machinery of state, to manipulate information and crack down on dissent, has been characterised as 'sharp power'.[79] This makes it difficult to disentangle cooperation and positive engagement with China from the party's efforts at infiltration and coercion. As a general principle, the CCP always links China's international political, economic and even scientific-research collaboration to its core agenda. According to Turnbull:

> China's policy towards other countries was thoroughly integrated. If a foreign nation disappointed China – for instance by criticising its conduct in some manner – then it could expect both criticism and economic consequences. Ministerial visits would be stopped or curtailed, trade deals would be frozen or

not followed through, Chinese tourism would drop off, foreign businesses in China would be boycotted.[80]

Australia's policy approach to countering interference has emphasised transparency as a guiding principle, beginning with the federal Foreign Influence Transparency Scheme (FITS) in 2018, on the basis that efforts by authoritarian regimes to influence democratic societies can be countered, provided these efforts are overt. FITS does not outlaw lobbying on behalf of Beijing or Chinese state organs, but introduces a legal requirement to register foreign-influence work and lobbying activity conducted at the federal level. This leaves a loophole to lobby at the state and local levels, which may be the focus of current UFWD efforts. FITS has also been criticised for including an overly broad category of 'communications activity'.[81] While FITS may have functioned initially as a deterrent against certain paid activities by retired politicians and officials, the lack of FITS-related cases brought to court so far has revealed the scheme to be a weak instrument.

Although concern about the CCP's activities within Australia provided the primary impetus for a concerted shift in government policy, Canberra has framed its initiatives for countering 'foreign interference' in country-agnostic terms, so as to avoid the appearance of discriminating against China. Canberra's decision to rescind Victoria's MoU on the Belt and Road Initiative marks a significant step towards asserting the federal government's foreign-policy writ by targeting cases where the Chinese state has already found subnational purchase among Australia's state governments and institutions. However, the downside of country agnosticism is that it has tended to blunt the government's focus on the preponderant threats and challenges posed by China's party-state.[82] The wisdom of this approach continues to be questioned within Australia.[83]

Australian universities have thus far chosen not to view activities by Confucius Institutes that are hosted on Australian campuses as falling within the scope of FITS legislation; none have been closed down. The federal government has attempted to engage and build awareness among university leaders on the dangers of foreign interference by engaging them in a joint government–university task force. Senator James Paterson, former chair of the Parliamentary Joint Committee on Intelligence and Security, chaired a public inquiry which brought greater scrutiny of Australian universities' relationships with their Chinese counterparts.[84] In March 2022, the inquiry delivered its report and recommendations, which included a specific recommendation that the foreign minister use 'her existing veto powers under the Foreign Relations Act to make determinations in the national interest, including in relation to Confucius Institutes'.[85] Some universities have responded by increasing their due-diligence efforts. Even though the perception gap between university leaders and Canberra over China remains wide in some cases, the Chinese-student boom that fuelled a significant expansion of Australia's university sector appears to be coming to an end under the cumulative weight of the coronavirus pandemic, official discouragement to study in Australia by the Chinese authorities and Beijing's own large-scale investment in domestic higher education.

The federal government has exercised its new counter-interference powers sparingly, sometimes resorting to de facto expulsions of foreign residents rather than legal prosecutions. Arguably, this approach focuses on putting out spot fires rather than building a broader response grounded in public awareness and civil-society vigilance. Prosecutions against Australian citizens have been approached extremely cautiously.

The Department of Home Affairs has identified five 'pillars' for its counter-interference strategy:

- enhance capability to meet current and future needs
- engage at-risk sectors to raise awareness and develop mitigation strategies
- deter the perpetrators by building resilience in Australian society
- defend directly against foreign interference activity through a coordinated government response
- enforce [counter-interference] laws, by investigating and prosecuting breaches.[86]

While the former Liberal-led coalition government made progress in some of these areas, it was less attentive to building public awareness about the nature of the foreign-interference threat from China, leaving it to the media and off-the-record briefings by senior officials and parliamentarians to communicate policy. This lapse did not help the evolution of an informed public debate on China, which instead oscillates between extremes, including on the vexed questions of foreign interference and how to respond to it. Federal ministers have, until very recently, shied away from publicly identifying China as a threat to Australia's domestic institutions or attributing cyber attacks and intrusions to China. Such reticence may be motivated by a desire to minimise the diplomatic fallout or to avoid stigmatising Australians of Chinese ancestry. Nonetheless, Australia's public China debate has become increasingly divorced from internal policy debates in Canberra, where the Turnbull administration's 'pushback' settings are likely to remain in place as the basic template despite the change of government in 2022. Official reticence has tended to undermine the government's objective of 'building resilience in Australian society', allowing the CCP and certain Australians to allege Sinophobia, McCarthyism and racism as a pressure tactic to discredit legitimate counter-interference measures.[87] As Turnbull warned presciently after leaving office, 'we should never get sucked into the false premise that any criticism of or concern about China and its ruling Communist Party is "anti-Chinese" or racist'.[88]

Building governmental resilience is one thing; societal resilience is another matter. The weakest link in Canberra's domestic communications strategy to counter CCP interference is its lack of engagement with Australian-Chinese communities. This is mainly attributable to the federal government's limited reach and risk aversion. The dominance of pro-CCP Chinese-language media has been a particular problem in this respect, handing the party an advantage to influence first-generation migrants from China to Australia.[89] Engaging with the Australian-Chinese community has been designated as a priority activity for the new National Foundation for Australia–China Relations, set up by DFAT in 2020 to replace the previous business-oriented council.[90]

Conclusion

Australia's policy record of countering CCP influence operations and interference is imperfect and incomplete. While Australian laws have provided models for other countries to draw on, their implementation and the absence of any obvious guiding China strategy leave much to be desired. Nonetheless, Canberra's pushback has demonstrated that a relatively small country in demographic and economic terms can exercise considerable agency to protect itself against penetration by the CCP, despite asymmetries in power and China's economic pull. CCP-led interference has not subverted Australia's liberal democracy. Remedial countermeasures in this area have been relatively straightforward to implement, though they were initially made possible only by a critical media spotlight and the catalytic efforts of a small number of people within government.

Beijing no longer appears to see Australia as an easy target for influence operations. Instead, it has settled on a campaign of deliberate coercion and ostracism, primarily to demonstrate to other countries in the region the costs of defiance. However, Beijing's overtly hostile treatment of Australia in the diplomatic and economic domains almost certainly does not spell an end to the CCP's covert influence activities in Australia, especially within the ethnic-Chinese community. Indeed, it is likely that the worse bilateral relations become, the more the CCP will attempt to use coercive, covert and clandestine levers of influence in Australia. Moreover, the recent appointment as the new PRC consul-general in Brisbane of a former vice-president of a think tank run by China's foreign ministry suggests that Beijing has not given up on influencing opinion in Australia.[91] The Chinese government's resort to hostage diplomacy, in the cases of Yang Hengjun and Cheng Lei, is symptomatic of a disturbing trend, though these cases have attracted less public attention than those of two Canadian nationals who were detained in China between December 2018 and September 2021.

As a guiding principle, transparency helps to mitigate the CCP's domestic interference in Australia, but it needs to be supported by a coherent, clearly communicated strategy and a willingness to enforce compliance. Without a more holistic Australian government response, covert activity will remain extremely difficult to deal with. Beijing's current modus operandi is likely to be more difficult to detect in the future, especially within the Australian-Chinese community, where the language barrier makes scrutiny by intelligence agencies and law enforcement more difficult. Australia has some distance yet to travel to improve its societal resilience. However, its experience suggests that the foundations for a successful policy towards China must be anchored at home.

CHAPTER THREE

The political economy of Australia–China relations

This chapter focuses on the major features and drivers of economic relations between Australia and China, examining the interplay between trade, investment and security. It explores China's decision to initiate a campaign of trade coercion against Australia in 2020 and assesses its impact on Australia's economy. It charts the development of Canberra's policy responses towards China in the economic domain, including instances when Australia has taken the lead among Western countries in acting to prevent Chinese interference, enacting measures to mitigate risk and protect itself, such as the decision in 2018 to ban Chinese telecoms firms from participating in Australia's 5G network.

Structure of trade

For most of Australia's history since European settlement, economic connections with China were negligible, except for a brief period during the early colonial era when Australia became a diversionary waypoint for merchant ships bound for Chinese ports, and again in the 1850s, when a large but temporary influx of Chinese labour helped to underpin Australia's gold rush.[1] Australia's trade with China only reached a significant scale in the 1990s, and even then it continued to lag well behind trade with Japan. The watershed for an exponential expansion of bilateral trade was Beijing's accession to the World Trade Organization (WTO) in December 2001 and the commodities boom that followed. By 2007, China had overtaken Japan as Australia's principal trade partner. Australia's exports of goods and services to China expanded from A$8.8 billion in 2001 to A$77.1bn in 2011.[2] Two-way trade has continued to grow, despite the impact of the coronavirus pandemic and China's restrictive trade measures against Australia, reaching A$267bn in 2020–21 and A$285bn in 2021–22.[3]

Australia is typical in the Indo-Pacific region in having China as its leading trading partner. But its level of trade dependence is unique among the advanced economies: in 2020, 39% of Australia's exports of goods and services went to China. More than a quarter of the value of Australia's two-way trade is with China, whereas Australia accounts for less than 2% of China's total trade.[4] Given such asymmetry, Chinese academics have expressed the view that 'middle powers' like Australia would hesitate to resist China for fear of losing economic gains.[5] In fact, China does not automatically enjoy leverage over Australia, given the latter's dominant position as a global supplier in some key commodities. However, psychological perceptions of dependence on Australia's part are another matter.

The foundation for the rapid shift in the structure of Australia's international trade was an intense phase of structural complementarity between the two economies, framed by high demand from China for raw materials, food and energy, and Australia's position as a leading exporter of those commodities. Australia is the world's largest producer of bauxite, rutile and zircon, the second largest of gold, lead, lithium, zinc and manganese ore, and the third largest of uranium. Moreover, Australia holds the largest or second-largest reserves of bauxite, copper, gold, iron ore, lead, lignite, nickel, niobium, rutile, tantalum, uranium, zinc and zircon.[6] Its minerals, which China needs for construction and advanced manufacturing, are often purer than those found elsewhere, including iron ore and coal found in China. In consequence, Australia emerged as one of the clearest beneficiaries from the global, once-in-a-generation commodities boom sparked by China's entry to the WTO, helping it to stave off recession during the 2007–08 global financial crisis, a unique feat among members of the Organisation for Economic Co-operation and Development (OECD). The well-established trade in Australian coal to China is in long-term decline as China shifts to alternative sources and fuels,[7] with the exception of high-grade metallurgical coal, which China still needs to import from Australia and North America in order to make steel. However, Australia has more recently become a major exporter to China of liquefied natural gas (LNG). Moreover, China is likely to remain dependent on imported foodstuffs for the foreseeable future, largely because of its chronic water shortage. Both Australia and New Zealand are important food suppliers to China. Yet New Zealand has no 'ace in the pack' comparable to Australia's dominant role as a supplier of iron ore. Wellington's primary exports to China, mainly dairy, meat and forestry products, are all agricultural and, in contrast to minerals markets, there are abundant alternative suppliers.[8] New Zealand's vulnerability to coercion by China has not been put to the test but is potentially much higher than Australia's. In the service sector, until the coronavirus pandemic disrupted mass travel, China was also a major source of tourists and foreign tertiary-level students in Australia.

During previous bouts of political tension between Australia and China, in 2010 and 2017, trade was largely unaffected. Indeed, bilateral trade continued to strengthen even as diplomatic relations atrophied from 2018 onwards, highlighting both the strength of bilateral economic complementarity and Australia's strong position as a stable, dependable supplier of commodities. To replace imports from Australia, China largely faces an unpalatable choice between paying higher prices and accepting greater political risk from less reliable providers. But the kernel of economic complementarity has remained China's demand for commodities, above all iron ore, Australia's most important export by value. In 2019–20, iron ore, coal and LNG accounted for 43% of Australia's total exports worldwide.[9] Australia provides approximately 60% of China's iron-ore imports and 40–45% of its LNG.[10] In 2019, Australia supplied over 40% of China's coking-coal imports and 57% of its thermal coal.[11] Around 80% of Australia's iron-ore earnings originate in China.[12] Demand from China has remained obstinately high even as its GDP growth has tapered off, owing to Beijing's unwavering commitment to stimulus spending, which narrowly targets construction and heavy industry rather than consumer-led growth in domestic consumption. Geopolitical factors aside, China's current high demand for Australian iron ore and other commodities is nearing the end of a long, somewhat artificially prolonged cycle, especially as the extent of debt and overcapacity within China's construction sector becomes clear.[13] This does not signal the end of complementarity between the Chinese and Australian economies. But, even if political relations were normal, Australia's commodity exports to China would be likely to continue declining for macroeconomic reasons.

The zenith of bilateral economic relations in policy terms was the China–Australia Free Trade Agreement (ChAFTA), signed in November 2014 after many years of negotiations and entering into force in December 2015. The agreement, according to Allan Gyngell, was 'more comprehensive and ambitious than any China had previously negotiated with a developed country'.[14] For many Australian economists, policymakers and politicians, the complementarity that ChAFTA represents was perceived as open-ended and peerless. Downside risks, to the extent they were perceived at all, were seen as a product of US–China rivalry rather than direct animus by the Chinese Communist Party (CCP) towards Australia.

In 2016, a major policy report published by the Australian National University (ANU) recommended a further deepening of all facets of economic relations, with the aim of ultimately nesting these within a bilateral treaty of cooperation.[15] The underlying assumption was that China would follow the same economic path as Japan, on a much larger scale, progressing from mineral imports, to a more diverse pattern of trade, then investment. The speech given by Chinese President Xi Jinping before the Australian parliament in November 2014 referred to Australia and China in similar terms to the ANU-published report, as partners 'not burdened by historical problems' with 'every reason to go beyond a commercial partnership to become strategic partners who have a shared vision and pursue common goals'.[16]

Even as political tensions leached into the core of the Australia–China relationship, those professionally focused on economic outcomes saw this as a bug rather than a feature. The belief remained that economic factors should and would ultimately drive political dynamics. In 2020, one of the ANU-published report's authors, Professor Peter Drysdale, was still warning that the 'Australia–China relationship desperately needs adult supervision'.[17] Business has adopted similar sentiments, hence former prime minister Malcolm Turnbull's blunt reflection that an 'Australian prime minister who ends up in conflict with China cannot expect any support or solidarity from the Australian business community … they'll always blame the government if problems arise – even if the problems have nothing to do with government policy'.[18] During the recent, prolonged diplomatic freeze, Australian business groups lobbied for the resumption of high-level dialogue with Beijing through the use of backchannels and private go-betweens. Individual business leaders have criticised the federal government's policies on China as overly antagonistic or pro-American, sentiments sometimes echoed on the opposition front bench.[19] In October 2021, iron-ore magnate Andrew 'Twiggy' Forrest was still urging Australia and China to 'take it behind closed doors, let's all sort it out as adults and let's remove the seemingly unproductive issues between us'.[20] Canberra's 'pushback' against China has never been embraced in the major commercial centres of Sydney and Melbourne, or by the business elites in Australia's other state capitals.

Coercion campaign

Long before China unleashed its punitive campaign against Australia, it had acquired a track record of economic coercion, including restricting salmon imports from Norway, fruit imports from the Philippines and rare-earth-metal exports to Japan.[21] More significant, though, in economic terms, was a 2017 boycott targeting South Korea's Lotte conglomerate in retaliation for Seoul's decision to host a US missile-defence battery on land owned by Lotte.[22]

Before 2020, Beijing had imposed small-scale, mostly symbolic costs on Australian exporters. According to Turnbull, 'there were some trade interruptions designed to send us a message – delays in approving meat exporters, for example. But it wasn't substantial.'[23] Shipments of coal and barley to China also incurred arbitrary regulatory delays. What set China's 2020–21 economic campaign against Australia apart from previous punishment efforts was its systematic and overt nature. The nominal trigger for Beijing's decision to step up trade coercion was Australian foreign minister Marise Payne's call in April

2020 for an international enquiry into the origins of the coronavirus pandemic. Shortly afterwards, China's ambassador to Canberra, Cheng Jingye, said in a media interview that the call for an enquiry was 'politically motivated' and inspired by the United States.[24] Asked how China might respond, Cheng went on to warn that the 'frustrated, dismayed and disappointed' Chinese people may no longer wish to send their children to study in a 'hostile' country like Australia, and might also stop eating Australian beef and drinking Australian wine.[25] The ambassador's comments set the stage for Beijing's campaign of punitive trade measures across a variety of sectors in Australia; these, however, excluded some priority commodity imports.

Within weeks of Payne's comments, China's government began systematically targeting Australian exports including barley, beef, coal, copper, LNG, wine and wool.[26] The first major step, in mid-May 2020, was the imposition of an 80% tariff on Australian barley, trade worth A$591 million in 2019 (around half the normal value, due to drought conditions).[27] Also in May, China suspended export licences for several Australian abattoirs, affecting around one-third of Australia's beef exports to China, which were valued at A$2.6bn in 2019. In August 2020, China imposed 'anti-dumping' duties of between 107% and 212% on wine imported from Australia. Australian wine exports to China were worth over A$1bn in 2019. Around the same time, China's authorities began to target Australia's two biggest service-sector exports – tourism and education – issuing travel warnings that falsely alleged 'a significant increase in racist attacks' against People's Republic of China (PRC) citizens and the number of 'arbitrary searches' conducted by Australian law-enforcement agencies. Education and tourism earnings from China were respectively worth A$12bn and A$16bn in 2018–19. Further tariffs on cotton were introduced while Chinese state-owned enterprises (SOEs) in steel-making and power generation ceased purchases of Australian coal, worth A$13.8bn in 2019. In November 2020, copper, lobsters, timber and wool were among Australian commodities added to China's de facto boycott list. The outstanding exception to this wave of import restrictions was iron ore, despite it being far and away Australia's biggest export commodity to China by value and volume. In fact, iron-ore exports and prices surged for the duration of China's punitive campaign. While Beijing was willing to mete out damage to Australia by denying access to China's market across a broad range of export industries, Australia retained its position as China's predominant supplier in the most lucrative sector of all. Beijing's decision to restrict coal imports from Australia also notably backfired; China's domestic coal production was unable to ramp up in time to prevent a wave of power cuts across the country in late 2021, and the price of coal imported from other countries increased.[28]

The potential economic losses that would result from a full-scale Chinese trade boycott of Australia were estimated in 2021 as equivalent to 6% of GDP.[29] However, according to the preliminary damage assessment of Australia's former treasurer Josh Frydenberg, the overall fallout for Australia from China's 2020–21 campaign was 'relatively modest'.[30] In most sectors directly affected, Australian exporters were able to identify substitute markets that partly or wholly offset the lost direct access to China's market.[31] Even Australian lobsters found ways of infiltrating into the Chinese market, via Hong Kong.[32] According to Australian academic Jeffrey Wilson, while the loss in trade to China amounted to approximately A$5bn in the first year of sanctions, the net loss in earnings was limited to only around A$1bn, when the successful diversion of A$4bn worth of trade is factored in.[33] Some sectors undeniably suffered commercial pain. However, Beijing's coercive activities have advertised to Australian export industries a need for diversification in the face of mounting political risk, helping to persuade a sceptical business community that the threat of economic coercion from China is real and best mitigated by finding alternative markets. Economic coercion was previously dismissed as unlikely, while looking for alternatives to China's market was deemed too difficult to try. Now, even proponents of close Sino-Australian economic ties admit that market substitution has succeeded in mitigating the economic repercussions of China's sanctions.[34]

China's concerted effort to use trade as a political weapon to punish Australia has had mixed results in terms of imposing economic pain. But there can be no reasonable doubt about its deliberate political purpose. After more than a year of formal and informal trade sanctions against Australia, in July 2021, China's Ministry of Foreign Affairs spokesman Zhao Lijian said: 'We will not allow any country to reap benefits from doing business with China while groundlessly accusing and smearing China and undermining China's core interests based on ideology.'[35]

Investment

China's investment profile in Australia is much smaller than that of trade. Even in 2019, China and Hong Kong accounted for only 5% of total direct-investment inflows.[36] Chinese investments in Australia were initially focused in mining, including an unsuccessful 2009 bid by the large SOE Chinalco for a stake in Rio Tinto.[37] China's interest in acquiring Rio Tinto reportedly resurfaced in a meeting between China's finance minister and his Australian counterpart in 2013.[38] The arrest by Chinese authorities of Rio Tinto's chief negotiator, Stern Hu, in July 2009 was an early indicator of Beijing's propensity to intervene coercively when its economic objectives are frustrated. China's direct foreign investment in Australia subsequently broadened to include agriculture and services, and Chinese buyers contributed to a post-millennial property boom in Australia's major cities, although their influence is commonly exaggerated.[39]

Tighter capital controls in China, introduced from 2016 and associated with Xi Jinping's anti-corruption clampdown, have had a dampening effect on investment flows from China. Since then, some high-profile proposed investments, linked directly or indirectly to China, have been rejected by Australia's Foreign Investment Review Board (FIRB). Chaired by the former director general of the Australian Security Intelligence Organisation, David Irvine, from 2017 until his death in March 2022, the FIRB has stepped up its oversight of proposed foreign investments on national-security grounds, particularly where there have been demonstrable, risky links to critical national infrastructure. Chinese investment in Australia started to fall significantly in 2017.[40] Portfolio and property investment flows from China and Hong Kong have declined dramatically since 2020.[41]

Despite China's relatively small footprint as an investor in Australia, individual cases of Chinese investment have triggered controversy and had a significant impact on bilateral relations, particularly when there have been clear links to national-security considerations. The best-known case was the Landbridge Group's acquisition in 2015 of a 99-year lease of Darwin Port for A$506m.[42] This acquisition was sensitive for several reasons. In the first place, the case invited scrutiny because of Darwin's significance as an Australian naval base, the nearby rotational presence of the United States Marine Corps and Landbridge's documented ties to China's People's Liberation Army.[43] Second, this was one of the first China-related issues to become a point of tension between Australia and the United States. US president Barack Obama raised it with Australian prime minister Malcolm Turnbull in person on the sidelines of the Asia-Pacific Economic Cooperation summit in November 2015, reportedly chiding his Australian counterpart to 'let us know next time'.[44] Third, the decision by former trade minister Andrew Robb to take up an advisory position with Landbridge soon after stepping down from Turnbull's cabinet, in spite of the potential for conflicts of interest given Robb's previous roles in government, embarrassed the governing coalition.[45] The Darwin Port acquisition was the harbinger of other subnational cases, such as Victoria's 2018 memorandum of understanding on the Belt and Road Initiative, highlighting the risk that the prospect of large-scale investments from China could expose dissonance and internal incoherence within Australia's federal governance structures.

The decision to approve the sale of Darwin's commercial port to Landbridge, after a competitive bidding process, was staunchly defended by Dennis Richardson, then secretary of Australia's Department of Defence, who rebutted suggestions that the change of ownership posed potential national-security threats, including espionage.[46] In 2015, China was not so obviously coercive as it was in 2020. Critics have nonetheless highlighted the deal's potential to drive a wedge between the federal and Northern Territory governments, labelling it a 'classic example of parochial short-term thinking winning out over what is in the national interest of all Australians across the country for the long term foreseeable future'.[47] Even more significant was the tension the episode generated between Canberra and Washington. Seven years after the deal was concluded, the Darwin Port controversy rumbles on. Landbridge has held on to its lease despite expectations that the deal would be annulled by the Morrison government before the federal election of May 2022.[48] Since the Darwin Port case, a number of proposed investments involving Chinese SOEs or Hong Kong-linked consortia have been rejected on national-security grounds, mainly but not exclusively relating to critical infrastructure.

An even bigger internal 'wake-up call' to the risks around investments by Chinese-linked entities in Australia's critical infrastructure was the FIRB's last-minute intervention in August 2016 to stop the planned A$10bn sale of a majority stake in Ausgrid, a major power provider and distributor in New South Wales, to a consortium including China's state-owned behemoth State Grid.[49] Previous sales of Australian utilities to State Grid had been allowed to proceed without triggering a security alert because these involved power generation, rather than the more sensitive sector of power transmission – a potential vulnerability compounded by Sydney's importance as Australia's main commercial and financial hub. Poor communication between federal and state levels was initially blamed for the late nature of the intervention. Turnbull vaguely attributed this late intervention in his memoir to 'certain national security concerns'.[50] But this was an oblique reference to the belated discovery that Ausgrid owned a secure fibre-optic cable connected to the highly sensitive Australia–US joint intelligence facility at Pine Gap. The shock of this revelation, recounted in a 2018 media report, was such that it single-handedly triggered the establishment of the Critical Infrastructure Centre 'to make sure it never happens again'.[51]

Another important case, particularly influential at the international level, was the Turnbull government's August 2018 decision to exclude Huawei and ZTE from participating in Australia's 5G network. This provided an unambiguous signal that national security would take precedence over commercial and even diplomatic considerations with regard to China. The decision, at the eleventh hour of Turnbull's premiership, was the first of its kind among the Five Eyes intelligence partners. Some of these partners, including the United Kingdom, were then at variance with Australia's threat assessment of Chinese vendors and 5G, instead favouring a mitigation-based approach rather than a ban.[52] The Australian decision was announced in a deliberately 'low key' manner, but was nonetheless 'bitterly resented in Beijing, which has put enormous pressure on other countries – especially the United Kingdom – not to follow suit', according to Turnbull.[53] The announcement did not identify China, Huawei or ZTE by name, referring in general terms to telecommunications vendors 'likely to be subject to extrajudicial directions from a foreign government'.[54] However, Turnbull later described it as the first formal ban on Huawei and ZTE in the world.[55]

A major influence on Canberra's 5G decision was China's 2017 national-intelligence law and, specifically, mounting evidence that Beijing applies PRC law extraterritorially, including but not necessarily limited to PRC nationals overseas[56] – notwithstanding the insistence of Huawei's Australian subsidiary that it operates independently of the Chinese government.[57] Turnbull's categorical view after leaving office was that 'if the Chinese Communist Party called on Huawei to act against Australia's interests, it would have to do it'.[58] Intelligence-based concerns about Huawei's potential pliability to the demands of the Chinese state predated Turnbull's leadership. Julia Gillard's Labor government (2010–13) sidelined the company from competing for Australia's national broadband network.[59] Subsequently, however, Huawei's market presence as a telecoms hardware provider in Australia grew rapidly.

The problem was that the transition from 4G to 5G communications posed a transformative level of risk: 5G is a platform connecting not only communications devices but potentially whole swathes of civilian national critical infrastructure. In the run-up to the Turnbull government's decision on whether to allow Chinese telecoms providers already present in Australia to bid for the project, the Australian Signals Directorate (ASD) ran an extensive 'red team' exercise designed to stress-test 5G's potential vulnerabilities. Of concern was not simply the breadth of 5G's functionality, but also the risk that 5G could empower an 'adversary with a permanent beachhead in an economy's most important enabling platform technology'.[60] According to Turnbull, this would give an adversary 'the ability to make all or parts of the network – or devices and institutions within it – unavailable and unresponsive'.[61] Australia's future 5G network was given priority status on ASD's critical-infrastructure list because 'shutting down a 5G network … could throw the country into chaos'.[62] According to Australian intelligence officials, had Huawei or ZTE been given proprietary control over the design of Australia's future 5G network, the 'cost of entry' for China's intelligence agencies would have been 'greatly reduce[d]'. Ultimately, the Australian intelligence community concluded that a Chinese provider, present in Australia and potentially taking instructions from Beijing, was a risk that could not be mitigated. In Turnbull's words, 'our approach was a hedge against a future threat: not the identification of a smoking gun but a loaded one'.[63] Reinforcing such fears, in late 2021, a Bloomberg report said that 'former national security officials' had 'confirmed' that a Huawei software update installed on the network of a major Australian telecommunications provider in 2012 was embedded with code designed to record data and relay this to China.[64]

The 5G decision represents an important threshold crossed in Australia's intragovernmental China policymaking. It helped to set the tone for subsequent initiatives and influence the mandate for new government bodies, including the Critical Infrastructure Centre established in 2017. As the final policy act of the Turnbull government, it may have constrained China-related policy under Turnbull's successor as prime minister, Scott Morrison. Morrison has also claimed credit for the 5G ban, in his joint capacities as both treasurer and acting minister for home affairs when it was implemented on Turnbull's final day in office.[65]

The international significance of Australia's 5G decision was as a precedent for other countries to exclude Chinese providers from their 5G networks. These countries include bigger players such as India and Japan, smaller countries such as New Zealand and Singapore (both of which have avoided formal bans), as well as Australia's Five Eyes intelligence partners, the US and the UK, the latter of which, in mid-2020, de facto reversed its previous policy of permitting Huawei's participation in parts of its 5G network.[66]

Responses

As the academic Jeffrey Wilson observes, 'as a medium-sized and open economy, Australia is highly exposed to risks from the geoeconomic strategies of major powers'.[67] It must find a balance between economic openness and national-security considerations. However, until exposed by China's punitive trade sanctions, Australia's economic policy settings were 'poorly configured' to respond to coercion.[68] Canberra's economic policy default has been to rely on multilateral institutions to uphold Australia's interests in the rules-based order. Recourse to the WTO remains useful but is not as dependable as it once was. China's 2020 economic-coercion campaign did not occur in a vacuum. Under the Trump administration, the United States confronted China and several of its own allies across a smorgasbord of trade conflicts, some highly divisive and political. At the same time, Washington simultaneously pursued policies aimed at undermining the WTO, the multilateral organisation purpose-built to maintain an international trading regime designed to serve small, middle and major powers alike.[69]

Nonetheless, the WTO remains a key plank in Australian trade and foreign policy. In 2020, Canberra filed an official complaint to the global trade body concerning China's imposition of tariffs on imports of Australian barley. A second case was lodged in June 2021 disputing China's allegation that Australia was dumping wine in China.[70] Then, at the WTO transparency review in October 2021, Australia accused China of 'undermining agreed trade rules … [and] the multilateral trading system on which all WTO members rely' and of engaging in coercive actions that are 'motivated by political considerations'. Canberra's WTO representative contended that China's tactics included 'arbitrary border inspections', 'unwarranted delays' for import licences and 'the imposition of unjustified anti-dumping and countervailing duties'.[71] This naming and shaming is consistent with Canberra's long-standing approach of using multilateral institutions to build a like-minded coalition. Concordant interventions during a WTO transparency review by Canada, the European Union, India, Japan, the UK and the US have demonstrated international support for Australia's efforts to highlight China's discriminatory trade practices. Australia also received support for its stand against economic coercion at the June 2021 G7 summit.[72] According to Wilson, Australia's relatively small size means it cannot 'realistically expect to "win" trade wars or investment races against larger players'. However, multilateral forums like the WTO continue to provide Australia with the opportunity to muster international support where China's coercive trade practices breach agreed rules and norms.[73]

Australia has thus managed to avoid South Korea's uncomfortable position, in 2017, of being isolated at the receiving end of China's economic coercion. Rather than inducing a submissive posture, coercion has hardened Australia's stance.[74] Under the Biden administration, the United States has vocally supported its ally. In May 2021, US Secretary of State Antony Blinken said that the 'United States will not leave Australia alone on the field … in the face of economic coercion by China'.[75] Just how far the US is prepared to go, in material terms, to buttress the economic security of its allies and

close partners is unclear. The Australia–United Kingdom–
United States (AUKUS) security partnership and supportive
messaging on supply-chain resilience via the Australia–India–
Japan–US Quadrilateral grouping indicate that the US will
provide more than rhetorical support in the Indo-Pacific.
However, Washington continues to lack an obvious economic
and trade strategy for the region. Meanwhile, the narrative,
favourable to Beijing, that US exporters to China are deliberately benefitting at Australia's expense is taking hold,[76] and
it appears clear that the Biden administration will not recon-
sider Donald Trump's decision to stay out of the 11-nation
Comprehensive and Progressive Agreement for Trans-Pacific
Partnership (CPTPP).[77] Some commentators have suggested
that the US and its treaty allies conclude a binding treaty-type
agreement as a framework for mutual support in future cases
of economic coercion from China, or others.[78] This could act
as a deterrent to authoritarian states to single out individual countries for trade coercion. However, the prospects for
such an agreement are at best uncertain because even long-
standing treaty allies compete vigorously for commercial
advantage and are prone to protectionist pressures.

Apart from India and Japan, few regional countries have
– so far – been willing to voice public support for Australia's
position at the WTO.[79] This relatively small caucus of support
within Australia's immediate region suggests that while
Beijing's economic campaign has failed in the narrow objective of coercing Canberra, it has had a chilling effect on smaller
countries, particularly in Southeast Asia, in spite of their own
dependence on a multilateral rules-based economic order.
This matters because, while Beijing's economic-punishment
campaign against Australia may have little prospect of making
Canberra more subservient, most governments in Southeast
Asia are likely to be more easily persuaded.

Apart from exploiting opportunities in the multilateral arena, Australia's major response has been to diversify its international markets. The CPTPP, of which Australia is a founding member, is the biggest regional free-trade agreement (FTA) without China as a member. However, without the US on board, the CPTPP's ability to set international standards is likely to remain limited because it lacks sufficient economic heft.[80] Diversification beyond CPTPP members is limited by high levels of protection in markets such as those of Indonesia and India. Canberra has nonetheless accelerated its efforts to conclude bilateral trade agreements with Jakarta and New Delhi. The Indonesia–Australia Comprehensive Economic Partnership Agreement (IA-CEPA) entered into force in July 2020. Indonesia is only Australia's 13th-largest trading partner, with bilateral trade worth A\$18bn in 2018–19, but the IA-CEPA signals mutual intent to deepen bilateral economic relations.[81] Australia and India signed an interim Economic Cooperation and Trade Agreement in April 2022.[82] Australia has other FTAs beyond the Indo-Pacific, including one pending with the EU and one agreed in December 2021 with the UK, which is bidding to join the CPTPP.

It is significant that, even while Beijing shunned bilateral contact with Australian trade officials and ministers, Canberra continued to hedge its economic engagement with China, not only through ChAFTA, but also by maintaining its membership of multilateral groupings that include China, particularly the Regional Comprehensive Economic Partnership (RCEP) led by the Association of Southeast Asian Nations (ASEAN). Australia is also a member of the Asian Infrastructure Investment Bank (AIIB), a multilateral financial institution that funds regional infrastructure projects. While the membership of both the RCEP and AIIB is broad, both institutions are widely seen as China-centred and the US is not a member of either.

China's potential for trade coercion is not limited to denying access to its market. Australia (along with many other advanced economies) bears significant vulnerability to a disruption of supply from China in critical import categories, such as communications and information-technology equipment, as highlighted in a 2020 study by a British think tank, the Henry Jackson Society.[83] The need to build greater resilience into Australia's supply chains is a policy challenge that straddles the international and domestic arenas. Increasing the diversity of suppliers offshore can be complemented by investing in the onshore production of critical products and commodities, especially given the continental-scale resource allocation and well-educated workforce at Australia's disposal. For example, Australia will soon have just two oil refineries to serve its national needs.[84] To prevent Australia from becoming more dependent on overseas supplies of refined petroleum products, including those imported from China, a case can be made that Canberra should invest in refineries because of their importance for Australia's defence sector and economic resilience.

Conclusion

Beijing's first line of effort in forging overseas influence is usually economic. Australia presented a unique opportunity for the CCP in this regard, given the intense complementarity between the two economies, arising from China's rapid growth and high demand for commodities. This fuelled a two-decade-long expansion of mutually beneficial trade that propelled China into pole position as Australia's leading trade partner, including as a major consumer of service exports. Bouts of political tension in bilateral relations in 2010 and 2017 were almost entirely insulated from the economic relationship.

In May 2020, however, China crossed the Rubicon from informal and mostly symbolic trade retaliation for Canberra's policies it deemed to be against China's interests to a full-scale campaign of economic coercion, including formal tariffs. The campaign was overtly and matter-of-factly justified by Beijing in political and ideological terms. China most likely sought to inflict overt economic pain on Australia in order to send a message to other countries, especially in Southeast Asia, that defiance attracts punishment – or 'killing a chicken to scare the monkey', according to the Chinese aphorism.

To the surprise of many, Australia has discovered that, by standing its ground politically and developing other markets, it has been able to weather such a punitive campaign without suffering serious economic damage, even to its overall exports to China – due in large part to the continuing trade in and rising price of iron ore. This has demonstrated the crux of the bilateral economic relationship.

In investment, as in trade, 'Australia's liberal approach ... puts it at a decisive disadvantage when responding to the surge of geoeconomically driven investment from Chinese SOEs'.[85] Strengthening the FIRB's powers of scrutiny and review has at least reduced Australia's potential vulnerability to this aspect of China's predatory economics. But Australia still faces the trickier problem of attracting investment from alternative sources on a scale sufficient to support its revival as a high-value manufacturing base.

There is also a case to be made that Australia needs, for national-security reasons, to restore a civilian manufacturing base that has been significantly hollowed out since the 1990s. At the same time, the technical-skills base of Australia's working population has atrophied. Future Australian governments should consider devoting significantly greater resources to relevant education and publicly funded research and development. However, these investments would doubtless require difficult budgetary trade-offs – including for defence spending.

CHAPTER FOUR

The China factor in Australia's defence strategy and alliance posture

This chapter addresses the military and defence aspects of the Australia–China security dynamic. It examines how China's growing military power is influencing the development of Australia's defence posture, which seeks to counter direct and indirect military threats that could arise in the future. In the context of Australia's alliance with the United States, this chapter explores the growing role that Australia plays in US military strategy towards China. It considers how Canberra is likely to adapt its defence strategy, capability and force structure to meet the future challenge from China, including the extent to which the Australian Defence Force (ADF) can achieve more self-reliant deterrence against potential threats from the People's Liberation Army (PLA). Finally, it grapples with the vexed questions of whether Canberra can deter Beijing without nuclear weapons and under what circumstances, and how Australia might decide to acquire its own *force de frappe*.

Bilateral defence relations

Between 1997 and 2019, Australia maintained low-key military-to-military ties with the PLA, primarily to build mutual confidence and establish communication channels. The anchor for the bilateral defence relationship was high-level defence talks, inaugurated in 1997 and convened annually until 2019. The ADF and PLA also engaged in regular bilateral and multilateral exercises; for example, the People's Liberation Army Navy (PLAN) sent a warship to take part in the Royal Australian Navy's (RAN) major multilateral exercise, *Kakadu*, for the first (and only) time in 2018.[1] Bilateral defence contacts have since fallen precipitously, in tandem with chilling diplomatic relations. Following the Australian general election of May 2022, the first high-level contact between China and the new Labor government was a bilateral meeting between defence ministers on the sidelines of the IISS Shangri-La Dialogue, in Singapore, early the following month.

Bilateral relations between the Australian and Chinese armed forces have been most developed at the navy-to-navy level, characterised by reciprocal port calls and bilateral gunnery and passage exercises, though all on a modest scale.[2] The most recent visit to China by an Australian warship was for the PLAN's 70th-anniversary fleet review at Qingdao in April 2019. A PLAN flotilla last visited Australia in June 2019. Apart from navy-to-navy ties, *Exercise Kowari* – a small-scale three-way endurance and survival exercise, involving ground forces from Australia, China and the US – was held on six occasions in northern Australia between 2014 and 2019.[3] Less cordially, but in conformity with freedom of navigation under international law, specialised PLAN intelligence-gathering vessels have sailed to Australia in order to monitor the biennial US–Australia *Talisman Sabre* exercise, taking up stations outside Australia's territorial waters off northern Queensland.[4]

China as a strategic concern

Beijing's strategic intentions are diversely interpreted and hotly debated, notably with regard to the basic question of whether China harbours expansionist and hegemonic ambitions across

Asia and the Pacific, or is more reactive, less capable than feared and defensively motivated.[5] But at a fundamental level, for the first time since the rise of imperial Japan in the 1930s, Australia faces an ascendant Asian hegemon with growing military capabilities that have already altered the regional balance of power, and with declaratory intent to revise the regional territorial status quo. In addition to threatening to annex Taiwan, China actively disputes land- or sea-based boundaries with several neighbouring states, including India, Japan, Malaysia, the Philippines and Vietnam. Beijing's readiness to carry out coercive military activities simultaneously on multiple fronts, from the disputed mountain frontier with India to the Taiwan Strait and East China Sea, accelerated after the start of the coronavirus pandemic in 2020.[6]

Since 2013, China has constructed or substantially enlarged bases on seven reefs or rock-like features in the Spratly Islands in the South China Sea, extending the PLA's strategic perimeter more than 1,000 kilometres south of Hainan to Mischief Reef, which is located within the Philippines' exclusive economic zone (EEZ). China has also upgraded its base on Woody Island in the Paracels and actively asserts its claims to sovereignty and jurisdiction throughout the area circumscribed by its 'nine-dash line'.[7]

Mischief Reef is one of three Chinese-controlled features in the Spratlys with a 3,000-metre runway, which could potentially accommodate any aircraft in the PLA's inventory.[8] The construction of hardened shelters and underground fuel reservoirs, as well as surface-to-air missile systems, on some of these features points to their likely purpose as forward platforms from which to support sustained air and naval operations. China's South China Sea outposts have also extended the PLA's surveillance and electronic-warfare network across much of the South China Sea, providing China's military commanders with tactical awareness of sea and air movements there and in the surrounding region.[9] Whether their primary purpose is to serve as a defensive bulwark for China's sea-based nuclear deterrent, or as stepping stones to project the PLA's air and sea power beyond the South China Sea, or as part of its military strategy against Taiwan, the PLA's island bases have elevated the operational risk for other countries' armed forces that continue to operate in the South China Sea, including Australia's as well as those of the US.

It is commonplace to assume that China's strategic behaviour is geared towards 'winning without fighting', using grey-zone tactics to achieve its aims.[10] However, military power is clearly a national priority for the Chinese Communist Party leadership, given Beijing's massive investments in force modernisation over the past two decades, including the development of power-projection capabilities that place Australia and its neighbourhood within reach of the PLA's conventional forces. The PLA's 'over the horizon' presence – out of sight but still potentially on hand if a crisis escalates – also reinforces China's grey-zone activities.

Although the PLA remains primarily focused on the US and other nuclear-weapons states, as a close US ally that hosts the important signals-intelligence Joint Defence Facility at Pine Gap, which tracks ballistic-missile launches, Australia is a potential nuclear target for China. Australia has been within range of China's relatively small but fast-expanding arsenal of nuclear weapons ever since the PLA Rocket Force began fielding intercontinental ballistic missiles in the early 1980s. Long-range conventional strike, including hypersonic glide vehicles and cruise missiles, poses a more novel set of PLA capabilities, which Canberra's defence planners and intelligence analysts must now factor into their assumptions.[11] The 'K' variant of China's H-6 bomber can carry the long-range CJ-20 air-launched cruise missile (ALCM).[12] This potentially brings Darwin and other parts of northern Australia within range of missiles launched from H-6Ks operating from the Spratly Islands.

As well as long-range conventional-strike capabilities, the PLA is also developing expeditionary amphibious forces, including a marine corps comprising six assault brigades as well as a flotilla of eight Type-071 amphibious ships. The first two of a larger class of Type-075 vessels have been constructed and are in service. These amphibious forces would have direct utility for an invasion of Taiwan, but their dispositions and capabilities also point to a wider expeditionary potential.[13] China's military build-up, force-structure design and naval-deployment patterns suggest power-projection ambitions across the Indo-Pacific region.[14]

While the Australia–China relationship has become openly hostile in the diplomatic and trade domains, the prospect of armed conflict between the two countries is difficult to envisage without a dramatic deterioration of the regional security environment. Australia's military-security concerns about China are far less acute than those of India or Vietnam. The distance between the two countries, Australia's alliance defence guarantee from the United States and the ADF's existing capabilities combine to make China's direct use of force against Australian territory seem improbable, at least for as long as the US armed forces remain forward-deployed in strength in the Western Pacific. Canberra's 2017 Foreign Policy White Paper assessed the prospect of a direct military threat to Australia to be 'low'.[15] Even in the worst-case scenario, it is hard to imagine the PLA invading the Australian mainland, though Australia's outlying Christmas Island and Cocos Islands in the Indian Ocean would be more vulnerable to attack.

It is somewhat easier to imagine the harassment of Australia's forward-deployed naval and air assets in the South

China Sea escalating into a skirmish. As far back as 2015, China's *Global Times* newspaper issued a lurid threat to shoot down Australian aircraft.[16] While the PLAN has avoided any significant confrontation with Australian warships, generally maintaining a safe distance, in 2020, a Royal Australian Air Force (RAAF) reconnaissance flight was unsafely intercepted over the South China Sea, prompting a diplomatic protest by Canberra.[17] Moreover, Australia's defence department publicly reported that, in late May 2022, a Chinese J-16 fighter unsafely intercepted an Australian P-8A *Poseidon* maritime-surveillance aircraft over the South China Sea, releasing 'chaff' that was ingested by one of the Australian aircraft's engines.[18] The Australian government clearly considered an armed clash to be possible; after stepping down as prime minister, Malcolm Turnbull revealed that the risk of an Australian warship being attacked was a major factor behind his decision not to engage the Australian navy in US-led freedom-of-navigation opera-tions (FONOPs) in the South China Sea during his 2015–18 term in office, despite US pressure to do so.[19] A similar level of caution towards FONOPs prevailed under the administration of his successor, Scott Morrison, suggesting that the Australian government treated this risk seriously. Current Australian naval movements in the South China Sea tend to occur either in the form of small task groups or embedded vessels within US Navy (USN) deployments.[20] Single-ship Australian deploy-ments are now rare.

The use of the PLA for coercive signalling, or even what the US strategist Thomas C. Schelling termed 'compellence', is another scenario.[21] As China's expeditionary forces mature, demonstrative deployments by the PLA in Australia's immedi-ate region and near its outlying islands are likely to increase. In February 2022, according to Australia's defence department, one of two Chinese warships transiting eastwards through the

Arafura Sea, immediately north of Australia and within its EEZ, used a laser to 'illuminate' an RAAF P-8A aircraft. The incident prompted a diplomatic protest by Canberra to China's foreign and defence ministries, alleging dangerous and unprofessional conduct. One possibility, although not confirmed by either of the official Australian or Chinese accounts of the incident, is that a PLAN submarine was operating ahead of the two Chinese warships and was detected by the Australian P-8A. This incident is additionally noteworthy because it occurred close to Australia.[22]

Other potential scenarios involving military forces could escalate tensions between Australia and China. If civil order broke down in a country on Australia's periphery, leading to violence against the resident ethnic-Chinese population, Beijing could order the PLA to intervene. Alternatively, a Chinese military intervention to provide humanitarian assistance and disaster relief (HADR) or to restore order could open the door to a longer-term PLA presence.[23] In either case, Australia could feel compelled to make some form of countervailing military response. A more linear scenario for armed conflict between Australia and China would be if Canberra ordered the ADF to participate in a US-led coalition to counter Chinese aggression against Taiwan or in the South China Sea. In the case of an attack on Taiwan, Australia's involvement could take the form of a direct ADF contribution, involving some combination of naval and air forces, to a US-led counter-invasion force or counter-blockade effort. Alternatively, Australia's contribution could be indirect, in the form of 'backstop' ADF deployments outside the main area of operation, in order to free up US combat forces. Australia's location would suggest a primary focus on covering Taiwan's southern approaches, including the southern portions of the South China Sea and the Indonesian archipelago. Australian fears in this regard are focused less on the immediate future and more on medium- to long-term scenarios in which the US forward-based military presence no longer credibly deters China. At that point, China's use of military force against Australia and other US allies and security partners in the region becomes more thinkable.[24]

Absent a full-scale economic shock or an unforeseen policy change, and assuming that new ships continue to be launched at present rates, China's ability to project military power beyond the first island chain, extending south from the Kamchatka Peninsula to the Indonesian archipelago, will continue to increase in the decade ahead.[25] At the same time, China's growing economic interests, especially to secure seaborne energy imports through the Indian Ocean, are impelling it to be a strategic actor on a broader stage. From Beijing's perspective, according to Singapore strategist Daljit Singh, the PLAN will 'be in the Indian Ocean as a matter of necessity, not choice'.[26] Deployments to the South Pacific are also likely as the PLAN seeks to establish a presence beyond the first island chain. In February 2022, the PLAN briefly deployed two Type-071 amphibious ships with escorts to the Southwest Pacific, including a flotilla on a HADR mission to Tonga and another transiting through the Coral Sea. At the same time, the PLA Air Force conducted long-range transport flights to both Tonga and Solomon Islands.[27]

The PLAN already operates ten times as many submarines and more than eight times as many principal surface combatants (cruisers, destroyers and frigates) as Australia.[28] If the current pace of construction continues, it could have around 100 principal surface combatants (compared with the present 86) in service by the early 2030s. The PLAN operates a large, eclectic force of 59 submarines, including six *Jin*-class ballistic-missile submarines (SSBNs) and six *Shang*-class nuclear-powered attack submarines (SSNs). It continues to grow in sophistication, with six more SSNs likely to be added by 2030.[29] For more than a decade, the PLAN has deployed task groups and submarines to the Indian Ocean. Since 2014, Chinese naval vessels have sometimes sailed close to Australia's outlying ocean territories.[30] In the future, building on its regular counter-piracy experience in the Gulf of Aden, the PLAN could expand its expeditionary deployments to the Indian Ocean to include larger vessels, such as aircraft carriers and amphibious ships.[31]

Indirect military pressure by China is another possibility. Australia has a relatively small population which depends on international trade for its prosperity and a seaborne supply of strategic commodities for its survival. It has continental resources to draw upon, giving it depth and potential resilience unlike most other island states. Yet it has done surprisingly little in practical terms to develop this potential to enhance its strategic resilience and remains critically reliant upon the long-distance supply of essential goods, including most of its refined petroleum and all of its aviation fuel, as well as on the largely seaborne transport of export goods to foreign markets. Australia could survive a very short conflict or blockade, temporarily forgoing export earnings. But in a more protracted war, if crucial imports were cut off, it would be difficult to maintain essential services and defence operations for long.[32] National fuel stocks amount to the equivalent of approximately three weeks' worth of normal consumption, far below the 90-day reserve recommended by the International Energy Agency.[33] In a crisis, Australia could be put under almost immediate pressure by the obstruction of its maritime approaches. This vulnerability is augmented by the nearly complete dependence on foreign-flagged merchant shipping, which cannot be compelled to sail to Australia if freight carriers deem the risk to outweigh the benefits. During the Second World War, Japan and Germany maintained offensive submarine patrols off Australia's western and eastern seaboard, with the latter sinking a ship as late as February 1945. Assuming that China's submarines are able to break out beyond the first island chain into open water, they could pose a formidable threat to naval and merchant shipping in Australia's environs.

Australia's main line of resupply and reinforcement in the event of a military crisis runs across the Pacific from North America as well as south from Japan and South Korea. This dependence helps to explain the enduring emphasis in Australian defence planning on Papua New Guinea and the scattered archipelagos of the Southwest Pacific: not simply as 'fragile' states that require external support for political and humanitarian reasons, but as strategic territories with the latent potential to support an adversary's sea-control or -denial strategies. Similarly, Australia perceives its defence and security as being connected to the defence and security of territories as far away as Singapore and the Malay Peninsula, in order to secure its northern maritime approaches.[34] Australia regards the South China Sea as an area of strategic interest, partly as a merchant-shipping route but also as a manoeuvre space within which the ADF has operated continuously since the Second World War – including through its participation in the Five Power Defence Arrangements with Malaysia, New Zealand, Singapore and the United Kingdom since 1971.[35] Indian Ocean sea and air routes to Australia's west are also important for supplies of fuels and, potentially, defence equipment from European suppliers, although these might be operationally more challenging for the PLAN to interdict because of the distance from Chinese bases.

Australia's main vectors of potential military threat lie in a broad arc to the north. But China has established an active scientific presence in Antarctica, where Australia has outlying islands as well as latent but expansive territorial claims equivalent to 42% of the continent's landmass. Resource exploitation, although currently proscribed by international treaty, is Beijing's most plausible long-term objective in Antarctica.[36] China's scientific expeditions to Antarctica have previously been supported by staging through Tasmania. As such, Beijing's Antarctic ambitions could be moderated by a perennial dependence on foreign support, although China's logistical ability to support its Antarctic presence independently continues to improve. The potential for China's distant-water fishing fleet to gain access to Antarctic fisheries is a related potential grey-zone concern for Australia. Australia's Heard and McDonald Islands contribute significantly to its EEZ, the world's third largest. Policing such a vast area of sea space is a challenge for Australia, given defence commitments elsewhere and the extreme conditions of the Southern Ocean. Antarctica is unlikely to develop into a zone of military competition for the same basic reasons, but it is still an arena where Australia has significant strategic interests that are likely to conflict with China's long-term goals.[37]

China and the US–Australia alliance

Australia's security dynamic with China is inextricably linked to its 70-year-old military alliance with the US, lending to it a triangular aspect. The Australia, New Zealand and United States Security Treaty (ANZUS) elevates Canberra's strategic significance in Beijing's world view. Australia's diplomatic and military activities are frequently ascribed to US orchestration in China's state media.[38] Equally, Australia's stock within US military strategy is rising as China becomes the primary focus of Washington's strategic attention. As the US intensifies its focus on China, so Australia's value to Washington in terms of its position and defence capabilities rises in parallel.

Australia's importance as an ally to the US is not based only on its record as a loyal, niche contributor to long-distance coalition operations: that became the norm in the 1990s, building on the precedent set by Australia's combat role in the Vietnam War three decades earlier. Australia's geostrategic value has revived after a period of post-Cold War latency, during which the US appeared to have no peer challengers – China had yet to assert itself as a major power – and countering terrorism was the designated priority for American and Australian strategists alike. Australia has a unique locational value as an island continent with coastal frontage on both the Pacific and Indian oceans and proximity to archipelagic Southeast Asia to the north. Australia remains a long way from East Asia's most obvious conflict flashpoints, but it is a politically secure, continent-sized staging ground from which to project US combat power into Asia or safely disperse it to the rear.

In spite of the centrality of the ANZUS alliance in Australia's strategic policy and Australian leaders' frequent claims to be Washington's closest ally, the US has not based sizeable military forces in Australia since the Second World War. The US alliance with Australia is exceptional in this regard. With a brief exception during the height of the Vietnam War, US forward-deployed military forces in the Pacific have been consistently and overwhelmingly based in Northeast Asia. Part of the domestic political subtext to ANZUS is that Australian governments, especially Labor ones, have been reluctant to offer bases to the US on a significant scale. The only permanent US presence left in Australia after the closure of the Cold War facilities at North West Cape and Nurrungar is the Joint Defence Facility at Pine Gap, near Alice Springs.

Australia's geostrategic potential within the alliance is therefore resurfacing as Washington's rivalry with Beijing intensifies. The Obama administration's decision, in 2011, to stand up a US Marine Corps (USMC) detachment near Darwin in the Northern Territory provided a foretaste. But it took almost a decade of sometimes difficult negotiations to build up to the modest target of a 2,500-strong task group for the USMC rotational deployment. For half the year during the dry season, the marines are seasonally dispatched to Australia, primarily for training purposes. Large-scale amphibious operations are currently not possible out of Darwin.[39] More consequential, in military terms, has been the US Force Posture Initiatives (USFPI). Commencing in 2011, the USFPI inaugurated a programme of regular US Air Force (USAF) deployments to Australia, including B-1B *Lancer*, B-2 *Spirit* and B-52 *Stratofortress* bombers, and F-22 *Raptor* fighter aircraft.[40] In 2022, four B-2s (constituting 20% of the total B-2 force) were temporarily deployed to RAAF Base Amberley in Queensland.[41] These deployments underline Australia's potential as a relatively secure forward-operating location, comparable in distance from the South China Sea as the US central-Pacific island bulwark of Guam, but endowed with continental depth – Darwin is equidistant from Melbourne and Singapore – and less under the shadow of China's land-based strike capabilities than Japan, South Korea or the Philippines.[42] The USFPI has so far focused on repositioning USAF and USMC deployments to Australia. It lacks a dedicated naval component, despite the fact that the US Navy is a frequent visitor to Australia and regularly participates in the bilateral *Talisman Sabre* exercise, which is normally staged off the coast of northern Queensland in alternate years.

From the perspective of US strategic planners, Australia combines forward position, relative security from China's growing missile force, and political stability. This makes it a natural choice for the US to disperse its forces from more vulnerable bases in Japan and South Korea, and to position reinforcements in the region in case of a protracted conflict. As US–China military competition looms, the Pentagon is likely to see Australia as a suitable location for US manoeuvre and strike forces, possibly including the future deployment of ground-based intermediate-range missiles, which the US military is no longer constrained from developing since withdrawing from the Intermediate-Range Nuclear Forces Treaty in 2019.[43] Northwest Australia and Cocos Islands are suitably situated as springboards to project American naval and air power in order to impede China's naval access to the Indian Ocean. Australia's potential as a basing location for the US Navy has sparked periodic bouts of interest in US strategic circles.[44] Reports first surfaced, around 2012, that Perth was being considered as a location for hosting a forward-deployed US aircraft-carrier group, but nothing eventuated.[45] Towards the end of the Trump administration, then-Navy secretary Kenneth Braithwaite proposed a new USN 'First Fleet' to supplement the Japan-based Seventh Fleet in the Western Pacific.[46] Little thought appears to have been given to which country would be willing to host the new fleet, beyond a cursory reference to Singapore.[47] However, the idea has failed to gain traction because the USN lacks sufficient ships and aircraft to justify establishing a new, shore-based fleet command; at the same time, a major increase in the US naval budget appears unlikely.

However, there are indications that the US force posture in Australia could soon be augmented significantly.[48] In March 2022, Australia's government announced that it will offer access to British and American SSNs at its existing submarine base, HMAS Stirling, located near Fremantle in Western Australia.[49] Earlier that month, Australia's government announced that a new submarine base would be constructed on Australia's eastern coast, most probably at Port Kembla.[50] Granting access to British and American SSNs is a logical step in light of the tripartite Australia–United Kingdom–United States (AUKUS) strategic technology-sharing agreement, announced in September 2021. A semi-permanent forward presence of British and American SSNs would help to supplement Australia's six conventionally powered submarines and kick-start Australia's own nascent nuclear-submarine programme through joint crewing and training. A submarine-basing accord would balance the US force posture in Australia, giving it a third, naval leg concentrated in undersea warfare, where the US still enjoys a clear edge over China. The fact that the USN operated submarines from Brisbane, in Australia's Queensland state, as well as Fremantle during the Second World War attests to the continuity of Australia's position for US military strategy in the Pacific.

China's growing military capabilities and increasingly coercive behaviour are the primary reasons behind recent shifts in Australia's military strategy. At the same time, Canberra's sense of strategic dislocation has been compounded by creeping doubts about the political willingness of the United States to act as a guarantor of regional security in the Indo-Pacific in the long term, and by concerns about US leadership and domestic political coherence in the meantime. Questions about the future of the alliance have been paralleled, paradoxically, by steadily intensifying military integration between the Australian and US armed forces. Their growing closeness derives from the complexity of their interactions through exercises, the embedding of senior officers and civilian officials in each other's defence and intelligence establishments, and the increasing commonality of the ADF's front-line platforms and those of the United States. Notwithstanding Canberra's vote of long-term confidence in the alliance in the form of the AUKUS agreement and the Australia–United States Ministerial Consultations (AUSMIN) joint statement in September 2021, it seems reasonable to assume that the increased emphasis on self-reliance and deterrence in Australian defence planning owes something to increased doubts about Washington's political reliability.[51] Additionally, it could reflect the influence of heightened US expectations about military burden-sharing amongst its treaty allies, a trend that has bipartisan support in Washington.

In spite of AUKUS, legal and political impediments continue to obstruct the transfer of some advanced military technologies from the US to Australia (among other allies and close partners).[52] This is a problem not only for US allies and partners, but potentially for Washington too. During the Cold War, the US innovated and invested largely autonomously in its national industrial and technological base. But China's technological base and overall industrial capacity are more advanced in comparison with those of the Soviet Union during the Cold War, so to remain strategically competitive, the US has greater incentive to leverage the technological strengths of its allies and partners, actively co-developing strategic technologies with some of them. Australia possesses research strengths in quantum computing, for example.[53] There are signs that the US government increasingly recognises the challenge: beyond funding Australian hypersonics-related research and development, AUKUS's focus on artificial intelligence, quantum technologies and advanced cyber capabilities, in addition to nuclear propulsion, suggests that Washington sees potential benefit in broadening the base of technological cooperation and co-development with its closest allies.

Responses

The ADF, which has slightly fewer than 60,000 regular personnel, has been described as a 'boutique' force.[54] In comparison with the armed forces of Asia's major military powers (China, India, Japan and South Korea) and even those of some Southeast Asian countries, it is small. Although well trained and highly capable, the ADF's force structure remains primarily configured to 'plug in' to a US-led military coalition rather than to conduct independent operations, other than on a limited scale. Ever since European settlement, Australia has always fought as part of a coalition, often in distant locations, and never independently. Its most famous battles were fought on land. These factors have combined to shape the Australian 'way of war', tending to project Australia's army to the forefront of national and strategic consciousness. For an island nation, surprisingly little thought (outside naval circles) has been given to maritime strategy or the defence capabilities that Australia needs against a primarily naval adversary.[55] This land bias appears to be breaking down within the ADF, as borne out by the large-scale investment in naval and air platforms over the past decade and the army's partial embrace of an amphibious role. But at the political level and in popular culture, there remains a lag in understanding the vulnerabilities that flow from being an island – even one that is continental in size.[56]

Although relatively small, Australia's armed forces possess some of the most advanced capabilities in their region. This is consistent with an unofficial but long-held force-planning objective of maintaining a capability 'edge' within Australia's neighbourhood. Hence, Australia's Department of Defence officially articulated its requirement, in 2015, for a 'regionally superior' future submarine.[57] Until the mid-1980s, Australia outspent the whole of Southeast Asia on defence. Yet even as Australia's economic weight declines relative to that of faster-growing countries in its region, the ADF's front-line equipment continues to undergo qualitative improvement. This is particularly true of the air force, which now deploys not only some of the same front-line platforms as the USAF and USN, but increasingly the same variants, as demonstrated by the current inventory of P-8A, F/A-18F *Super Hornet*, EA-18G *Growler* and F-35A *Lightning* II aircraft, as well as recent air-launched weapons acquisitions.[58]

The Defence Strategic Update (DSU) launched by the Australian government in July 2020, with an accompanying force-structure plan, signifies the biggest adjustment to Australia's defence policy settings since the 1980s, in effect superseding the 2016 Defence White Paper. An 'update' would normally carry less weight than a white paper. But the federal government's decision to circumvent the lengthy white-paper compilation process attests to the urgency of Canberra's assessment that the 'strategic environment has deteriorated more rapidly than anticipated'.[59] The gravity of the DSU was underlined by then-prime minister Scott Morrison and then-minister of defence Linda Reynolds, in their respective accompanying comments, the latter asserting that Australia is undergoing its 'most conse-quential strategic realignment' since the Second World War.[60]

The DSU posits three objectives for Australia's defence policy:

- 'to shape Australia's strategic environment'
- 'to deter actions against Australia's interests'
- 'to respond with credible military force, when required'.[61]

China is not specifically identified as a threat in the update. But the reference to countries that 'pursue their strategic inter-ests through a combination of coercive activities, including espionage, interference and economic levers' leaves little room for ambiguity that China is now the major strategic focus of Australia's defence planning.[62] The DSU also terminates one of Australia's longest-standing strategic policy settings: the assumption that Canberra would have a ten-year warning for emerging military threats. With the end of 'strategic warning time', the Australian government implicitly assumes that a military threat to Australia or its vital interests could materi-alise during the current decade. This aligns partially with the public prediction in 2021 by then-chief of the US Indo-Pacific

Command Admiral Philip Davidson that China could launch a military assault on Taiwan within six years.[63]

The defence update affirms a focus on potential threats to Australia and its 'immediate region', defined expansively from the northeast Indian Ocean, through maritime Southeast Asia to the Southwest Pacific, although notably excluding Northeast Asia. The update maintains the centrality of the US alliance, committing Australia to 'support the United States and other partners where Australia's national interests are engaged'.[64] In a more consequential shift, the update deems it 'essential that the ADF grow its self-reliant ability to deliver deterrent effects'.[65] Self-reliance is a theme with deep roots in Australia's defence policy, dating from the post-Vietnam War period and the 1976 Defence White Paper. As Australian strategist Stephan Fruehling has argued, self-reliance for Australia does not mean autarky in military affairs, which is unfeasible in light of Australia's deep dependence on the US for intelligence, technology and resupply. Instead, a posture of 'self-reliance in alliance', implying an ability to conduct military operations up to a certain threshold without direct combat support from the US, is a more realistic aspiration.[66] Such operations could be necessary in future: Washington's interests do not always align with those of Canberra. As was demonstrated during the Australian-led stabilisation operation in Timor-Leste in 1999, the two governments sometimes weigh the political costs of intervention differently.[67]

Australia is now developing a high-intensity conventional deterrence role for the ADF that focuses primarily on its own region. This represents a step change in defence strategy, albeit within the bounds of a deeper and more militarily integrated alliance with the US. This could be seen as a change to Australia's strategic personality, but perhaps more accurately, it represents a reversion to the outlook that prevailed in the mid-twentieth century, when Australia last faced significant regional military threats (from Japan during the Second World War, and from Indonesia in the 1960s). At the other end of the spectrum, the update refers to a need to develop deterrence against grey-zone threats, a reference that encapsulates the broad range of challenges that China poses to Australia's security below the threshold of armed conflict, including in the cyber domain. The Australian Signals Directorate (ASD) publicly attributed to China some recent cyber attacks, including a large-scale hack of Microsoft Exchange email-server software in 2021, which affected servers in Australia.[68] In addition, the ASD reportedly identified China's Ministry of State Security as the culprit behind an attack on Australia's parliament and its three largest political parties in the lead-up to the May 2019 general election.[69]

Capability enhancements

The capability enhancements mandated in the DSU reflect a basic judgement that Australia's armed forces lack the striking power necessary to deter attacks against Australia or challenges to its regional interests, as well as sufficient mass to respond effectively to grey-zone challenges. The DSU aims to transform Australia's strategic posture from one focused on continental defence and the relatively small-scale contribution of forces for coalition operations located far from Australia to deterrence focused on Australia's region. Funding of A$270 billion has been allocated for the 2020–30 period to strengthen defence capabilities, including those for long-range strike, cyber security and underwater surveillance.[70] The annual defence budget is set to rise from A$42bn in 2020–21 to A$74bn in 2029–30, with the share allocated to new equipment rising from 34% to 40%.[71] Whereas the DSU mandates only a modest increase of 800 personnel across the armed services, in March 2022 the federal government committed to a significant expansion of the ADF headcount from 60,000 to 'almost 80,000' by 2040.[72]

The ADF's force structure, which has remained remarkably constant since the 1960s, will not change significantly as a result of the DSU or China's growing military capabilities. But the government has committed to acquiring long-range strike weapons and boosting offensive cyber capabilities with the explicit intention 'to hold potential adversaries' forces and infrastructure at risk from a greater distance'.[73] An accelerated programme of major weapons acquisition has been rolled out in its wake. Australia's Department of Defence plans to procure several new systems, including the M142 High Mobility Artillery Rocket System (HIMARS) for the army, the AGM-158C Long-Range Anti-Ship Missile (LRASM) and the AGM-158B/B2 Joint Air-to-Surface Standoff Missile–Extended Range (JASSM–ER) for the air force, as well as the *Tomahawk* land-attack missile (TLAM) for the navy.[74] The defence update also emphasises the need for new sensors (including an integrated undersea surveillance system), enhanced secure satellite communications and logistics upgrades (including the supply and storage of specialised munitions and fuel).

Beyond these specific acquisitions, Australia is currently considering moves to expand its industrial capacity to produce advanced munitions and other defence equipment domestically.[75] The US Congressional Research Service has questioned the adequacy of precision-guided munition stockpiles,[76] and during wartime, Washington is unlikely to have sufficient industrial capacity to meet its allies' needs in addition to its own – a concern only reinforced since Russia's invasion of Ukraine.[77] A pre-AUKUS agreement with the US to jointly produce missiles could herald a trend towards deeper technological and industrial defence cooperation within the alliance.[78] While political obstacles to sharing technology between the US and Australia remain, the value of a US presidential endorsement for such sharing via AUKUS, in the full glare of global media publicity, could prove to be the key to creating more robust cooperation – including but not limited to the provision of US nuclear-propulsion technology.

Although the ADF will increasingly be well equipped under the plans set out in the DSU and the force-structure plan, the emphasis on maintaining Australia's qualitative edge in defence technology has, according to commentators such as Canberra-based academic Peter Hunter, created an 'exquisite' set of capabilities.[79] The resultant problem is that a small number of high-end defence platforms becomes too valuable to be risk-worthy in high-intensity combat, unless fighting as part of a traditional US-led coalition. The existing force could be expanded in a time of acute strategic tension or conflict, but concern is likely to remain that it is too small to deter threats credibly or to respond effectively if Australia is forced to fight alone or with only limited assistance from the US. However, the DSU recognises that upgrading defence capability, in isolation, is insufficient to meet China's strategic challenge. This recognition steers the DSU away from another prominent theme in Australia's strategic discourse, the notion that 'Fortress Australia' can be defended independently.[80] Acknowledging that Australia's regional military heft will remain limited, the DSU emphasises the importance of building defence relationships and security links with 'partners whose active roles in the region will be vital to regional security and stability, including Japan, India and Indonesia'.[81] Further to the DSU, in August 2022 the new Labor government led by Prime Minister Anthony Albanese announced a Defence Strategic Review, which is mandated to 'examine force structure, force posture and preparedness, and investment prioritisation, to ensure Defence has the right capabilities to meet our growing strategic needs'.[82] The review is scheduled to conclude and present its findings in early 2023.

The Australian navy and deterring China

The RAN and the RAAF are likely to bear primary responsibility for conventional deterrence against China. They are also the most obvious sources for any Australian contribution to a US-led military coalition in case of a major regional war involving China. The RAN is currently in the middle of its biggest re-equipment programme since 1945. It has acquired three *Hobart*-class air-warfare destroyers, based on a Spanish design and equipped with the US *Aegis* combat system. A total of nine new British-designed *Hunter*-class frigates, originally optimised for anti-submarine warfare (ASW), is slated to replace the German-designed *ANZAC*-class frigates first introduced in the 1990s but extensively modernised, including with the CEAFAR active phased-array radar.[83] Once introduced into service from the early 2030s, the *Hunter* class will be closer to destroyers in size and capability, with a reported displacement of 8,800 tonnes.[84] Dogged by design and displacement issues, however, the start date for the construction of the *Hunter* class has been delayed until at least 2024.[85] Once the new frigates are in service, in combination with their MH-60R helicopters, they promise to significantly boost Australia's ASW capability.[86] This is important for sea-control functions, including the protection of strategic supplies to Australia from submarine attack. The frigates would also allow Australia to contribute, along with the US and Indian navies, to an ASW division of labour in the eastern Indian Ocean. Such a strategy is already suggested by the pattern of multinational naval exercises in the region.[87] Australia operates P-8A maritime-patrol aircraft that are fully inter-operable with similar USN and Indian Navy aircraft. With important supplemental capacity from India, this arrangement would represent a return to a more traditional geographical division of labour in the naval arena, resembling a scaled-up version of the Radford–Collins Agreement of 1951, in which the US and Australian navies (the latter also representing the British Royal Navy and the Royal New Zealand Navy) agreed on a division of operational responsibilities along geographical lines within the so-called 'ANZAM' (Australia, New Zealand and Malaya) region.[88]

While the RAN's surface capabilities are increasing in terms of vessel tonnage and the potency of onboard systems, Australia's surface fleet has for several decades remained more or less constant in terms of the number of hulls and ship types. Australia's latest surface combatants carry a relatively small load of anti-air and anti-ship missiles, mostly in vertical-launch cells that cannot be reloaded at sea. They must traverse long distances from their main bases at Sydney and Fremantle to their likely areas of operation. Even Darwin is almost a week's steaming from each of those bases.

The RAN's capacity to engage in sustained high-intensity naval combat at a distance from Australia is heavily constrained. Australia's last aircraft carrier was decommissioned in 1980. Since 2015, the navy has operated two Spanish-designed *Canberra*-class landing helicopter docks (LHDs). Although these outwardly resemble light aircraft carriers, there are no plans to retrofit them to support F-35 operations (as has been partially completed for Japan's *Izumo*-class helicopter carriers).[89] Instead, Australia's two 'flat-tops' are likely to continue serving as helicopter-equipped amphibious assault ships. However, they could carry long-range armed uninhabited aerial vehicles (UAVs) in the future, which would go some way to make up for the RAN's lack of fixed-wing air cover beyond the range of land bases. Nonetheless, the survivability of Australia's LHDs in naval combat against the PLA's far bigger array of surface-, air- and submarine-launched anti-ship capabilities would still be in doubt.

The ADF's most survivable offensive arm in any high-intensity conflict involving China is its submarine force, which is characterised by substantial range and firepower and can be employed on anti-ship, ASW, intelligence-gathering (and, prospectively, land-attack) missions. The submarine's primary purpose is sea denial. Being highly complex and expensive to build, renewing the submarine force has been the most fraught area of the ADF's modernisation. These troubles date back to the development history of the *Collins*-class submarines in the 1990s, six of which eventually entered service between 1996 and 2003. From 2026, the *Collins* class will undergo a 'life-of-type extension' programme, intended to provide a further decade of service.[90] The current plan, which is the centrepiece of AUKUS, is to replace the *Collins* class with at least eight British- or US-designed nuclear-powered submarines. A consultation period of up to 18 months is now under way to settle on a US or British design and supplier. AUKUS triggered the abrupt termination of Australia's A$90bn 2016 contract to produce a bespoke, conventionally powered version of France's *Barracuda*-class SSN, to be known as the *Attack* class.

The Australian government's dramatic move to scale up its submarine requirement to nuclear propulsion was made primarily on strategic grounds in light of its assessment of China's growing threat to regional security and a concomitant desire to upgrade Australia's deterrent capabilities. The decision to rescind the French contract without a successor yet in place was Canberra's sovereign decision to make, but it was also arguably a sign of strategic desperation – a conviction that the ADF urgently needed a major boost to its offensive capabilities to deter Chinese aggression in the future. Much remains uncertain about Australia's future SSNs, not only whether the Australian government will opt for a British or US design, but also when the first SSN will enter service. The new Labor government has reconfirmed its intention to build the entire fleet in South Australia, despite the Australian defence industry's lack of experience with SSNs and continuing reliance on the US and/or the UK to supply the naval reactors and propulsion system for each boat. With an approximate launch date for the first new-built Australian SSN in the late 2030s, or possibly later, the risk of a submarine capability gap has increased, given that the *Attack* class was projected to begin entering service around 2035. Unless a new class of diesel-electric submarines, long-range uninhabited underwater vehicles or some other mitigating capability, such as US and UK submarines forward-based in Australia, is introduced in the interim, Australia will be reliant on the six ageing *Collins*-class boats as the mainstay of its maritime deterrent posture into the 2040s.

Nonetheless, the decision to commit to nuclear propulsion promises, eventually, to deliver a quantum leap in capability, allowing Australia's navy to project power across much of the Indo-Pacific, including within the first island chain, where China's navy would be concentrated and most vulnerable in the early stages of any major war. The primary combat mission of Australia's nuclear-powered submarines, according to French analyst Mathieu Duchâtel, is likely to be 'operations against Chinese surface ships and submarines, to exploit the weaknesses of the People's Liberation Army's (PLA) anti-submarine warfare technologies'.[91] This could potentially extend to a 'hunter–killer' role against the PLAN's fleet of SSBNs. It is possible that some of China's SSBNs would use deep waters close to the Philippines as staging posts on the way to launch areas in the Pacific during a crisis or in the early stages of a war.[92] Their JL-2 submarine-launched ballistic missiles do not currently possess the range to hit US continental targets from the South China Sea.[93]

Australia's conventionally powered *Collins*-class submarines can already operate in the South China Sea and further north, but their endurance is limited. Nuclear submarines will offer major advantages because their greater submerged speed will halve transit times to combat stations and they will be well suited to escort high-value assets such as aircraft carriers and amphibious assault ships. Their submerged endurance is practically unlimited, which also reduces risks of detection. The gains that an SSN brings in terms of time to, and time on, station are highly beneficial in view of Australia's geography. Nuclear-powered attack submarines, which are much larger (around 7,500 tonnes submerged for the Royal Navy's *Astute* class and 9,000 tonnes for the USN's *Virginia* class) than the cancelled 4,900-tonne *Attack*-class boats, would pack a formidable punch in terms of anti-ship and other weapons. It is likely that they will be armed with TLAMs or successor systems. Land attack was not originally a requirement for the cancelled *Attack*-class boats, but the acquisition of TLAMs for the *Hobart*-class destroyers, announced at the same time as AUKUS, appears to presage Australia's interest in developing a 'deep strike capability against Chinese military infrastructure'.[94] The overall capability enhancement that the future SSN force represents, in conjunction with their long-range missiles, could move Australia from a sea-denial posture to something significantly more ambitious, incorporating an element of deterrence by punishment against Chinese mainland targets.[95]

A fleet of eight Australian SSNs would also provide a substantial adjunct to the United States' undersea capabilities in the Indo-Pacific; the US Navy's own SSN inventory is projected to decline to a nadir in the early 2030s, when the *Los Angeles* class is retired.[96] Supplementing the USN's SSN fleet would fit within the traditional Australian template of coalition warfare should Canberra opt to support the US in a conflict against China over Taiwan or in the South China Sea. The obvious problem, however, is that Australia's SSN fleet may not be fully constituted until the mid-2050s. According to Duchâtel, Australia's decision to acquire SSNs signals a broader ambition to integrate Australia more closely within a US deterrence posture directed at China:

> By acquiring SSNs, the Australian government is clearly expressing its intention to operate far from the coast. The Australian Navy is consequently reconsidering its priorities. It is turning to power projection scenarios in the South China Sea and the Taiwan Strait, with the ambition to influence China's future strategic calculations. In other words, acquiring SSNs places the Australian Navy at the heart of the new deterrence posture that the United States is building in the Indo-Pacific.[97]

The main purpose of this heightened Australian deterrence posture is to influence the risk calculations of China's leadership about the use of military force. The ADF lacks the mass of Japan's Self-Defense Forces, but nuclear-powered submarines with the capability to interdict China's resource supply routes across the Indian Ocean, and/or to loiter undetected off China's coastline, sinking Chinese warships and submarines and striking PLA bases directly, might alter Beijing's calculus concerning the use of force to achieve national objectives. Canberra's decision to lock itself into a long-term strategic partnership with the US and UK on nuclear submarines signals the reinforcement of Australia's alliance with the United States. This signal appears to have been amplified by Canberra's decision to allow American and British attack submarines to operate from HMAS Stirling, among other enhancements to the US military posture in Australia.

In addition, Australia's SSNs would constitute a potent stand-alone offensive capability, in the unlikely, but not unthinkable, scenario that China exerts military pressure on Australia directly and US combat support is unavailable because of urgent commitments elsewhere. Whether US- or UK-supplied, the naval reactors that power Australia's SSNs will run on highly enriched uranium and so will not need to be refuelled. Australia would still rely on external through-life support for its submarines, but it is already highly dependent on US technical support for much of its front-line defence capability, as well as for intelligence. In almost all conceivable scenarios, even if the US stayed out of a conflict militarily, it would be very unlikely to withhold logistical and intelligence support from Australia. Canberra would therefore retain its operational autonomy to use submarines in self-defence against China or other potential adversaries.

The role of Australia's air force
Until 2010, the RAAF had a long-range strike capability in the form of its F-111C force, but its current front-line inventory, based on the F-35A, F/A-18F and EA-18G, is constrained by a more limited range and the vulnerability of its in-flight refuelling aircraft. Australia's relatively large fleet of 72 F-35As would provide a potent, fifth-generation aircraft capability in a future conflict involving China, but their limited range is an obvious constraint unless operating from forward bases within the first island chain. The EA-18G squadron provides a potent electronic-warfare capability; another squadron equipped with the E-7A *Wedgetail* operates in the airborne early-warning and control role. The air force has an integral role in maritime

warfare, as it operates Australia's 12 P-8A maritime-patrol and anti-submarine aircraft: these provide significantly improved capability over the AP-3C *Orions* that they replaced, including the ability to deliver AGM-84 *Harpoon* LRASMs and mines. The RAAF has operated P-8As from Brunei, Malaysia, the Philippines and Singapore, suggesting an operational focus on intelligence collection and forward-based ASW operations in the South China Sea. From 2023, the P-8As will be complemented in the maritime-patrol role by a small number of MQ-4C *Triton* high-altitude, long-endurance UAVs.

In the long term, one possibility for an aerial long-range strike capability could be the B-21 *Raider* bomber. If the US agreed to export this aircraft after inducting it into USAF service, which is by no means a foregone conclusion, it could conceivably be delivered to Australia earlier than the new submarines, ensuring that Australia has a front-line platform for long-range strikes within this decade. However, its huge cost and doubts about the long-term ability of large, airborne stealth platforms to evade detection make this option unlikely, especially now that Australia has committed itself to the Herculean task of acquiring SSNs.

Australia's army
Compared with the navy and air force, Australia's army is less relevant to the military equation with China. Over the past decade, it has developed a limited amphibious capability but, with only one battalion currently dedicated to amphibious operations and without any integral air support beyond attack helicopters, this capability appears more appropriate for relatively small-scale interventions in lightly defended environments such as the Southwest Pacific. This is not to say that the army will not operate or engage in combat in locations away from Australia, or that China and the PLA would be

irrelevant to future ADF stabilisation or humanitarian operations that involve a substantial land-based component in Australia's immediate neighbourhood. But army-led interventions in the Middle East or elsewhere beyond Asia seem likely to become rarer since the US-initiated withdrawal from Afghanistan in 2021. Instead, Australia's army, including its special forces, is likely to be assigned responsibility for long-range littoral defence and other maritime-linked missions – analogous to the role of and possibly in conjunction with the USMC, as it reconfigures to 'stand-in' forward operations in support of the USN within the first island chain.[98] Australia's planned acquisition of HIMARS, a system also used by the USMC, is instructive in this regard, as it seemingly points towards a similar logic for Australia's army. Since the DSU was released, Australia's defence department has allocated A$500 million for a separate land-based anti-ship missile system, suggesting that plans to integrate ground forces into the defence of Australia's maritime approaches and coastline are already well advanced.[99] The army will also play an offensive cyber role and continue to contribute special forces to joint operations.

Nuclear weapons

The DSU re-emphasises Australia's long-standing policy of relying on the United States for extended nuclear deterrence. The Morrison government made clear that, while Australia will acquire nuclear-powered submarines, it 'has no plans to acquire nuclear weapons' and will continue to be bound by its obligations under the Nuclear Non-Proliferation Treaty.[100]

US nuclear coverage was not explicitly extended to Australia during the Cold War. Compared with guarantees extended by Washington to Japan and South Korea, which face more immediate sets of nuclear threats, the United States' extended nuclear-deterrence commitments to Australia are still less clearly defined. This has not been a point of tension between Washington and Canberra for the most part, because nuclear threats to Australia have been perceived to be minimal.[101] During the 1950s, the government led by prime minister Robert Menzies considered acquiring nuclear weapons from the UK.[102] However, the nuclear option has been 'off the cards' since the 1970s due to strong domestic opposition in Australia, which has extended even to the development of a civil nuclear-power industry. Canberra has adopted a robust diplomatic line against nuclear testing and proliferation. Domestic anti-nuclear sentiment has recently lessened – public-opinion polls now suggest that there is close to majority acceptance of nuclear propulsion for Australia's future submarines.[103] However, there is no domestic consensus in favour of Australia acquiring nuclear weapons. The DSU says simply that 'only the nuclear and conventional capabilities of the United States can offer effective deterrence against the possibility of nuclear threats against Australia'.[104] However, if Australia faced a more clearly threatening security environment, involving either a direct military challenge or a threat of nuclear blackmail from China, or a wholesale collapse of confidence in the US as a security guarantor, domestic public and political opinion could change, as it already has with regard to nuclear propulsion.

Although Australia lacks a civil nuclear-energy programme, it has long maintained an experimental nuclear reactor at Lucas Heights in suburban Sydney. This is essentially a hedging of Australia's nuclear 'bets' in human-capital terms, given the long lead times necessary to assemble the scientific base required for the production of fissile materials, weapons design and development. Australia possesses uranium ore in abundance. But it lacks the capability to produce fissile material or a reliable means to deliver a nuclear weapon over distance. The Morrison government said that it had no interest in developing

a civil nuclear-energy programme. The new Labor administration appears similarly uninterested. Unique among SSN
operators, Australia plans to acquire nuclear-powered submarines without control over the nuclear-fuel cycle.

The Australian strategist Rod Lyon has estimated that it would
take Australia at least 15 years to acquire a nuclear-weapons capability independently.[105] This could be accelerated with assistance
from another nuclear-weapons state, such as the UK or the US.
The academic Hugh White has suggested that (as in the cases of
France and the UK) Australia would need four nuclear-armed
submarines equipped with either ballistic or cruise missiles to
ensure a sea-based second-strike capability and that the approximate annual cost of maintaining a sea-based national nuclear
deterrent would be A$20bn.[106] The start-up costs associated
with educating and training a nuclear workforce, and creating
the physical infrastructure for the production and handling of
fissile material would be a quantum higher. Australia's track
record of indigenous weapons development (for example, of
diesel-electric submarines and air-defence destroyers) bodes
poorly in terms of both the time and the money that would be
required. Australia might be able to reduce both the development time and the costs of a nuclear deterrent by avoiding the
'gold-plated' submarine-based option and choosing instead to
plan for a land-based, road-mobile missile system, which could
be adequate for Australia's needs given the country's abundant
strategic depth. Alternatively, some of Australia's future SSNs
could be repurposed with relative ease for a basic but functional
nuclear deterrence role *if* Australia acquired nuclear-tipped
cruise missiles, either developed indigenously or supplied by
the US. However earnest Australia's diplomatic assurances
about non-proliferation appear in the early 2020s, the potential
for its SSNs to serve as a rapid 'breakout' platform for nuclear
deterrence should not be dismissed.

Ultimately, the logic of Australia's ability to deter China with only a conventional military force depends on the continued credibility of nuclear deterrence being extended by the US to its allies. Australia's decision to join AUKUS in 2021 represented a 'doubling down' on the US alliance in military and technology terms. Nevertheless, a mature SSN programme, in the 2040s, could be a hedge against a strategic requirement for an independently operated Australian sea-based nuclear deterrent, potentially at short notice.

Conclusion

In the hard-security realm, China is increasingly the focus of Australia's defence planning. Canberra has recently reordered its defence and alliance policy settings in response to the rising potential for China to exert military pressure, indirectly or directly, against Australia's interests. Under the DSU, Australia has committed itself to boost its conventional deterrent capabilities significantly and to concentrate on the defence of its immediate region with an intensity not matched in more than half a century. However, China's challenge is sufficiently extensive that it is simultaneously playing out as a challenge to Canberra's statecraft in the two sub-regions of the Indo-Pacific that are closest to Australia and most central to its security: maritime Southeast Asia and the Southwest Pacific.

CHAPTER FIVE

Australia's Indo-Pacific statecraft and Southeast Asia

This chapter and the one that follows together consider how China is influencing Australia's external statecraft across the Indo-Pacific macro-region, focusing on the key, adjacent sub-regions of Southeast Asia and the Southwest Pacific. These chapters identify Australia's major regional interests with respect to geopolitical competition with China, as well as its principal policy levers. Australia's security and defence policy efforts in the region are considered at multilateral, minilateral and bilateral levels, and their respective efficacy is assessed in relation to the scope of China's challenge; those areas where Canberra's responses have been deficient are identified. This chapter proceeds with an overview of the Australia–China strategic dynamic at the macro-regional level, before focusing on Southeast Asia.

Australia, China and the Indo-Pacific

Canberra is substantially increasing defence resources and strengthening its military cooperation with the United States, driven by the assessment that Australia faces a pressing strategic requirement to deter China militarily and in the cyber domain. Australia's 2017 Foreign Policy White Paper (2017 FPWP) says that 'military strength is a deterrent against armed coercion'.[1] According to one Australian commentator, the 2020 Defence Strategic Update (DSU) 'recasts the country's defence strategy as a regional-order-defending enterprise'.[2] Yet Australia needs substantially more than the enhanced capabilities of the Australian Defence Force (ADF) and an invigorated US alliance to maintain a set of balances favourable to its interests across the vast and increasingly multipolar Indo-Pacific macro-region. In particular, Australia seeks not only to deter armed conflict but also to ensure that China does not prevail in the ongoing competition for influence in the 'nearer region' of maritime Southeast Asia and the Southwest Pacific. For the latter challenge, Australia requires broad-based statecraft, utilising all the tools at the government's disposal, including aid, economic diplomacy, defence cooperation and conventional diplomacy.

Australia needs to shape its regional security environment in order to support its national interests but, as a medium-sized state, it sometimes struggles to maintain influence in its neighbourhood. According to Australian academic Rory Medcalf, 'Australia's interests are simply too extensive for it to protect and advance on its own'.[3] This is a problem common to all countries, but is 'particularly acute' in Australia's case due to its small population, large landmass and cultural dissimilarity from most of its neighbours.[4]

The 2017 FPWP contains numerous references to 'coercion', generally understood as a code word for China. The White Paper further judges that in 'parts of the Indo-Pacific, including in Southeast Asia, China's power and influence are growing to match, and in some cases exceed, that of the United States'.[5] China's new-found economic and military power, coupled with a revisionist posture towards the geopolitical and normative status quo in the region, have added urgency and purpose to Canberra's external interactions, reinforcing the need to strengthen relations with what it refers to as 'like-minded' countries in the Indo-Pacific.[6]

Some of Australia's non-military external policy levers, such as aid, have attenuated in the past decade. There is a wide-spread view that Australia's diplomacy, as delivered by the Department of Foreign Affairs and Trade (DFAT), is under-resourced.[7] DFAT has also been criticised in some quarters for being slow to recognise China's coercive and aggressive turn under Xi Jinping and the swing of the pendulum of Australia–China relations back from economics to geopolitics.[8] Australia's Department of Defence has not escaped criticism for inefficiencies and procurement failures,[9] but in contrast to DFAT, it has seen its budget climb rapidly over the past five years. Accordingly, defence needs to be considered not simply in terms of military capabilities, but as an integral arm of Australia's strategic policy through expanded defence diplo-macy, a greater forward military presence and more operations in the surrounding region, as foreshadowed in the 2016 Defence White Paper (2016 DWP) and the 2020 DSU.

Domestic factors have sometimes inhibited Australia's influ-ence in the region. Parochialism, including a preoccupation with domestic politics, is hardly unique to Australia's political class, but it has not helped the development of a coherent or well-communicated strategy towards the region. One manifestation of this decline is that there have been very few foreign-policy speeches (on China or other topics) in parliament during the last decade in contrast with the Cold War period. Frequent leader-ship changes since 2010, afflicting both Labor- and Liberal-led governments, have further taken a toll on the conduct of Australia's foreign policy in a region that places a premium on interpersonal diplomacy between national leaders. One of the most egregious policy shortcomings of the Liberal–National coalition government, in power from 2013 to 2022, was its failure to invest in maintaining and developing Australian universities' teaching and research on the surrounding region, including contemporary China, at a time when such knowledge has never been more needed in parliament, the bureaucracy, business and across Australian society.[10] The leadership of Australia's universities bears a share of the blame for this intellectual atrophy, specifically in regard to the study of the Chinese Communist Party and the People's Liberation Army (PLA), which it has shunned partly out of commercial self-interest, for fear of damaging student recruitment from China.

There is an isolationist streak in Australia's strategic debate that manifests itself in a 'Fortress Australia' mentality towards defence and border security. But there is another strategic tradition that recognises Australia's heavy dependence on the international system and the need for statecraft to shape its surrounding region by building supporting coalitions.[11] If China succeeds in persuading enough countries in the Indo-Pacific to defer to its strategic interests and accept their allotted station in a China-centred hierarchy, Australia's freedom to manoeuvre, including in the economic domain, will be heavily circumscribed, regardless of whether China directly threatens the Australian homeland. Australia alone lacks sufficient heft to be a strategic price-setter.[12] Without the support of other states, particularly in Asia, Canberra may feel it has no choice but to adopt a price-taking position and accommodate China to the detriment of its own interests.

In 2013, Australia was the first state (long before its Quad partners) to adopt the 'Indo-Pacific' as its regional conceptual framework, replacing the prevailing 'Asia-Pacific' nomenclature. As Medcalf writes, Australia's 'policy elites have sought to link its domestic values (and national identity) as a multicultural and liberal democracy with pragmatic national interests in an Indo-Pacific order based on mutual respect and the sovereign equality of nations'.[13] Behind this reframing of the region's geography was a pragmatic desire to bring 'India to the Asia Pacific' as a counterbalance to China.[14] After decades of ambivalence and occasional bouts of strategic suspicion towards New Delhi, in the 2017 FPWP, Canberra upgraded India to 'the front rank of Australia's international partnerships'.[15] This process had started 12 years earlier, when Australia backed India's entry into the 18-member East Asia Summit (EAS) in 2005 to bring greater balance and diversity to that forum, which includes all of Canberra's key partners in the region. New Delhi's value as a defence partner to Australia is currently understood in the more limited context of India being 'the pre-eminent maritime power among Indian Ocean countries', and not a significant military player in East Asia in its own right.[16] However, India's broader value as a diplomatic counterweight to China is central to Australia's vision for and, indeed, definition of the Indo-Pacific.

Canberra's adoption of an Indo-Pacific grand-strategic framing has not pleased everyone in Australia. Some critics have bemoaned dropping the 'Asia-Pacific' formulation, charging that this devalues Asia's central importance within Australia's foreign policy.[17] Notwithstanding its strategic merits as an encouragement to power balancing, the appeal of the wider Indo-Pacific formulation to Canberra is not unconnected with the central position it confers on Australia as an island continent with coastal frontage on both oceans – an upgrade from a previous age when Australia was consigned to the periphery of the world map.[18] A streak of strategic narcissism also lurks within Australian security debates, but it arises from fear and a sense of neglect due to the country's remote location relative to Europe and the United States.

The 2017 FPWP identifies four Indo-Pacific countries as key partners: India, Indonesia, Japan and South Korea.[19] It also highlights trilateral security-cooperation agreements with the US and Japan. Japan is singled out for the 'values and interests' it shares with Australia, as well as its high level of defence capability and technology. Canberra supports Tokyo's efforts 'to play a more active role in the security of the region'.[20] Since 2014, Australia and Japan have upgraded their bilateral security ties at a steady rather than spectacular pace, and relations were set back by Japan's failed bid in 2016 to supply Australia's future submarines.[21] It took more than seven years to conclude a military reciprocal-access agreement, which must still be ratified by the legislatures of both countries before it can enter into force.[22] But ultimately, the symmetry between Japan and Australia as close allies of the US, their deep-rooted economic relations and – above all – converging threat perceptions of China's intentions have combined to make Tokyo Canberra's most important Asian partner. A bilateral joint declaration on security cooperation in October 2022 confirmed the interest of both countries in reinforcing that partnership.

Unlike Japan, the 2017 FPWP does not characterise Indonesia in terms of either common values or shared threat perceptions, a circumscribed assessment that reflects numerous false dawns in bilateral relations with Jakarta. Canberra's ties with Jakarta are instead framed by the practical necessity of maintaining stable relations with a large and important neighbour. Indonesia can be considered as a *sui generis* defence and security priority for Australia for political reasons. But Jakarta has never been Canberra's most trusted regional partner and remains largely unreceptive to external influence. Scope for Indonesia to counterbalance China in active cooperation with Australia is extremely limited. According to an IISS analyst, writing at a high point in the bilateral relationship in 2012, 'while both Indonesian and Australian defence planners might need to take into account a "Chinese threat", this cannot be used as a basis for practical bilateral military cooperation'.[23] Australian strategic analyst Andrew Davies is slightly more optimistic regarding the possibility for closer defence coop- eration with Indonesia, but notes this would 'probably require a major strategic shock, such as overt hostilities in the South China Sea or significantly increased Chinese pressure on Indonesian interests'.[24] Indonesia's relatively limited defence capability, though growing, is also a practical constraint on the potential for military cooperation with Australia, beyond basic confidence-building. Nonetheless, Australia has an endur- ing strategic interest in ensuring that the archipelago is well defended against the projection of military force by a hostile power through Indonesia's sea and air space.

South Korea is identified in the 2017 FPWP as a fellow 'trade-oriented' democracy, which shares with Australia a common ally in the US.[25] But South Korea's relatively cursory treatment suggests that it remains more of an aspirational partner to Australia as compared to India, Indonesia or Japan. Seoul's tendency to hedge between the US and China is likely to limit its cooperation with Australia to less contentious issues, such as supply-chain security. South Korea perceives China through the lens of its geopolitical and military focus on North Korea, and is reluctant to push back against Beijing's wider regional behaviour for this reason.[26] This constraint on cooperation continues despite Seoul's experience of economic coercion from Beijing and signs of Seoul's desire to strengthen bilateral relations, such as former president Moon Jae-in's visit to Australia in December 2021. Australian academic Lesley Seebeck asks 'why Australia has not done more in the region, particularly given our traditional focus on engagement in it'. Her own answer to this question is:

'The reality is that the region has not offered firm ground for deep foundations.'[27] While this is too sweeping to apply throughout Asia, it largely holds true with regard to Indonesia and South Korea.

Notably, although it was drafted in the context of rising concern about China, the 2017 FPWP mentions Taiwan only once – a geographical reference to the Taiwan Strait, not to Taiwan as a political entity and like-minded democracy with a population of 24 million, similar to Australia's.[28] Until as recently as 2020, Canberra approached relations with Taipei with great caution so as not to upset Beijing. This is now changing, in step with the greater willingness demonstrated by the US to engage Taiwan within the constraints of its 'one China' policy, which is similar to Australia's. Canberra is also showing greater inclination to highlight Taiwan's centrality to regional security. In November 2021, then-defence minister Peter Dutton said it was 'inconceivable' that Australia would not join the US if it acted to defend Taiwan.[29] The joint statements from '2+2' meetings of Australian and US foreign and defence ministers since 2020 have featured Taiwan conspicuously, referencing 'Taiwan's important role in the Indo-Pacific region' and including a commitment to strengthen ties with the island as 'a leading democracy and a critical partner for both countries'.[30]

Taiwan still tends to receive reductive treatment in Australia's public discourse as a potential *casus belli* between the US and China,[31] and hence is seen mainly through the lens of the Australia–US alliance. Yet Taiwan is Australia's 12th-largest trading partner and a critically important source of microchips. Australia's Taiwan debate is underdeveloped principally because of Canberra's deference to Beijing's sensitivities.[32] That it is no longer taboo for politicians to mention Taiwan in public is testament to the turnaround in Canberra's relations with Beijing. Fear of offending China has lost its sting for Australia, and Taiwan could feature more prominently in Australia's future defence and foreign-policy white papers, including under a Labor government.

'Shared values' are frequently invoked by Australian policymakers when articulating Canberra's approach towards cooperating with countries in the region, although the values in question are often left undefined.[33] The 2017 FPWP asserts an explicit values-based connection to other Indo-Pacific democracies.[34] By contrast, the 2016 DWP employed the phrase 'rules-based' over 50 times to describe the regional and global 'order', while not mentioning the word 'liberal' once.[35] This lacuna in the latter document reflects the reality that most of Australia's neighbours and near neighbours are not 'liberal' by any definition. Despite marked differences in political systems, though, Canberra has little choice but to partner with countries like Singapore and Vietnam that share their security interests – including preserving the regional balance of power.

Australia's preferences in the Indo-Pacific are also influenced by its predisposition towards multilateralism. The 2017 FPWP defines the EAS as 'the region's premier political and security forum', despite the fact that it has registered no obvious diplomatic accomplishments since it was set up in 2005 to foster 'strategic dialogue and cooperation' among the ten member countries of the Association of Southeast Asian Nations (ASEAN) and its eight dialogue partners: Australia, China, India, Japan, New Zealand, Russia, South Korea and the United States.[36] Canberra has maintained faith in the EAS because it assembles all the major Indo-Pacific players, including China and the United States. Canberra's declaratory commitment to a foreign-policy vision for the region based on inclusivity continues despite the fact that China is intent on revising the very order that Australia and others wish to preserve. This dissonance has pushed Australia to rely increasingly on minilateralism and key bilateral partnerships in the region. As Medcalf writes, 'Australia has taken a lead in crafting creative new "small groups" for trusted security talks, and … combining these "minilaterals" with big bilateral partnerships and the inclusive regional organisations that Australia has done so much to propel'.[37] Yet these regional organisations, mostly ASEAN-centred and including the ASEAN Defence Ministers' Meeting–Plus (ADMM–Plus), the ASEAN Regional Forum (ARF) as well as the EAS, have fallen far short of the declaratory expectations that Australian governments have continued to vest in them.

ASEAN is extremely diverse in terms of its members' size, political systems and security interests, and Canberra's bilateral partnerships in Southeast Asia vary accordingly. Collectively, however, the ten-member grouping has for decades been the institutional cornerstone of Australia's multilateral diplomacy in Southeast Asia and the wider region. Chinese scholars are alert to the geopolitical context of Australia's diplomatic and military influence in the sub-region, assessing that for China, Australia's cooperation with Southeast Asian countries brings a certain pressure.[38] Australia was among the first partner countries to appoint an ambassador to ASEAN, in 2008. It has been an enthusiastic participant in the ADMM–Plus framework, co-chairing working groups in such functional areas as maritime security and counter-terrorism.[39] Canberra's engagement with ASEAN broke new symbolic ground in March 2018 with the first ASEAN–Australia Special Summit, hosted in Sydney by then-prime minister Malcolm Turnbull.[40] Yet the same fundamental disjuncture between declaratory ambition and strategic reality applies with regard to Australia's deference to ASEAN's 'centrality' to regional security: ASEAN has persistently failed as an institution to acknowledge, let alone grapple with, the challenge to its members' security posed by the emergence of a powerful and revisionist China.

The Quad, which brings together Australia, India, Japan and the US for leader-level discussions, has emerged as the most important minilateral forum in which Australia engages. Since its revival in 2017, the Quad has progressed from ad hoc gatherings of senior officials to the first Quad Leaders' Summit, convened in Washington in September 2021.[41] Rather than using the Quad as a mechanism for coordinating efforts to counter-balance China militarily, the leaders of participating countries have settled on a broad policy agenda for the Indo-Pacific, encompassing pandemic recovery, supply-chain security and initiatives to mitigate climate change. Statements issued by Quad leaders have maintained deference to ASEAN's regional diplomatic convening function and 'centrality'.[42] However, the fundamental purpose of the Quad's existence is to counterbalance China, a role that ASEAN has no desire or capacity to play. The upsurge in China's military coercion across the disputed Himalayan frontier in 2020 largely explains India's increased willingness to participate in the Quad and to develop a bilateral defence and security partnership with Australia.[43]

Since 2017, the same year that Australia's counter-interference 'pushback' took hold, Canberra has committed itself to the Quad with renewed vigour, in reaction to China's increased coercive behaviour across the region. Beyond the various 'ASEAN–Plus' frameworks, the Quad is currently the closest thing there is to an Indo-Pacific concert comprising Australia's closest partners. According to Australian academic Ashley Townshend, 'while the Quad is not on a trajectory to become a collective-security arrangement, the densification of combined activities among its members is the most promising avenue for advancing collective deterrence and defence policy in the Indo-Pacific'.[44]

While the Quad is steering away from a narrow security agenda, the quadrilateral format remains important for strategic signalling in other contexts. In November 2020, Australia's navy joined its Indian, Japanese and US counterparts as a participant in the annual *Malabar* joint exercise in the Indian Ocean for the first time since 2007.[45] India's consent to Australia's return to the *Malabar* drills had become a litmus test of India's support for Canberra's participation in reconstituted four-way cooperation.[46] Quadrilateral symbolism aside, Australia's bilateral navy-to-navy exercises and relationship with India had already far surpassed *Malabar* in terms of their levels of trust and sophistication.[47]

Australia and China in Southeast Asia

Southeast Asia is located at the confluence of the Indian and Pacific oceans, giving it geostrategic value – according to the 2017 FPWP – 'at a nexus of strategic competition in the Indo-Pacific'.[48] The South China Sea, with Southeast Asian countries to its west, east and south, sits at the geographical epicentre of the Indo-Pacific construct. For these reasons, Southeast Asia is a prime location for Sino-American competition for influence. Maritime Southeast Asia includes the major approaches to Australia from the north and is assessed by some Chinese scholars to be Australia's main area for external defence.[49] Maintaining access through the archipelagic part of the sub-region and preventing it from falling under the influence of a hostile power is a first-order priority for Australia's security.

Southeast Asia matters further to Australia as a significant economic bloc in the form of ASEAN, which had a combined population of 666m and a GDP of US$3.4 trillion in 2021.[50] Southeast Asia harbours important minilateral and bilateral security partners for Canberra, particularly the Five Power Defence Arrangements (FPDA), which centres on the Malay

Peninsula and has two Southeast Asian members, Malaysia and Singapore. Given the prevailing tendency in Southeast Asia – just as in Australia itself – to look north and east to China and the US respectively, rather than south, Canberra needs actively to strengthen its diplomatic and economic influence in order to gain attention. Australia also requires access for its armed forces, and ideally those of its allies, to operate in the region, so that it is in a position to monitor and meet threats before they manifest themselves on Australia's horizon. Canberra cannot afford to fall back on the defence of its own continent as a foundation for its security. A hostile power able to control Australia's maritime approaches would be able to apply immediate economic pressure from a distance.

In Southeast Asia, Australia has maritime boundaries with Indonesia and Timor-Leste. The importance of maintaining and safeguarding access through the Malay Archipelago (the islands that make up Indonesia and the Philippines, together with Brunei, PNG, Singapore and Timor-Leste), including major straits used for international navigation, is an important national interest. Canberra's official strategic thinking sees Malaysia and Singapore as part of Australia's northerly defensive bulwark.[51] This continuity in Australia's strategic perceptions is underlined by the commitment to maintaining a forward military presence there since 1945.

In addition to its overall strategic concern with Southeast Asia, Australia has more specific security interests, both direct and indirect, in the South China Sea.[52] How China behaves there is particularly important from Canberra's perspective in terms of any impact it may have on the credibility of the United Nations Convention on the Law of the Sea (UNCLOS), a key multilateral regime that serves Australia's interests as a maritime state with the world's third-largest exclusive economic zone (EEZ) and an acute dependence upon freedom of navigation for both merchant and naval vessels through archipelagic waters. According to former member of parliament David Feeney, one of the Australian Labor Party's most knowledgeable defence experts, 'the risk now is that China's successful annexation of the South China Sea will serve as a precedent in other disputes, such as the India–China border, the East China Sea and Taiwan'.[53]

Australia has not altered its long-standing neutrality on territorial disputes, but it has voiced opposition to China's excessive claims more explicitly and forcefully than before. In July 2020, Australia became the first non-littoral country to submit a *note verbale* to the United Nations specifically rejecting China's maritime claims based on Beijing's assertions of 'historic rights' and interests in the South China Sea.[54] The *note verbale* presented Canberra's position that Beijing's use of straight baselines is inconsistent with UNCLOS and that artificial structures do not generate jurisdiction over surrounding waters. Canberra's diplomatic activism on the South China Sea rated a specific mention as one of Beijing's '14 grievances' against Australia in November 2020.[55]

Australia's links with Singapore and Malaysia, both bilateral and via the FPDA, can be thought of as constituting a first tier for Canberra's strategic defence engagement with Southeast Asia, along with Australia's ties to Indonesia. Indonesia demands priority consideration as the most important Southeast Asian country for Australia in geopolitical terms, although it is not Canberra's closest defence partner. A second tier includes Brunei, the Philippines and Vietnam; as Southeast Asia's claimants in the South China Sea, these countries have China-related security concerns that overlap with Australia's. Since a military coup in 2014, Thailand has drifted from the second tier closer towards the third, as it appeared to some observers that the country, while still a US ally, was more willing to accommodate

China as the region's rising power.[56] However, since the restoration of an elected government in 2019, Thailand's relations with the US and the West have marginally improved. Cambodia, Laos and Myanmar make up the third tier of essentially continental Southeast Asian countries that are less important for Australia's strategic interests.

Judging Australia's level of influence in Southeast Asia is subjective and contextual. Australia cannot compete on a par with China given the disparity in resources. According to the former head of the Australian Strategic Policy Institute, Peter Jennings, Canberra has been 'caught flat-footed with the volume of Chinese money' in Southeast Asia and is losing influence because its diplomacy is under-resourced.[57] Foreign Minister Penny Wong, whilst in opposition as the shadow foreign minister, accused Scott Morrison's government of 'constant neglect' towards Southeast Asia that 'undermines our own national interest'. She further warned that aid 'for Pacific partners shouldn't come at the expense of an ongoing step down in Southeast Asia'.[58] Some Australian think-tank analysts have echoed Wong's charge that Canberra's policy 'step up' in the South Pacific has diverted resources that could have been used to bolster Australia's influence in Southeast Asia, a more geopolitically consequential sub-region.[59] Australia's government has also been criticised for being slow to furnish pandemic-related assistance to Indonesia and other Southeast Asian countries, drawing negative comparisons with China's prompt provision of vaccines and active pandemic diplomacy.[60]

Recent developments, however, suggest a different trajectory. In November 2020, at the ASEAN–Australia summit, then-prime minister Scott Morrison announced an aid package of US$383m for Southeast Asia.[61] This followed significant commitments already pledged under the May 2020 'Partnerships for Recovery' initiative supporting pandemic-relief efforts across the Indo-Pacific.[62] The record of recent Australian ministerial and senior-official visits suggests a considerable investment in high-level diplomatic engagement with Southeast Asia across the gamut of foreign-policy concerns. The coronavirus pandemic sharply curtailed official travel overseas, but several ministers, including the prime minister, visited Southeast Asia in 2020–21. Then-trade minister Dan Tehan travelled to the sub-region in September and November. The defence and foreign ministers attended a '2+2' meeting in Jakarta in September 2021, before flying on to New Delhi, Seoul and Washington. And Australia's vice-chief of the Defence Force travelled to Jakarta, Singapore and Kuala Lumpur, as the prime minister's personal envoy, for consultations following the announcement of the Australia–United Kingdom–United States (AUKUS) security partnership. Prime Minister Anthony Albanese visited Southeast Asia twice during his first six months in office, while Penny Wong and other cabinet ministers have travelled frequently to the sub-region.

Minilaterals and bilaterals

The FPDA, in place since 1971, anchors Australia's defence engagement and forward commitment in Southeast Asia and is the sub-region's longest-established minilateral defence-cooperation framework. Although the FPDA has a low public profile, including in Australia, its persistence over half a century, as a 'non-provocative form of hedging and confidence building', underlines its usefulness to all its parties, including as an enabler for Australia's military access to Southeast Asia and the South China Sea.[63]

The FPDA is not a treaty, but a deliberately less formal set of 'arrangements' to encourage consultation in case of an armed attack on peninsular Malaysia or Singapore. Beyond designated FPDA exercise areas, it does not extend formally to East Malaysia or the South China Sea. The FPDA provides a political context for Australian access to Butterworth air base in Malaysia's Penang state and facilities in Singapore, as well as a framework for Australia to consult with the defence establishments of Malaysia and Singapore at senior-command and intelligence levels. According to a 2020 joint statement by the FPDA's defence ministers, its 'core focus' remains on conventional warfare.[64] The FPDA's schedule of regular exercises brings together the armed forces of all five member countries to focus on combined-arms activities in ground, sea, air and now cyber domains.[65] Following the end of the United Kingdom's forward-defence presence in Southeast Asia (apart from its garrison in Brunei) in 1976, Australia's relative military weight in the FPDA became more significant.

The FPDA was originally based around a common air-defence framework for peninsular Malaysia, but since 2000 has broadened into the Integrated Area Defence System (IADS). The multinational headquarters of the IADS is at Butterworth and is headed by a two-star Australian air-force officer; an Australian Army rifle company provides base security.[66] Under a bilateral arrangement with Malaysia dating back to 1980, Australia's *Operation Gateway* involves surveillance flights over the eastern Indian Ocean and South China Sea from Butterworth air base.

Australia also benefits from access to Singapore's Paya Lebar air base, and naval berths and a logistics facility at Sembawang, operated by the British Royal Navy.[67] Under the auspices of the FPDA and through bilateral security arrangements, boosted since 2015 by the Australia–Singapore Comprehensive Strategic Partnership, Australia uses Singapore as a Southeast Asian forward-operating location that complements Butterworth. Since 2020, Paya Lebar has become more important as a facility supporting Australian reconnaissance flights by AP-3C electronic-intelligence aircraft as well as P-8A *Poseidon* maritime-patrol aircraft.[68] These flights are helping the ADF and its partners to maintain their picture of the growing PLA (and, particularly, PLA Navy) presence and activities in the South China Sea, including its forward bases in the Paracels and Spratlys. This intelligence-based picture supports the operational deployment of Royal Australian Navy ships and submarines to the South China Sea on presence patrols, sometimes sailing with US Navy task groups.

Australian maritime-patrol aircraft have also operated under bilateral arrangements with Brunei and the Philippines – in the latter case, since Australia provided non-combat operational support to the Philippine armed forces during the battle for Marawi City in 2017.[69] In 2020, an Australian maritime-patrol aircraft and, for the first time, a submarine visited Brunei.[70] In 2021, the first navy-to-navy talks took place between Australia and Brunei, spanning regional deployments and exercises, logistics and training. Australia and the Philippines concluded a bilateral logistics agreement in August 2021, and Australia is the only country apart from the US to have a status-of-visiting-forces agreement with the Philippines.[71]

This thickening web of access arrangements has enabled the ADF to operate from multiple locations around the South China Sea, so as to maximise its mission flexibility and avoid overstressing individual Southeast Asian partners. This applies in particular to Malaysia, which has sometimes shown ambivalence towards FPDA exercises within its EEZ, as well as marked diplomatic caution wherever China's perceived sensitivities are concerned.[72] Moreover, Malaysia is likely to continue distancing itself from any perceived counterbalancing against China. Former defence minister Hishammuddin Hussein's equivocal reaction to the AUKUS announcement in September 2021 highlighted the difference in strategic outlook between Canberra and Kuala Lumpur, Australia's oldest partner in Southeast Asia. Former prime minister Ismail Sabri Yaakob suggested that AUKUS would raise tensions and spark a regional arms race, in terms strikingly similar to those employed by China.[73] Soon after the AUKUS announcement, Hishammuddin said he would travel to Beijing for consultations, although these ultimately happened virtually.

Malaysia is also a territorial claimant and occupant of the Spratly Islands and, despite its sometimes accommodating approach towards Beijing, has found itself increasingly on the receiving end of China's maritime assertiveness, including illegal oil- and gas-exploration activity within Malaysia's EEZ, off the coast of Sarawak state. In May 2021, a formation of 16 Chinese military-transport aircraft flew close to Sarawak's coastline, in a possible instance of coercive signalling, probably triggered by Malaysian energy exploration in waters claimed by China.[74] Meanwhile, Malaysia's armed forces – lacking long-range maritime-patrol and electronic-intelligence aircraft of their own – continue to depend on shared Australian intelligence from *Operation Gateway* flights.[75] It is in Malaysia's continuing interest to maintain close defence relations with Australia through the FPDA and bilaterally. Bilateral defence links with Australia remain generally strong and the ADF seconds an officer to the Malaysian Armed Forces headquarters to help organise a joint programme of exercises and training. Australia is the only country to have such an arrangement with Malaysia.

Australia's July 2020 DSU reaffirmed the direct connection of maritime Southeast Asia to Australia's defence. Subsequently, the ADF has accelerated the tempo of its deployments to the sub-region in parallel with Canberra's intensified diplomatic outreach. Then-defence minister Linda Reynolds visited Southeast Asia in October 2020, followed by her successor,

Peter Dutton, in September 2021.[76] During that month, as part of the ADF's annual *Indo-Pacific Endeavour* activity, a maritime task group composed of three ships visited Brunei, Malaysia, Singapore, Thailand and Vietnam.[77] Australia's *Indo-Pacific Endeavour* expeditionary activity started in 2017, following the 2016 DWP's promise to strengthen Australia's engagement with Southeast Asian armed forces.[78] Other Australian warships and aircraft deployed across the wider Indo-Pacific, including Southeast Asia, in 2020–21, exercising with forces from Canada, India, Japan, New Zealand, Singapore, the UK, the US and others. That the ADF sustained this effort despite the successive distractions of the 2020 domestic bushfire crisis (which required the mobilisation of a substantial part of the ADF), followed by the coronavirus pandemic, demonstrates the seriousness of Canberra's defence-engagement effort in Southeast Asia.

Australia's most important strategic relationship in Southeast Asia is with Indonesia, by virtue of that country's proximity to Australia, as well as its size and potential power. There is a clear rationale – founded in good part on the two countries' overlapping concerns about China – for Australia to pursue a close security partnership with its large neighbour, and there has been a succession of bilateral agreements to that end, since the conclusion of the 2006 'Lombok Treaty', officially known as the 'Agreement Between Australia and the Republic of Indonesia on the Framework for Security Cooperation'.[79] Relevant regular high-level official contacts now include '2+2' ministerial talks and an annual bilateral meeting involving the defence-force chiefs and heads of service.

Although the two countries have moved a long way towards overcoming mutual suspicions, bouts of political volatility continue to plague bilateral relations. The prickly reaction of Indonesia's foreign ministry to the AUKUS initiative points to the limits of potential strategic alignment,[80] despite the fact that China's maritime encroachments close to Indonesia's Natuna Islands in the South China Sea pose a more direct security concern for Jakarta than any faced by Canberra.[81] Indonesia is unlikely to grant preferential access to the ADF beyond what Jakarta legally guarantees in transit rights to all foreign navies and air forces through its archipelagic sea lanes and air space. However, Jakarta also probably understands that Australia's defence build-up and new initiatives such as AUKUS are not aimed at Indonesia. Defence Minister Prabowo Subianto's comment at the 2021 IISS Manama Dialogue that Indonesia understands and respects Australia's decision to enter into the AUKUS arrangement should allay Canberra's anxieties in this regard.[82]

The 2016 DWP recognised Singapore as Australia's 'most advanced' defence partner in Southeast Asia: uniquely in the sub-region, Singapore's armed forces possess capabilities that, overall, are comparable to the ADF's.[83] This makes Singapore an important defence partner to cultivate, in addition to its role as a host for forward-deployed ADF assets. Cooperation on intelligence and cyber security, as well as joint science and technology ventures, provides depth to bilateral defence and security relations. However, as a majority ethnic-Chinese city-state, Singapore has been cautious in relation to China, adopting a low-key posture of official reticence on the South China Sea since 2016, when it came under pressure from Beijing over its previously vocal diplomatic stance on the need to uphold international law and freedom of navigation. In that year, a number of Singapore Army armoured vehicles were impounded by authorities in Hong Kong during their shipment back to Singapore on a commercially chartered merchant ship, following training in Taiwan.[84] It is widely assumed that the Hong Kong authorities acted at Beijing's behest on this matter.

However, Singapore's most important strategic value to Australia is its facilitation of the ADF's forward presence, by providing access as well as a substantial degree of operational latitude to Australian and US forces staging through the city-state. Singapore thus tacitly supports the US and Australian contributions to maintaining the balance of power vis-à-vis China in Southeast Asia and the South China Sea, despite assuming some strategic risk in the process. From Australia's perspective, it is a highly beneficial arrangement. Singapore has a reciprocal interest in training its armed forces in Australia and, to that end, has funded a significant expansion of military facilities in Queensland that it has used since the 1980s.[85] Above all, Australia offers Singapore ample space to train and exercise its forces together in ways that are not possible elsewhere.[86]

The Australia–Philippines security relationship prospered to a surprising degree under the mercurial presidency of Rodrigo Duterte from 2016 to 2022. This was in part due to Australia's ability to present itself as a like-minded, regional US ally, without the historical and strategic baggage of the United States. Canberra's offer of military training and intelligence support to Manila during the 2017 siege of Marawi City was an effective example of Australia using counter-terrorism as a foundation on which to strengthen strategic ties, including access to facilities for visiting ADF ships and aircraft. Reflecting these deep ties, in September 2021, then-foreign affairs secretary Teodoro Locsin Jr endorsed Australia's decision to acquire nuclear-powered submarines. In remarkably candid terms by contemporary Southeast Asian standards, he suggested that the 'enhancement of a near abroad ally's ability to project power should restore and keep the balance rather than destabilise it', and admitted that 'ASEAN member states, singly and collectively, do not possess the military wherewithal to maintain peace and security in Southeast Asia'.[87]

Among Australia's other defence and strategic relationships in Southeast Asia, the one with Vietnam has been among the fastest growing, albeit from a low starting point. In 2018, the Royal Australian Air Force flew Vietnamese peacekeeping troops to South Sudan, Vietnam's first such deployment. This airlift support has since continued.[88] Bilateral cooperation includes a naval and non-military maritime-security component, including visits by Australian warships as well as joint training activities involving the two countries' navies and special forces.[89] Despite Vietnam's perception of the Chinese threat to its interests in the South China Sea, where no other Southeast Asian claimant is as vulnerable, Hanoi's emphasis on strategic self-reliance tempers the possibility of extensive defence cooperation with Australia or other countries. Hanoi imposes a low ceiling on the level of defence cooperation that it is willing to undertake with the US and its regional allies, such as Australia, partly to avoid provoking China. Basing of foreign military forces in Vietnam remains anathema. Nevertheless, Vietnam tacitly supports Australia's contribution to maintaining the existing balance of power and is prepared to cooperate with Australia diplomatically and, to a lesser extent, militarily.[90] Australia's defence relationship with Thailand has deeper roots than that with Vietnam, and Australian forces participate regularly in the annual Thai–US *Cobra Gold* military exercises; however, this relationship lacks the strategic underpinning of shared threat perceptions towards China.[91] In comparison, Canberra's security ties with Cambodia and Laos are more limited, while defence cooperation with Myanmar was suspended shortly after the February 2021 military coup in Yangon.

Finally, Timor-Leste fits within the geographical definition of Southeast Asia, though it still sits peculiarly outside ASEAN. It holds significance for Australia's security as its closest neighbour in Southeast Asia, just 650 kilometres from Darwin. The two countries share a maritime boundary in energy-rich waters, which was successfully renegotiated in March 2018.[92] Timor-Leste's importance was underscored by Canberra's decision to intervene militarily – at substantial risk to its relations with Indonesia – after the 1999 referendum vote in favour of independence and ensuing violence by pro-Jakarta militias. Despite Australia being instrumental in Timor-Leste's independence from Indonesia, the relationship with Dili has since proven to be one of Canberra's trickiest to manage in Southeast Asia. In 2017, Timor-Leste accepted an offer from Australia to join the Pacific Maritime Security Program, including the donation of two *Guardian*-class patrol vessels, which are expected to enter service in 2023.[93] Previously, Dili had leaned diplomatically towards Beijing and purchased patrol boats from China. Beijing has reportedly offered to strengthen the small country's transport infrastructure.[94]

Conclusion

Southeast Asia is strategically the most important sub-region in Australia's immediate neighbourhood. Maintaining physical access and political influence there is essential for Australia's security. Although Canberra lacks the means to maintain a favourable balance of power in Southeast Asia without active US participation, Australia is sometimes preferred by countries in the sub-region that see it as a less censorious and demanding partner than Washington. India, Japan and the US have also affirmed their commitment to cooperate with Australia in Southeast Asia bilaterally, trilaterally and through the revived Quad.

There is a danger that Beijing's cold-shouldering of Canberra could stigmatise Australia to some extent in Southeast Asia, by raising the risks of association with a pariah in Beijing's view.

However, ASEAN is not a synonym for Southeast Asia and there is no overall Australian security relationship with the sub-region. Australia's most active security relationships remain those with Indonesia, Malaysia and Singapore. However, the potential for some Southeast Asian governments to distance themselves from Australia because of a perceived risk to their relations with China, combined with the ever-present potential for volatility in Australia–Indonesia relations, means that Canberra has no choice but to develop a broad base for its strategic policy towards the sub-region. Doubts about the political reliability of the US and mounting concerns about China's strategic intentions towards Southeast Asia have boosted Australia's standing with partners with which it has not in the past had strong defence and security relations: Brunei, Vietnam and especially the Philippines, which is moving closer towards first-tier status and is of particular geostrategic importance with regard to possible contingencies in Taiwan and the South China Sea. However, the significant gains in influence that China has made across Southeast Asia over the last two decades are unlikely to be reversed easily, and will continue to complicate and constrain Australia's more limited effort at statecraft in the sub-region, even in coordination with its Quad partners.

CHAPTER SIX

Competing with China in the Southwest Pacific

The Pacific Ocean, while including the scattered island groups of Melanesia, Micronesia and Polynesia, mostly comprises open water. The Southwest Pacific sub-region includes all of Melanesia, Australia's eastern and northeastern approaches, and major trade routes and lines of communication to North Asia, New Zealand and the United States. It is the closest sub-region to Australia's major population centres of Sydney, Melbourne and Brisbane. By this measure, Australia belongs more to the Southwest Pacific than to Southeast Asia. For several decades after the Second World War, Australia and New Zealand were the predominant states in this sub-region, but now their influence is being challenged by China. The Southwest Pacific matters critically to the Australia–China strategic dynamic because Beijing and Canberra compete more here than anywhere else. This is where they are most likely to clash directly.

The scattered Pacific archipelagos are separated by profound distances. Under the United Nations Convention on the Law of the Sea (UNCLOS), island states have acquired vast exclusive economic zones (EEZ) and, in some cases, archipelagic

seas that far exceed their land area. Ensuring maritime security is an imperative shared by island states in order to support
their economic viability, as well as to protect their defence
and security interests. Yet very few of the sub-region's states
independently possess the means to police their waters against
illegal fishing and other predations.

Southwest Pacific countries are not all micro-states. Papua
New Guinea (PNG) has a population of nine million, a large
landmass, a sovereign archipelagic sea and abundant natural
resources. Fiji has 900,000 people and is host to the secretariat of the Pacific Islands Forum (PIF), the most important
sub-regional grouping, among other multilateral institutions.
Pacific island countries have demonstrated in the past some
ability to exploit geopolitical rivalry to their advantage, and
micro-states such as Nauru and Tuvalu still have agency. But
the capacity of even the largest states in the Southwest Pacific is
extremely limited by their small size and relative remoteness.

Latent potential

For most of the period since 1945, the Southwest Pacific's strategic potential has lain dormant. During the Second World
War, much of Melanesia and Micronesia was the scene of
intense fighting between the United States and Japan, as both
sides employed island-hopping strategies, jostling for position within the second island chain, which extends from Japan
to New Guinea through the Northern Marianas, with Guam
as its centrepiece. Australia and its armed forces were deeply
implicated throughout this struggle, from the bombing of
Darwin, in February 1942, to the defensive battles of New
Guinea and the Coral Sea, to the final amphibious advance
into Southeast Asia.

The distances separating territory in the Southwest Pacific
impose onerous logistical burdens on all powers seeking to

maintain a military presence there. Even in peacetime, the strategic value of Pacific island territory remains strong, if latent. While Melanesia's positional importance was already waning towards the end of the Second World War – as the US pushed forward its strategic perimeter all the way to the first island chain – Guam and Micronesia continue to underpin the forward deployment of the US armed forces in the Western Pacific, as well as its long-range missile tests. Guam is the United States' defensive lynchpin in the second island chain and the most important US territory west of Hawaii. In 2020, Palau, which maintains close links with the US under a Compact of Free Association, indicated that it may agree to host new bases.[1] Washington's interest in buttressing its strategic position in the second island chain is steadily intensifying. Australia and the US have announced joint plans to upgrade and operate from PNG's existing naval facility at Lombrum on Manus Island, which was a US Navy fleet base during the Second World War. That Manus, at the foot of the second island chain, is again considered strategically important speaks volumes about the seriousness of China's perceived challenge to American paramountcy in the Pacific.

In the post-war era, Australia 'saw itself having particular responsibilities' in the Southwest Pacific, according to former director general of Australia's Office of National Assessments Allan Gyngell, in 'an informal division of allied labour'.[2] Even more so than in Southeast Asia, Washington 'look[s] to Australia to provide leadership' and maintain stability in the sub-region, argues former Australian member of parliament (MP) David Feeney.[3] The Pacific islands have not been immune to geopolitical competition since 1945, but it has been mostly non-military in nature. The longest-running manifestation of this competition has been the tug of war for exclusive diplomatic recognition between China and Taiwan. The Pacific islands currently account for four of Taiwan's 14 diplomatic allies: Marshall Islands, Nauru, Palau and Tuvalu. This is a bigger concentration of states that maintain diplomatic relations with Taiwan than in any other region. However, Beijing has recently made diplomatic gains: Solomon Islands switched diplomatic allegiance from Taiwan to China in 2019, followed swiftly by Kiribati, which has twice abandoned Taipei in pursuit of a better deal from Beijing. China also has diplomatic relations with Cook Islands, the Federated States of Micronesia, Fiji, PNG, Samoa, Tonga, Tuvalu and Vanuatu.

The Pacific islands are sometimes referred to colloquially in Australia as its 'backyard' or 'patch'.[4] Papua was a colony of Queensland even before Australia became a federation, while the larger territory of PNG (incorporating the former German New Guinea colony) remained under Australian rule until 1975. Australian governments, whether conversative- or Labor-led, continue to invoke a familial connection between Australia and neighbouring island states in the Southwest Pacific.[5] The sub-region has also been dismissed as a strategic backwater, although this deprecation has waned as a number of major powers have shown increased interest – not only China and the US but also India, Russia and the larger European states.[6] Pacific island countries are often characterised as 'fragile' states, part of an 'arc of instability' that makes up Australia's strategic periphery.[7] To critics, such terminology betrays patrician and hegemonic Australian attitudes.[8] Others view Australia as having neglected the sub-region,[9] focusing instead on threats and opportunities in Asia or on the alliance with the US. As hegemons frequently discover, the 'sweet spot' between devoting too much strategic attention and too little is elusive for Canberra in the Southwest Pacific.

Perceptions of condescension or neglect notwithstanding, Canberra still regards itself as the preponderant security provider in the sub-region, as demonstrated by the Australian-led, 14-year intervention in Solomon Islands (which then-prime minister John Howard ordered in 2003 over his foreign minister's objections), as well as the decision to reintervene to reinstate order, following riots in Honiara, the capital, in November 2021. When Australia has interceded militarily in the Southwest Pacific, it has usually been because broader factors were in play, including considerations regarding the US alliance. Howard decided to commit Australia's armed forces to Solomon Islands partly because of a perceived – in retrospect, wildly overblown – risk that al-Qaeda-linked terrorists could lodge themselves in failed states on Australia's periphery.[10] Less dramatic than intervening militarily, Australia has a long tradition of seconding officials, law-enforcement officers and jurists to Pacific island nations. Canberra has maintained its profile over many decades as the Southwest Pacific's largest aid donor, despite cutbacks to Australia's overseas assistance to other regions.

New Zealand, Australia's only formal treaty ally apart from the United States, is Canberra's most important defence and diplomatic partner in the Southwest Pacific, and the primary security and aid provider in parts of Polynesia. Australia and New Zealand are both founding members of the PIF. Wellington has been implementing its own Pacific 'reset' since 2018.[11] However, regarding China, Canberra's and Wellington's threat perceptions and policy settings are different. New Zealand, by and large, continues to 'hedge' between China and the United States, whereas Australia's behaviour is now firmly driven by the logic of power balancing. For example, New Zealand's then-prime minister Jacinda Ardern contended in July 2022 that 'China has a crucial role to play' in upholding the post-war international order, and that 'trade is a means of upholding shared values'.[12]

Australia has seen its influence in the Southwest Pacific ebb gradually over the past three decades, as Canberra's strategic and foreign-policy attention has been focused elsewhere and its relative economic weight has declined. Australia has never completely taken its eyes off the sub-region, participating in regional summits and maintaining continuity in defence engagement and maritime-security capacity-building. Malcolm Turnbull attended every PIF summit during his tenure as prime minister from September 2015 to August 2018. His successor, Scott Morrison, failed to attend in 2018, just as concern was intensifying in Australia about China's rising influence in the Southwest Pacific.

The perception that the sub-region has been overlooked by Canberra has proved impossible to staunch. In May 2018, then-deputy leader of the opposition Richard Marles criticised Australia's lack of leadership in the Pacific as the 'biggest blind spot' in Australia's national-security policy.[13] In a major speech, delivered six months later in Townsville, facing the Coral Sea, Morrison acknowledged that 'Australia cannot take its influence in the Southwest Pacific for granted. And sadly I think too often we have.'[14] As Morrison's term in office progressed, he invested more policy attention and committed more resources to the Pacific islands than his predecessor.

Shadow-boxing

China's profile in the Southwest Pacific, as a trading partner, source of investment and concessional lender, has grown rapidly from a low base. Until around 2015, in the context of flourishing bilateral Australia–China ties, Canberra viewed China's economic interest in (and also Chinese migration to) the Pacific as largely benign – more of an organic phenomenon than one centrally directed. On occasions when anti-Chinese violence broke out in the sub-region, as happened in the capitals of both Solomon

Islands and Tonga in 2006, Beijing's reliance on Australia's and New Zealand's assistance to evacuate People's Republic of China nationals appeared to augur a template for future security cooperation rather than the seeds of strategic competition. However, since then, serious questions have been asked about Beijing's strategic motivations in the sub-region, as well as Chinese Communist Party (CCP) attitudes towards the ethnic-Chinese diaspora in the Southwest Pacific. Graeme Dobell's 2018 assessment that 'Australia judges that Beijing has decided it wants to remake the order in the South Pacific' appears prescient.[15]

China's initial inroads, in terms of influence in the Southwest Pacific, came in Fiji following the military coup there in 2006. After Canberra imposed sanctions on the government led by Commodore Frank Bainimarama, Suva initiated a 'Look North' approach that maximised intergovernmental links with China. While Australia and New Zealand pared back their official contacts with Fiji, Beijing rapidly emerged as Suva's largest donor in the period 2013–15.[16] From around 2016, China began to intensify ties with other Pacific island states. Vanuatu became the object of particular attention from Beijing. In mid-2016, the renovation of the office of Vanuatu's prime minister was funded by a Chinese grant.[17] China also paid for the construction of the headquarters in Port Vila of the Melanesian Spearhead Group, an association of Pacific countries, excluding Australia and New Zealand, that includes security in its agenda and actively pursues cooperation with China.[18] Vanuatu became an early and enthusiastic supporter of China's Belt and Road Initiative (BRI) and conspicuously voiced support for China's position against the arbitral tribunal award obtained by the Philippines in the South China Sea, in July 2016.[19] In 2019, on his first official visit to China, Vanuatu's then-prime minister Charlot Salwai met President Xi Jinping and then-premier Li Keqiang, proclaiming that 'we can't wait for grants to come'.[20]

China has pursued defence relations with all three Southwest Pacific states possessing armed forces – Fiji, PNG and Tonga – as well as with Vanuatu, which has a paramilitary Mobile Force. Within the past three years, China has appointed military attachés to PNG and Fiji.[21] China has constructed new buildings and infrastructure, including for the Vanuatu government, and instituted training and officer exchanges across the sub-region. Chinese warships have made port calls, while the People's Liberation Army Navy's (PLAN) 'Peace Ark' hospital ship visited Fiji, PNG, Tonga and Vanuatu in the second half of 2018, ahead of Xi's visit to Port Moresby for the Asia-Pacific Economic Cooperation (APEC) summit. In a few cases, China has donated military equipment. In November 2017, China gave 54 military vehicles to the PNG Defence Force.[22] In late 2018, China donated a hydrographic research vessel to Fiji's navy.[23] It is not clear whether and on what basis data from survey operations will be shared with China, or whether its maritime authorities have any influence over the activities of the vessel.

Beijing has also sought close ties with Pacific island states in law enforcement; for example, Fiji concluded a cooperation agreement with Beijing's Ministry of Public Security in 2011 that encompasses training in China for Fiji's police officers. The desire to extradite fugitive Chinese citizens has pushed Beijing's law-enforcement cooperation efforts in a more assertive direction.[24] In February 2022, a detachment of China's People's Armed Police (PAP) arrived in Solomon Islands to provide anti-riot training to the local police, under a bilateral agreement concluded in late 2021, following a serious outbreak of violence in Honiara, which targeted the local ethnic-Chinese community. According to the Chinese embassy in Honiara, the PAP unit will 'cooperate with the embassy to conduct visits, and safety training for overseas Chinese and

Chinese-funded enterprises, so as to effectively protect the legitimate rights and interests of Chinese citizens and overseas Chinese'.[25] China is also funding the construction of a new police academy in Samoa.[26]

China's activities in the Southwest Pacific are a good barometer of its strategic ambition. Chinese military analysts have noted that because of their geography connecting the Indian and Pacific oceans, the Pacific island countries have a profound impact on the construction of the 21st Century Maritime Silk Road, which is an important part of the larger BRI strategy.[27] A 2017 Chinese government document, cited in the Pentagon's annual report on China, lays out three corridors under the BRI; these include a spur extending from China to the South Pacific.[28] China's state media and regional representatives often describe Southwest Pacific countries, such as PNG and Vanuatu, as joint participants in the BRI.[29] A number of development reports published since 2016 have highlighted Chinese investments targeting ports, airports and associated transport infrastructure in at least five Southwest Pacific states: Kiribati, PNG, Samoa, Solomon Islands and Vanuatu.[30] Unlike the core Eurasian elements of the BRI, however, there is no obvious economic or commercial rationale for China's interest in modernising transportation infrastructure in the sub-region, possibly suggesting an ambition to secure access to infrastructure that is potentially capable of servicing future PLA deployments in the Southwest Pacific.

The maximalist strategic objective that can be imputed to China is to gain a foothold in the second island chain from which to threaten lines of supply and communication between Australia and Japan, or Australia and the US. Chinese think-tank experts have identified a requirement to break through the first and second island chains in order to enable military operations in more extensive sea waters.[31] This resonates with what David

Feeney calls Australia's 'enduring concern' that a 'hostile power could establish a military base in the region from which to challenge our control of Australia's air and sea approaches or even project force against us'.[32] There are more innocuous potential explanations for seeking military access: for example, to support China's space operations or as a logistics hub for evacuating Chinese nationals in case of outbreaks of violence against ethnic-Chinese people in Pacific island countries.[33] These do not exclude more strategic ambitions; Chinese security scholars have postulated these and other rationales in favour of a PLA presence in the Southwest Pacific.[34] According to Qin Sheng of the Chinese Academy of Social Sciences, the region is viewed as an important setting for competition among major powers.[35] Beijing's diplomatic and military focus on the sub-region has unquestionably sharpened within the past five years.

Cat and mouse

The PLAN's apparent interest in overseas bases in Australia's environs could have been stimulated by the operational challenges it experienced in 2014, when a Chinese flotilla was sent to search for the downed Malaysia Airlines flight MH370 in the Indian Ocean and had to depend on Australia to provide logistical support.[36] Following this experience, Chinese experts noted in February 2015 that enhancing cooperation with Pacific island states could help to address a prominent lack of supply depots for China's navy.[37]

Any Chinese 'base' in the Southwest Pacific need not necessarily take the form of a fortified facility resembling the PLA base in Djibouti (established in 2017) or even be reserved exclusively for military use.[38] In order to facilitate regular Chinese naval and air deployments in the surrounding area, the minimum requirement for the PLA would be to obtain host-country consent for the use of a convenient and relatively secure location to provide logistical support, including food, fuel and other essential items. Over time, such a 'dual-use' commercial and military facility could evolve to become more like a conventional military base. But in the generally low-threat environment of the Southwest Pacific, a hybrid facility could continue to serve China's peace-time needs for some time as a logistics 'toehold', supporting an expeditionary PLA presence without the need for fortified, garrisoned bases. Most of the regional locations that have been identified in media reports over the past five years as potential sites of interest for Chinese investment involve commercial ports or airfields. Such reports, sometimes citing unnamed Australian government officials, were generally met with scepticism by academic experts on the Pacific, who pointed to a lack of hard evidence behind China's alleged military-basing ambitions.[39] The fact that no Chinese military facility has yet materialised in the Southwest Pacific has reinforced their suspicions that Beijing's intentions have been exaggerated or misinterpreted.

A pronounced cleavage between academic and government perceptions regarding China's intentions has been a feature of Australia's public debate on the Southwest Pacific, though recent developments in Solomon Islands and elsewhere have added considerable credence to the Australian government view. In March 2022, then-prime minister Morrison said that China has been 'very clear' about its aspirations to acquire a military base in the Pacific islands.[40] That Australia's prime minister commented publicly about China's intentions in such unequivocal terms bears out an assessment within the Australian intelligence community, from 2016 onwards, 'that China was looking at sites for a naval base in the South Pacific'[41] and seeking to develop transport infrastructure in the sub-region with a view to facilitating access for the PLA.

China's official confirmation in April 2022 that it had concluded a security agreement with Solomon Islands has significantly shifted the terms of the debate.[42] While the terms of that bilateral agreement remain secret, Beijing's intentions to pursue an overt security role and presence in the Southwest Pacific are no longer in doubt, despite continuing denials from Solomon Islands' government that the agreement will lead to basing arrangements for the PLA.[43] A purportedly leaked draft of the agreement, widely circulated in the media, stipulates that Solomon Islands can 'request China to send police, armed police, military personnel and other law enforcement and armed forces … to assist in maintaining social order, protecting people's lives and property'. It further states that 'China may, according to its own needs and with the consent of Solomon Islands, make ship visits to, carry out logistical replenishment in and have stopover and transition in the Solomon Islands'.[44] Reports of Chinese interest in investing in large-scale transportation-infrastructure projects in Solomon Islands began to emerge around the time of Prime Minister Manasseh Sogavare's announcement in September 2019 that Honiara was switching diplomatic recognition from Taipei to Beijing. The *New York Times* initially reported that 'a Beijing-based company with close ties to the Chinese Communist Party' had secured a deal with a provincial governor in Solomon Islands to lease 'the entire island of Tulagi and its surroundings', in order to build a fishery facility, an operations centre and 'the building or enhancement of the airport'.[45]

Media reports alleging Chinese interest in basing locations in the Southwest Pacific have been circulating for several years. In April 2018, the *Sydney Morning Herald* claimed that China was pursuing a military-access agreement with Vanuatu. This source cited Australian officials' concerns that 'Beijing's plans could culminate in a full military base'.[46] Both the Vanuatu and the Chinese authorities 'strenuously denied' that plans for a base were discussed.[47] The supposed infrastructure deal centred on the wharf at Luganville (Vanuatu's second city) which, according to Vanuatu's government, was meant to be significantly lengthened and refurbished by a Chinese firm, Shanghai Construction Group, with an original targeted completion date of 2017.[48] In 2017, a Chinese academic published an article in a scholarly journal specifically suggesting that China should develop strategic pivot ports at Luganville, as well as Apia, Port Moresby and Suva, for both civilian and military uses, such as 'materials supply, staff rest, and vessel repairs'.[49] However, as of the end of 2022, no work had commenced at Luganville Wharf.

Chinese infrastructure providers are increasingly competing with Australian and New Zealand companies in PNG,[50] including Lombrum on Manus Island, which is a particularly attractive site from a naval viewpoint given its unobstructed location and deep draught. In 2016, China Harbour Engineering Company (CHEC) signed a contract to upgrade Momote airport on Manus Island.[51] CHEC is also listed as a contractor for the Lae Port Development Project.[52] Manus Island's prime location was first appreciated by the Imperial Japanese Navy during the Second World War. A major US naval base was set up at Lombrum in 1943 following the capture of Manus Island from Japan. However, Manus Island became less important to the US in the latter stages of the war, as military operations in the Pacific moved closer to Japan. Subsequently abandoned by the US Navy, the base was operated by the Australian navy from 1950 until PNG's independence in 1975. As a measure of its renewed significance in Australian eyes, China's reported interest in developing Lombrum prompted Turnbull to make an Australian counter-offer to then PNG prime minister Peter O'Neill in July 2018 to develop the base jointly.[53] In January 2022, then-prime minister Morrison further announced that Australia would commit A$580m to upgrade PNG's principal commercial ports, including Lae Tidal Basin, Kimbe on the north coast of New Britain, Lorengau on Manus Island, Kavieng in New Ireland, Vanimo in West Sepik and Wewak in East Sepik.[54]

In November 2020, it was reported that China's Fujian Zhonghong Fishery Company had signed a memorandum of understanding (MoU) with PNG's central government and provincial authorities to build a A$200m 'multi-functional fishery industrial park' on Daru Island in PNG's Western Province.[55] Daru overlooks the Torres Strait, an important shipping lane used for international navigation, in intimate proximity to Australian territory. Yet the surrounding waters are not known for their abundance of fish.[56] While the strategic value of a Chinese-owned port facility so close to Australia would be limited by its military vulnerability in any conflict, its potential to support a Chinese maritime-militia presence (on the pretext of fishing around northern Queensland) would expose Australia to the risk of grey-zone operations and hostile intelligence collection.

In 2018, Canberra beat off a rival bid from China to upgrade the Fijian armed forces' Blackrock Camp as a regional police and peacekeeping training centre. Fiji reportedly accepted the Australian offer, which included a training component, on grounds that it was more comprehensive.[57] While details of the Chinese bid have not been made public, Canberra's fear was that it would have laid the relational foundations, over time, for the PLA to acquire access to and influence over military officers and other personnel from across the sub-region. Earlier, in 2015, the Chinese ambassador to Fiji had expressed China's willingness in principle to support the construction of a new naval base, following the conclusion of a bilateral defence MoU during Xi's visit to Fiji in November 2014.[58]

Following Kiribati's decision in 2019 to recognise Beijing rather than Taipei, it was reported in May 2021 that China's government had funded a feasibility study for the potential redevelopment of an abandoned US-built airstrip on Kiribati's Kanton Island; this raised concerns, in Australia and beyond, that China intends to build a runway for potential military use, though Kiribati's authorities have denied this to be the case.[59] In another move widely imputed to China's influence and specific interest in expanding access to fisheries in the Southwest Pacific, the Kiribati government controversially decided in November 2021 to open up a large marine reserve to commercial fishing, de-gazetting it as a World Heritage site.[60]

China operated a space-tracking facility on Kiribati's South Tarawa island from 1997 until the Kiribati government's decision to switch recognition from China to Taiwan forced the facility's closure in 2003. Its purpose was primarily to support China's crewed space programme, although Tarawa's proximity to the US ballistic-missile testing range at Kwajalein, in the Marshall Islands, is widely suspected to have provided a secondary, eavesdropping motivation for China's tracking facility.[61] Since the closure of this facility on Tarawa, the PLA has periodically deployed satellite-tracking ships to the South Pacific to provide support to China's crewed space flights.[62] Beijing's renewed interest in Kiribati has been linked to its space ambitions, and the construction of a new fixed facility would obviate the need for expensive tracking-ship deployments to the region.[63] Finally, Samoa, under the previous administration of prime minister Tuilaepa Sailele Malielegaoi (1998–2021), was associated with a controversial China-backed plan to develop a new port costing US$300m, despite the Asian Development Bank saying there was no commercial case for the project.[64]

China's persistent interest in investing in ports, airfields and related infrastructure across the Southwest Pacific has led to 'cat and mouse' competition with Australia (and, to a lesser extent, the US). However, it is unclear to what extent China's association with port and airport infrastructure projects in the sub-region indicates offensive strategic intent or more mundane logistical considerations to do with boosting the PLA's regional presence and supporting China's space operations, or is even a bluff on Beijing's part. A bluff might be explained as a Chinese effort to keep Canberra absorbed and off-balance by triggering repeated diplomatic interventions and expensive counter-offers to forestall a feared PLA operating location within Australia's maritime environs. Alternatively, China's apparent interest in Southwest Pacific infrastructure could be intended to signal China's willingness to match Canberra's parallel pursuit of military-access arrangements and presence in Southeast Asia. Another plausible explanatory factor is that Pacific island elites have learned to exploit the sub-region's heightened geopolitical value for material gain by deliberately courting Chinese interest in commercially questionable investment projects with a view to leveraging this for more tangible infrastructure-related counter-offers from Australia or other Western countries.

Canberra has established an Australian Infrastructure Financing Facility for the Pacific (AIFFP), which became operational in July 2019. The aim of the AIFFP is to partner with Southwest Pacific governments (and Timor-Leste) and the private sector in funding important infrastructural projects, including ports, airports and submarine cables, so as to ensure that alternatives to Chinese-funded infrastructure are available to governments in the sub-region.[65] Australia's Department of Foreign Affairs and Trade (DFAT) and Export Finance Australia are also cooperating with the Japan Bank for International Cooperation and the US International Development Finance Corporation under the Trilateral Infrastructure Partnership, which is financing a submarine cable from the United States to Palau for its first project.[66]

There has been vigorous competition between Australia and China over the supply of submarine fibre-optic communications cables to Southwest Pacific states. In some cases, Chinese telecommunications firms have emerged successfully as the suppliers.[67] On other occasions, Australian companies, with government subsidies, have successfully outbid Chinese providers, as with a submarine cable across the Coral Sea to Solomon Islands that was approved in June 2018.[68] Nauru has also expressed interest in a connecting spur to this project. In a competition for regional influence, submarine cables are the crown jewels of communications infrastructure, given their near monopoly over the flow of international communication. Due to their centrality to public and private information and attendant importance for cyber security, seabed cables carry a special premium, which has prompted Canberra to back counter-offers from Australian private-sector providers to Pacific island countries. In October 2021, Australia's Telstra outbid competition from China to acquire Digicel Pacific, a key communications provider in the South Pacific, in a deal largely funded by the Australian government, with additional credit guarantees provided by Japan and the United States.[69] Additionally, cyber is an area of chronic weakness for Pacific island states, leading Australia to establish a Cyber Cooperation Program for the Pacific and to cooperate with PNG in jointly establishing national computer-emergency response teams in the run-up to its hosting of the 2018 APEC summit.[70]

Despite growing strategic competition between Australia and China in the Southwest Pacific, Beijing has not sought to foment local conflicts in the sub-region. But Beijing could, in the future, be tempted to distract Canberra's strategic attention by stirring up trouble in the Southwest Pacific. One concern among senior Australian military officers and defence officials is that much of the deployable strength of the Australian Defence

Force (ADF), and particularly the army, could be absorbed by a protracted stabilisation deployment in the sub-region. The estimated cost of the Australian-led 2003–17 civilian and military mission to restore order and rebuild institutions in Solomon Islands was A\$2.6 billion.[71] During its military phase, which terminated in 2013, a total of 7,270 ADF personnel (including 2,112 reservists) were deployed to Solomon Islands.[72] If, hypothetically, PNG became seriously destabilised, the scale and costs of an ADF deployment would likely be significantly higher, in a potentially open-ended and sapping commitment. For China, it would be a relatively cost-efficient way to tie Australia down militarily, making it harder for the ADF to deploy expeditionary forces to parts of the region of more direct military interest to China, such as Taiwan.

Regardless of China's motivations, geopolitical calculations are becoming increasingly intertwined with local politics. In November 2021, Australia joined Fiji, New Zealand and PNG in contributing to a police and military contingent to restore security in Solomon Islands' capital, Honiara, following violence partly directed against the ethnic-Chinese community. An important contributory factor behind the riots was the build-up of popular anger, also voiced by opposition MPs, about the growth of Chinese influence in Solomon Islands following the Sogavare government's decision to switch diplomatic recognition from Taiwan to China.[73] Australia's decision to intervene followed a direct request from Prime Minister Sogavare under the 2017 security treaty between Australia and Solomon Islands.[74] However, Canberra's desire to be a 'partner of choice'[75] in the Southwest Pacific may increasingly be influenced by the possibility that governments there could call upon Beijing to help restore order during times of crisis. The new security agreement between Beijing and Honiara has significantly increased the probability of this happening in Solomon Islands. It appears likely that Sogavare perceives paramilitary or military assistance from China as a means to suppress domestic opposition and buttress his regime's security. His government has already moved to postpone a general election due in 2023.[76]

Responses

Preserving influence and protecting its security interests against rising competition from China have necessitated Canberra adopting a calibrated, broad-spectrum policy approach towards the Southwest Pacific.[77] Canberra's principal response has been to initiate a DFAT-led 'Step-up' in sub-regional engagement. The Pacific Step-up originated in then-prime minister Turnbull's announcement ahead of the September 2016 Pacific Islands Forum, pledging to boost Australia's engagement in the sub-region.[78] The Step-up continued and was amplified under Turnbull's successor, Scott Morrison. In January 2019, DFAT established a dedicated Office of the Pacific, staffed from across government and led by a deputy secretary, 'to support Australia's deepening engagement with the Pacific, to enhance whole-of-government coordination and to drive implementation of our regional activities, consistent with the priorities of Pacific countries'.[79]

Aid is arguably a more effective and influential policy tool for Australia in its relations with Pacific island states than in Southeast Asia, given the former's modest size and serious socio-economic challenges. Despite the truncation of its overseas aid programme in the past decade, Australia has remained the Southwest Pacific's largest donor by some margin, owing in part to a successful effort by former foreign minister Julie Bishop (2013–18) to protect aid to the sub-region from cuts that severely pared back Australia's overall development-assistance budget. Between 2011 and 2017,

Australia funnelled $US6.5bn into aid projects across the sub-region.[80] In 2019–20, Australia committed a record sum of A$1.4bn in development assistance.[81] Australia's fear of being eclipsed by China has occasionally led Canberra to over-promise, as demonstrated by the lofty and probably unrealisable pledge, during the 2018 APEC summit, to extend electrification to 70% of PNG by 2030.[82]

China's profile as a Pacific donor has grown rapidly, although, as in other parts of the world, Beijing's follow-through on pledges of assistance is patchy. In 2018, China's assistance to the Pacific, in the form of grants and concessional loans, totalled US$246m.[83] In 2019, China's aid dropped to US$169m. This drop of around one-third, year-on-year, has been ascribed to various factors. First, peaks and troughs in China's aid dispersal tend to correlate with visits by senior officials and leaders. Xi's visit to PNG for the APEC summit in November 2018 coincided with a pronounced peak. Second, China's lending to BRI countries has generally declined in the past five years, becoming less generous in the process as the proportion of grant aid to loans has decreased. In 2021, China announced a 'China–Pacific Island Countries reserve of emergency supplies'.[84] Yet initial indications suggested that Beijing provided significantly less pandemic-specific assistance in comparison with most other Pacific donors, Australia included.[85] Third, Pacific island states have become warier of concessional lending from China, as awareness has grown of its potentially predatory conditionality and as the terms Beijing offers have become much less attractive. Compared with countries in some other regions prioritised by the BRI, Southwest Pacific states are at less risk of Chinese 'debt-trap' diplomacy because their exposure to Chinese debt is generally lower.[86] Samoa and Tonga are currently most exposed, with debt to China accounting for 30% and 35% of GDP, respectively, although Tonga's real level of debt is thought to be substantially higher.[87]

Aid from China has declined, but this does not equate to reduced economic influence. The lines between Chinese investment in and aid to the Southwest Pacific have blurred, as they have in Southeast Asia. China's emphasis has moved away from policy lending and towards investment by state-owned enterprises (SOEs), which have expanded their footprint in PNG particularly, whilst aid has fallen. Under Xi, SOEs are now more closely controlled by the CCP. According to Australian-based analysts Jonathan Pryke and Alexandre Dayant, writing in 2021: 'It might … be that Chinese aid has served its purpose. Chinese loans have been used as a vehicle to get [SOEs] into the region. These SOEs have now put down deep roots and are competing in commercial activity across the board.'[88]

Pryke and Dayant cite Chinese statistics showing that, by 2017, Chinese SOEs' construction activity across the South Pacific was already 'almost six times greater than its foreign aid activities'.[89] These companies serve to expand China's presence and influence in the region.[90] Pryke has also highlighted the risk of elite capture as a means for China to pursue basing and other ambitions throughout the region.[91] Small states have sovereign agency, but elite capture can be considered an endemic vulnerability for Southwest Pacific island countries, in light of their small populations, low levels of development, propensity towards 'strongman' politics, as well as their diplomatic value as a United Nations voting bloc. China and Taiwan have engaged in long-running competition for diplomatic recognition, and they continue to vie for influence among Pacific island political elites.[92]

China has become Canberra's primary competitor for influence in the sub-region, not simply by virtue of the scale of its economic activities but because Beijing has preferred to operate unilaterally, beyond the reach of the sub-region's established multilateral institutions, thus limiting opportunities for cooperation. Australia has attempted to pursue cooperation with China where opportunities arise, including through the coordination of a handful of insignificant aid projects.[93] But China's preference for bilateralism and the essentially competitive nature of its efforts to build regional influence have relegated such opportunities to the margins.

Over the past two decades, climate change has emerged as a common security challenge and rallying cry for Pacific island states as they seek international assistance. Countries such as Kiribati and Tuvalu face the possibility of wholesale population relocation due to rising sea levels and intensifying storms. Climate increasingly dominates the security perceptions of Pacific islanders, as borne out in the Boe Declaration on Regional Security, endorsed by PIF members (including Australia) in September 2018. Because of the Morrison government's controversial stance on climate change, it became a bone of contention between Canberra and Southwest Pacific countries, despite Australia's continuing efforts to pursue climate-related cooperation with Pacific island states.[94] This tension has eased since the Labor government came to power in May 2022 and raised climate higher up Canberra's policy agenda for the Southwest Pacific.[95] China has been more willing than Australia to pay lip service to the climate concerns of national leaders in the Pacific. Pacific island politicians and civil-society leaders emphasise an expanded concept of security, including human security, humanitarian assistance, environmental and resource security, and protection from transnational and cyber crime.[96] From Australia's perspective, though, there are equally valid concerns about China's strategic motivations towards the Southwest Pacific, its interest in gaining access to militarily useful facilities, elite capture and China's generally deleterious influence on governance.

Ministers and senior officials from the Pacific islands have directly experienced China's strong-arm tactics. For example, in 2018, Nauru's then-president Baron Waqa accused China's representative at the PIF summit of engaging in bullying behaviour and demanded a formal apology.[97] The Boe Declaration itself pointedly emphasises 'the sovereign right of every Member to conduct its national affairs free of external interference and coercion'.[98] China's diplomatic attempt in May 2022 to conclude a broad-based deal with ten Pacific island countries represented a significant break from Beijing's previous bilateral approach in the Southwest Pacific and can be seen as an overt effort to create a new multilateral architecture that excludes Australia and New Zealand in the sub-region. China's efforts have thus far failed to gain traction because the majority of Pacific island governments held firm to the principle of consensus.[99] Nevertheless, China continues to promote an alternative institutional architecture oriented towards countries that officially recognise Beijing. This alternative architecture includes a China–Pacific island countries 'poverty reduction and development cooperation centre' as well as a China–Pacific island countries fisheries cooperation and development forum.[100]

Defence cooperation is important to Canberra's Step-up, in relation to Australia's ambition to remain the sub-region's preferred security provider, vis-à-vis China, as well as to maintain the ADF's forward presence. As part of Australia's long-standing Defence Cooperation Program (DCP) with states in the Southwest Pacific as well as Southeast Asia, an ADF Pacific Support Force was established in 2019.[101] PNG is the largest Southwest Pacific recipient of DCP assistance, which focuses on training and capacity-building for the 3,600-strong PNG Defence Force (PNGDF), and particularly on strengthening its Maritime Element, which numbers only around 200 personnel and relies heavily on Australian assistance.

Australia's 2017 bilateral security treaty with Solomon Islands, a legacy of the Regional Assistance Mission to Solomon Islands (RAMSI) intervention, is also important from the viewpoint of facilitating access, providing a legal basis for ADF deployment in response to a request from Honiara.[102]

Australia's Pacific Maritime Security Program (PMSP) has 12 participant countries in the Southwest Pacific, and also includes Timor-Leste.[103] The PMSP has A$2bn allocated to it for 30 years from 2018 onwards. Between 2018 and 2023, Canberra plans to deliver 21 *Guardian*-class patrol vessels to participant states, replacing smaller boats donated in the 1980s.[104] Under the programme, patrol boats are handed over to recipient countries as sovereign assets, with naval personnel from Australia and New Zealand embedded in their crews. The boats are principally used to counter illegal fishing. In most cases, they are the only physical assets effective for maritime surveillance and law enforcement that are available to Pacific island states. Australia is further providing a A$10m aerial-surveillance package under the PMSP, involving up to 1,400 hours of coverage per year, provided by civilian-operated aircraft based in the sub-region.[105] The patrol-boat programme further serves to augment Australia's surveillance of its eastern and northeastern approaches, including keeping watch over the activities of China's long-distance fishing fleet and the increased presence of Chinese naval vessels. These forces – though small – represent an extension of Australia's maritime-surveillance network in peacetime and a potential source of reinforcement to the ADF in times of crisis and conflict, an important factor given the challenges that Australia currently faces in recruitment for its armed forces.[106] Maintaining institutional and interpersonal connections with Southwest Pacific defence forces is important for their latent auxiliary potential for Australia's defence and security.

In this light, the dispatch of 1,500 ADF personnel to PNG to help provide security for the November 2018 APEC summit in Port Moresby was significant as an experiment in what was, by the ADF's contemporary standards, a large-scale forward military deployment to the Southwest Pacific. *Operation APEC Assist* demonstrated that Australia could deploy forces to assist its closest neighbour for a short-term, clearly defined purpose. It could be considered a successful trial for potential future ADF task-force deployments to PNG or elsewhere in the Southwest Pacific. Before the summit, the ADF sent a special-forces team to work with the PNGDF on establishing a joint headquarters and Joint Security Task Force.[107] During the summit, the Australian air force provided airspace security, including a mobile air-defence radar near Port Moresby and F/A-18 aircraft operating from Townsville in northern Queensland.[108] The Australian navy provided maritime-security support with the amphibious-assault ship HMAS *Adelaide* acting as a floating command centre. The operation included the use of amphibious troops from the Australian army, a deployment of navy and army helicopters operating from HMAS *Adelaide*, and the first deployment of the Currawong Battlespace Communications System.[109] Although the APEC summit was an unusual event for PNG, the ADF contribution and its close working relationship with the PNGDF could have enduring value as a model for Australia to adapt in the future as it moves to a stronger forward defensive posture.

Australia has also frequently deployed the ADF for humanitarian-assistance and disaster-relief missions in the sub-region, including *Operation Fiji Assist* in the aftermath of Cyclone Winston in 2016. Beyond their humanitarian purpose, such missions provide benign capability demonstrations for the ADF, opportunities for the various Australian services to operate jointly in a forward environment, and contexts in which to forge closer relations with political and military leaders in the Southwest Pacific. Over the past five years, the Australian navy has started to undertake more regular deployments to the sub-region, including a small task group sent in alternate years under the auspices of the *Indo-Pacific Endeavour* activity, inaugurated in 2017. An Australian submarine made an emergency visit to Solomon Islands in June 2019 to relieve sick crew members, possibly a sign that Australia is stepping up patrols of its northeastern approaches.[110]

In September 2019, Canberra launched a new, specialist Australia Pacific Security College at the Australian National University, providing major government funding. The college is focused primarily on training officials from the sub-region, and aims to provide 'a venue where the countries of the Pacific can collaborate and learn from each other'.[111] A likely ancillary aim is to restore Australia's interpersonal links with those governing Pacific island countries, ties that have slowly atrophied over the past 30 years. In addition, one of the first security-related initiatives announced under Canberra's Step-up was the creation of a new, Australian-funded Pacific Fusion Centre, to provide assessments of security topics to Pacific island leaders and policymakers.[112] The centre was initially located in Canberra, but commenced operations in Port Vila, Vanuatu, in December 2021.[113]

One of the most potentially significant moves in Australian defence policy towards the Southwest Pacific was the decision announced in November 2018 to establish a PNG–Australia naval base at Lombrum on Manus Island. This joint facility could potentially elevate Canberra's defence relations with Port Moresby to a new level. The plans to upgrade the PNGDF Lombrum facility are designed primarily to buttress its existing role as a base for PNG's *Guardian*-class patrol vessels and, theoretically, to provide a forward-operating base for the

Australian navy's new offshore-patrol vessels in the future. As of 2021, Australia had committed A$175m to modernising the wharf and other facilities at Lombrum.[114] The modernised base at Lombrum should deliver national maritime-security benefits for PNG, helping it to better police its archipelagic waters and surrounding EEZ. It could also function as a hub for training, exercises and possibly joint maintenance with other Pacific island states.

The involvement of the US Navy with third-party access to the joint base at Lombrum promises to facilitate a more regular, if initially modest, US naval presence in the Southwest Pacific. Over the last five years, PNG has received a succession of high-level US visitors, including the secretary of the Navy and the commander of the Indo-Pacific Command. In 2021–22, a US Naval Construction Battalion assisted in the upgrade of Lombrum.[115] However, progress has been slow, and the refurbished base's capacity is likely to remain relatively limited and will be unsuited to accommodating or resupplying larger US or Australian warships. The nearby airfield at Momote, refurbished by CHEC, is not currently available for defence purposes, despite its clear potential to boost the strategic value of Manus Island.[116] The main purpose of Australia's reactive 'counter-offer' at Lombrum appears to have been to prevent China from constructing a commercial port and airfield that might subsequently have been adapted to facilitate access for the PLA.

Conclusion

During 2022, the strategic dynamic between Australia and China in the Pacific moved out of the shadows and entered an overtly competitive phase with the advent of China's bilateral security agreement with Solomon Islands and failed multilateral initiative. Australia's status as the de facto sub-regional hegemon means that Beijing and Canberra compete more intensely and directly in the Southwest Pacific than in other parts of the Indo-Pacific. This gives the sub-region wider significance as a strategic bellwether and bilateral point of tension.

A growing anxiety about China's potential strategic footprint in the Southwest Pacific has driven Canberra to resource its policy Step-up in the sub-region on a significant scale. But Australia has been playing 'catch up'. Even in its own Southwest Pacific 'backyard', Australia has struggled to restore influence lost to China's allure. To succeed, Australia will need to work in conjunction with its partners in the sub-region, including France, Japan, New Zealand, the United Kingdom (which in 2019 began stepping up its commitment to the sub-region, albeit on a much smaller scale) and the United States, which is belatedly directing more attention towards Pacific island countries.[117]

It would be overly reductive to attribute Australia's Pacific Step-up entirely to China's recent gains in influence. The relative decline in Canberra's influence in the sub-region has older and broader origins than China's rise. Australia has lost sway, due partly to its own neglect of the sub-region, but its relative power is still significantly greater in the blue expanses off its eastern flanks than in the more populous Asian archipelagos and continent to the north. Despite diminished influence, Canberra retains greater policy leverage and options in the Southwest Pacific than in Southeast Asia.

A Chinese threat to Australia via the Southwest Pacific is unlikely to appear over the horizon in the short term, in part owing to Canberra's successful reactive diplomacy. Not everything China does in the Southwest Pacific is strategic. But Beijing's persistent efforts to gain access to and ownership of infrastructure suggest an underlying military interest in the sub-region, beyond the limited potential economic and diplomatic gains that are available. Canberra's ongoing cat-and-mouse game with Beijing may not prevent China from eventually gaining a firmer foothold somewhere in the sub-region, especially where local political elites see Beijing's largesse as an acceptable trade-off for material benefits for their countries and, in the particular case of Solomon Islands, regime security. Kiribati could be the next island state where China makes gains, though China, too, faces competition, as well as mounting scepticism from within the sub-region regarding its intentions. Canberra's diplomatic interventions and counter-offers have reduced the options available to Beijing. Still, a base or quasi-base for the PLA in the Southwest Pacific could put significant pressure on the ADF and constrain Canberra's options in crisis or wartime and could mean that fewer assets would be available for forward deployment elsewhere. Growing competition with China in the sub-region has forced Canberra to devote greater attention and resources to its neglected periphery. That, in itself, is not necessarily a bad thing for Australia and the Southwest Pacific.

CHAPTER SEVEN

Learning to live in China's shadow

The contours of a more austere Australia–China bilateral dynamic emerged in sharp relief in the early 2020s. A frictional, if not yet fully adversarial, trend in bilateral relations had been discernible for most of the previous decade, but this dynamic only clarified fully during 2020–21, as Beijing's behaviour towards Australia became openly hostile in the economic and diplomatic domains. Since the start of the coronavirus pandemic, China has tilted towards hardline policies and has accelerated the political tightening that was already well advanced under President Xi Jinping. As a result, China has entered a period of prolonged self-isolation, trading bitter accusations and counter-accusations with many countries, including Australia, over the origins of the coronavirus and Beijing's subsequent management of the outbreak.

Adversarial relations between states are not cast in stone. But any improvement in Canberra–Beijing ties appears likely to be confined to the margins, irrespective of the change of government in Australia in May 2022, or even a meeting between the two countries' leaders in November.[1] Prime Minister Anthony Albanese's new Labor administration has so far maintained continuity in Australia's strategic policy. Its communications style is likely to differ from that of its predecessor, but the Labor government strongly supports Australia's alliance with the United States and related initiatives, such as the Australia–United Kingdom–United States (AUKUS) trilateral security agreement, which are in large part motivated by the desire to balance against China's rising power.[2] Albanese travelled to attend the Quad Leaders' Summit in Tokyo only a day after winning power, while his new defence minister, Richard Marles, was quick to endorse AUKUS and signal basic policy continuity on China and the US alliance, despite ordering a Defence Strategic Review.[3] A change of leader in Beijing would be more consequential for the course of Australia–China relations, but this is highly improbable in the short to medium term now that Xi has secured a third term as general secretary of the Chinese Communist Party (CCP). Fundamental political change in China is unlikely for as long as the CCP itself remains in power. Any attempt by an Australian government to recast relations with China in more positive terms would have to contend with the reality that the paradigm undergirding the relationship has swung back from economics to geopolitics and will not swing back again quickly. A competitive, largely adversarial framing is more likely to define the future of Australia's relations with China than one based on expanding cooperation. The important question for Canberra is how to prevent further deterioration in relations with Beijing while, at the same time, investing in ties with 'like-minded' states to uphold a favourable set of balances (military, economic, even psychological) in relation to China that supports Australia's strategic interests in its immediate environment of Southeast Asia and the Southwest Pacific, as well as in the wider Indo-Pacific and, indeed, globally.

Until as late as 2016, China seemed to have identified Australia's international loyalties as being potentially in play, perhaps understandably given Canberra's mixed diplomatic signals in the past. Today, it is clear that China's leadership has failed to coax Australia into its strategic orbit, or even to obtain a more neutral Australian posture towards Taiwan or the South China Sea, or to secure its official silence on Hong Kong and Xinjiang. Instead, Beijing has settled for making an example out of Australia, to demonstrate to other states, especially in Asia, that countries pursuing policies deemed hostile to or at variance with the CCP's core interests will incur punitive costs.

Of greater international relevance than Beijing's recent efforts to mete out punishment to Australia are the positive lessons that Australia holds out as a resilient, if somewhat ruffled, canary emerging from the coal mine. Australia's course correction on China has not been cost-free, but Canberra has demonstrated the will to protect its sovereignty and the ability to cooperate with others facing similar challenges. Other countries in Australia's region, as well as in other parts of the world, are grappling with comparable difficulties in their interactions with Beijing, ranging from coercive trade practices, political interference, grey-zone operations and cyber predations to higher-order military threats (for those countries on China's periphery such as India, Taiwan and Vietnam), as well as a widespread challenge to the principle of sovereign equality in the international system. Countries as far away as those in Europe are using Australia–China relations as a benchmark for their own experiences and China-policy choices.

This comparative aspect is frequently missed in Australia itself, where tensions with China are more often perceived in a bilateral context or else viewed through the prism of the alliance with the United States. This blinkered outlook ignores the fact that many states have experienced similar treatment from China in recent years. With increasing bluntness, China is seeking to use a combination of economic rewards and punishments to condition other countries into conforming to a Sino-centric international hierarchy. China's state media has sought to characterise Australia's approach as provocative, alleging that 'current tensions in China–Australia relations ... are the result of hostile political decisions made by the Australian government'.[4] China's official media and 'wolf warrior' diplomats have lambasted Canberra for failing to pursue 'independent' policies and have depicted Australia as an adjunct to a US-led containment strategy.[5] Although Australia has been confined by China to the diplomatic 'freezer', that is an increasingly 'crowded place', as Rory Medcalf observes.[6] Accepting that the primary cause of Australia's deteriorating relations with China is Beijing's own behaviour has proved especially difficult for Australians who have been professionally or personally invested in a China-centred vision of the future.

Australia falls short of being a China-policy paragon. Canberra's policies are obviously tailored to a specific set of national interests. Australia's financial resources, military capability and international political capital are limited, while the execution of policy towards China has been imperfect and sometimes contradictory. Frequent changes in political leadership have not helped in that respect. Australia still lacks an overarching China strategy, much less a grand strategy. But China has awoken Australia to a need for statecraft that is significantly more ambitious in scope than its customary reliance on great and powerful friends.

Nevertheless, Australian policy towards China offers a useful comparator, especially for small and medium-sized states. Canberra's policy responses in the face of increasingly hostile behaviour from Beijing suggest the possibility of a loose template for other states seeking to protect themselves against a similar combination of political interference, coercive trade and investment policies and other forms of pressure. There is enough experiential overlap for other countries facing increased pressure in their relations with China, particularly among the advanced democracies, to draw general lessons and calibrate policy responses appropriate to their own circumstances. There are several policy areas where Australia's policies have exemplar value.

The first lesson is that an effective China policy starts at home. Threats that manifest themselves domestically are inherently easier to manage in policy terms than external challenges, for the simple reason that governments enjoy jurisdiction within national borders, even if they do not always have a monopoly over governance at all levels. Australia's experience demonstrates that effective protection against the divide-and-conquer, or just divide-and-disrupt, tactics of the CCP requires both a vertical (federal to municipal) and a horizontal approach across departmental policy silos that goes beyond the mantra of 'whole of government'. No country's counter-interference policies will be effective unless its government adopts an integrated approach that reflects China's own efforts to project a unified stance. Attempts to bring together the various dimensions of external policy towards China are unlikely to succeed unless prior progress has been made on the home front.

Australia offers particular pointers for other federal systems. The freedom of states and territories to make their own trade and investment deals with Chinese state-controlled entities has highlighted vulnerabilities in Australia's constitutional model. The CCP has been able to bypass Canberra and build relations, at lower levels of government and across society, which are receptive to forging commercial links with China but have neither the capacity nor sometimes the inclination to apply a national-security filter to their decision-making.

Despite China's official claims of 'tangible benefits', the Victorian government's 2018 memorandum of understanding on the Belt and Road Initiative brought about no concrete financial commitments from China;[7] indeed, its only observable output was public rancour between Melbourne and Canberra. The federal government reacted belatedly to this and earlier cases by giving itself new powers to scrutinise foreign deals negotiated by subnational institutions, including universities, which have often pursued prestigious Chinese partners without exercising proper diligence about potential institutional links to China's military and intelligence organisations. Elite capture by China has developed to a worrying degree within Australian academia. Australia's university sector presents elements of a national case study in microcosm and is a harbinger of the risks that attach to a China-dependent business model, raising broader questions around this model's corrosive effects on academic freedom and open debate within democratic societies. Universities could still play a useful role by rebuilding national expertise on the mechanics of China's contemporary party-state, helping to educate Australia's future business elite, political leaders, diplomats and intelligence analysts – most of whom will have to deal with China in one form or another during their careers. Alternatively, the government could choose to fund research on the Chinese party-state directly by creating a new institution dedicated to that purpose.

The success of China's pull overseas depends primarily on its economic strength, which gives the CCP substantially more influence in democracies than the Soviet Union had. The benefits of economic engagement with China have helped persuade many among Australia's elite to tell China's story well. The assumption, for many years, was that Western countries were doing the influencing, and that China was becoming more like them. Australia's experience over the past decade has shown that, without greater precautions, influence is likely to flow in the opposite direction.

Contrary to perceptions that Canberra has followed Washington's lead with regard to China, Australia has sometimes found itself ahead of the US and other states in developing self-protection measures. Canberra's 2018 counter-interference legislation and 5G ban against Chinese telecoms firms were both groundbreaking. The 5G decision stands out, since it was domestically controversial at the time and Australia's intelligence community was also out in front of its Five Eyes partners in terms of its risk assessment. Canberra's cautionary stance on admitting Chinese firms into any part of the 5G network has been validated by similar policies adopted by the other Five Eyes countries. In May 2022, Canada became the last among the Five Eyes partners to exclude Chinese providers from 5G.[8] France and Japan have also edged towards a de facto 5G ban. If the UK had not followed Australia's important self-protection precedent on 5G, it is unlikely that a strategic-technology-sharing and co-development initiative like AUKUS could have materialised.

Australia's government has been criticised domestically for making itself a lightning rod for Chinese anger by adopting strong public positions. These criticisms can be debated on a case-by-case basis, but Australia's experience suggests that declaratory policy is integral to the success of countering foreign interference, in terms of both raising domestic public awareness about the potential threats posed by the CCP's influence activities and building intra-governmental consensus behind an integrated policy approach to China. Transparency has become the bedrock principle informing Australia's domestic responses to predations by China's party-state, on the basis that 'sunlight is the most reliable disinfectant'.[9] The alternative approach, whereby private understandings were sought with Chinese interlocutors behind closed doors, has not served Australia well. Australia has not always lived up to the transparency principle in practice, especially in terms of suspected political-interference cases and clear messaging to the Australian-Chinese community. But its internal- and external-signalling value is clear, including to Beijing as the source of the threat.

Bipartisanship on China policy still holds in Australia's parliament, although it has frayed and was tested to an unusual degree, on defence and security in particular, in the run-up to the general election of May 2022.[10] Former Labor prime ministers Paul Keating and Kevin Rudd have accused the conservative coalition government of mishandling China, while former Labor foreign ministers Gareth Evans and Bob Carr have adopted a similar line.[11] During its first month in office, the Albanese administration successfully restored high-level contact with China, with a bilateral meeting of defence ministers on the sidelines of the June 2022 IISS Shangri-La Dialogue in Singapore, followed by a meeting between Albanese and Xi on the sidelines of the G20 summit in Bali, Indonesia. Yet the new government has remained firm in its pursuit of Australia's defence and security interests in the region, without offering concessions to China.[12] Marles asserted Australia's right to overfly the South China Sea following a reportedly dangerous People's Liberation Army Air Force intercept of a Royal Australian Air Force P-8A aircraft near the Paracel Islands in the South China Sea just days after Labor's election victory.[13] In Australia, the most significant divide on perceptions and policy approaches towards China runs not along party-political lines, but generational tracks. Younger people – including politicians from both left and right – tend to be more sceptical towards China because of their lived experience, which in Australia's case now includes prolonged exposure to wolf-warrior tirades, trade sanctions, hostile intelligence operations and political interference. The new Labor government includes its share of China sceptics, who are cautious about the prospects for a rapprochement.

As a result of Canberra's pushback, Beijing no longer sees Australia as easy prey for influence operations. Nonetheless, the CCP, its United Front Work Department, the People's Liberation Army and China's intelligence agencies are all learning organisations. In the future, the CCP could rely on covert tactics and focus on disruption and coercion as more achievable aims than persuasion. It could decide to focus more on the Australian-Chinese community. The Australian government's reluctance to use counter-interference legislation to prosecute beyond a handful of cases thus far may have eroded deterrence. Canberra's record of introducing new legislation to counter foreign interference is let down by its poor performance on follow-through.

Australia's experience demonstrates the disproportionate impact that key individuals can have on China policy. Without a small cohort of highly motivated government advisers and investigative journalists, as well as persistent warnings about China from the intelligence community, the 'pushback' initiated under Malcolm Turnbull would probably not have acquired critical mass. There was nothing preordained about the turnaround in Australia's China policy, which took place around 2016–17. Indeed, given how deeply invested much of Australia's political and commercial establishment was in maintaining a close partnership with China, it is remarkable that the pushback happened at all. Five years on, Australian public opinion has become much more cautious with regard to relations with China, with recent survey results revealing a marked deterioration in China's image and a corresponding increase in the public's perceptions of threat.[14] This trend chimes with a broader international trend, as corroborated by data from Japan, South Korea and Sweden.[15]

Australia's experience shows that the economic relationship with China cannot be separated from politics, because Beijing consciously links them. Political behaviour by a trade partner that China perceives as undesirable can be expected to trigger economic retaliation.[16] China's decision to punish Australia economically in 2020 was not spontaneous but, rather, a cumulative reaction to Canberra's willingness since 2017 to call out the CCP's interference in Australia's domestic affairs and to protect its critical national infrastructure from the growing threats of espionage, data theft and data manipulation.

Australia's ability to withstand punitive trade measures without suffering significant economic damage has sent a powerful signal to other countries that they need not compromise their foreign policy or sovereignty for the sake of commercial interests. According to John Fitzgerald, 'far from Australia misunderstanding China, as its critics allege, China got Australia very wrong. Beijing's miscalculation may portend others under the sway of its "wolf warrior" polemics.'[17] Economics is the foundation of national power, but it should not be allowed to dictate national strategy. China's coercive treatment of Australia since 2020 has delivered a sharp reminder that politics and geopolitics ultimately trump economics in the conduct of foreign policy. Contrary to Beijing's expectations, Australia has become more assertive and willing to bear risk in the face of economic punishment. Fear of offending China has waned. Beijing's failure to compel Australia to adopt a more compliant posture via overt restrictions on trade demonstrates the limits to China's power. According to Denny Roy of the US-based East-West Center think tank, 'Canberra's refusal to capitulate may serve as an inspiration for other governments under Chinese economic pressure over a political disagreement, diminishing the usefulness of this tactic'.[18] In fact, Australia was a remarkably poor choice by China's leadership to demonstrate the old Chinese idiom of 'killing the chicken to scare the monkeys', not least because it is the market-leading exporter of iron ore, which China needs for its economic growth. Australia's willingness to stand its ground in the face of economic retaliation by its leading trade partner may embolden other countries, many of which are less exposed to the Chinese market, to follow suit.

In the realm of defence, Canberra has responded to the perception of a more threatening China by significantly boosting its military spending, enhancing its conventional deterrent with new, longer-range strike capabilities and strengthening military integration within the US alliance. By jettisoning its ten-year 'strategic warning time' as a basis for defence planning, Canberra has indicated that it sees China as a potentially serious military threat emerging within that time frame. Australia's 2020 defence update sent a clear message that it is time to prepare in earnest. The biggest problem now confronting Australia's defence policy, and specifically its mission to deter Chinese adventurism, is the glaring disjuncture between the end of the strategic warning time and the introduction of new military capabilities that are currently planned for the Australian Defence Force (ADF). This 'capability gap' applies most conspicuously to the future Australian-built nuclear-powered submarine fleet.[19] Increased forward-basing of US forces – including nuclear-powered attack submarines (SSNs) – in Australia is the most obvious solution to short-circuit the looming capability gap. The US alliance would thus retain its strategic centrality to Australia – another own goal for China's resort to open coercion.

Converging threat perceptions regarding China are also bringing Australia into closer strategic alignment with Japan and India. Japanese Prime Minister Kishida Fumio has promised to raise Japan's defence spending significantly. Like Australia, Japan is considering the acquisition of new strike capabilities. Australia's defence and security partnership with Japan is the closest and most important with any Asian partner. New Delhi may not cooperate with Canberra with quite the same intensity, but India's primary external threat is no longer Pakistan, but China.[20] Early indications from the new Labor administration suggest that Canberra will pursue deeper defence and security relations with New Delhi, an objective that is shared by Prime Minister Narendra Modi's government.[21]

Canberra's revamped defence policy, especially since the release of the Defence Strategic Update in 2020, includes the objective of 'shap[ing] Australia's strategic environment' – a nod, beyond military capabilities, to the importance of statecraft.[22] For Australia to meet the scale and complexity of the challenges that China poses, a broad-based and sustained effort will be required across the Indo-Pacific to boost Australia's influence and achieve a defence posture that contributes to a favourable balance of power and facilitates the forward deployment of the ADF. To this end, Australia needs to look beyond its enduring focus on Association of Southeast Asian Nations (ASEAN) multilateralism and maximise its regional partnerships through bilateral and minilateral cooperation, including the quadrilateral partnership with India, Japan and the United States. Engaging closely on regional security with major European countries – primarily the United Kingdom, but also France and Germany – will also be worthwhile.

The Australia–China power dynamic plays out differently in Australia's two key neighbouring sub-regions, Southeast Asia and the Southwest Pacific. In maritime Southeast Asia, Australia is still a first-class military power and, in some countries, is regarded as a more palatable security partner than the

US. However, it is increasingly overshadowed in economic terms by China, which has cultivated deep influence among elites. China has resources and touch points that Australia will find hard to match, except as part of a like-minded coalition with other major regional players, particularly its Quad partners.

In the Southwest Pacific, Canberra's influence is constrained by a recent history of relative neglect. China's growing presence on Australia's Pacific periphery has brought home sharply the extent to which Canberra has lost ground, including in Pacific-island states where Australia and New Zealand have historically been the dominant security providers. A blanket Australian objective of strategic denial towards China in the Southwest Pacific no longer appears tenable. The decision by Solomon Islands to pursue a bilateral security agreement with China in April 2022 highlights the shifting balance. Nonetheless, Canberra still has a better prospect in the Southwest Pacific than in Southeast Asia 'to shape Australia's strategic environment', provided it is sensitive to the security concerns of Pacific island nations and responsive to their economic needs. Foreign Minister Penny Wong, who dedicated several overseas visits to the Pacific islands during her first months in office, has demonstrated that the new Labor government remains concerned about the Pacific islands, despite its pre-election promises to prioritise relations with Southeast Asia.

Some of the key deficits in Australia's geopolitical toolkit are non-military in nature, owing to Canberra's under-resourced diplomacy and to domestic political factors that have obstructed a coherent strategy towards its region. The decline in real terms of Australia's aid budget since 2013–14 may have detracted from Canberra's influence marginally in Southeast Asia. But aid counts much more centrally to shaping the security environment in the Southwest Pacific. On balance, it makes sense for Canberra to focus its limited resources and interpersonal links there, where they have greater impact.

Australia has provided an imperfect but useful exemplar of how governments can effectively meet China's spectrum of security challenges through an integrated set of responses. This loose policy template suggests that addressing domestic vulnerabilities and building resilience at home can serve as the foundation for external China-policy settings that maintain sovereign independence, in cooperation with similarly minded partners. Australia, too, can gather confidence from the fact that other countries are going through their own learning processes on China, resulting in varying degrees of pushback. Australia appears destined to live in China's shadow for many years to come. But it is hardly alone. Shadows, moreover, are often bigger than the objects that cast them. The best counter to an overshadowed existence is to embrace sunlight, a commodity that Australia possesses in abundance.

NOTES

Chapter One

1. Defined for the purpose of this book as Brunei, Indonesia, Malaysia, the Philippines, Singapore, Timor-Leste and Vietnam. Cambodia, Myanmar and Thailand can be considered partly maritime from a geographical standpoint, although they are predominantly continental countries.

2. Defined for the purpose of this book as the Pacific islands east of Australia: American Samoa, Cook Islands, Fiji, French Polynesia, Kiribati, Nauru, New Caledonia, New Zealand, Niue, Papua New Guinea, Samoa, Solomon Islands, Tonga, Tuvalu, Vanuatu, and Wallis and Futuna Islands. This should not be confused with the broader, Allied definition of 'Southwest Pacific' used during the Second World War.

3. Geoffrey Blainey, *The Tyranny of Distance: How Distance Shaped Australia's History* (Melbourne: Sun Books, 1966), p. 24.

4. For two official views, see Australian Government, Department of Foreign Affairs and Trade, '2017 Foreign Policy White Paper', November 2017, https://www.dfat.gov.au/sites/default/files/2017-foreign-policy-white-paper.pdf; and Australian Government, Department of the Prime Minister and Cabinet, 'Australia in the Asian Century White Paper', October 2012, https://apo.org.au/node/31647.

5. Graeme Dobell, *Australia Finds Home: The Choices and Chances of an Asia Pacific Journey* (Sydney: ABC Books, 2000), pp. 1–15.

6. Donald Horne, *The Lucky Country: Australia in the Sixties* (Sydney: Angus and Robertson, 1964), p. 98.

7. Australian Government, Department of Foreign Affairs and Trade, 'Australia's Trade in Goods and Services 2021–22', https://www.dfat.gov.au/trade/trade-and-investment-data-information-and-publications/trade-statistics/trade-in-goods-and-services/australias-trade-goods-and-services-2021–22.

8   John Fitzgerald, 'Old Hu's "Gum" Attack on Australia a Clear Sign of China's Global Mindset', *Crikey*, 1 May 2020, https://www.crikey.com.au/2020/05/01/old-hus-gum-attack-on-australia-a-clear-sign-of-chinas-global-mindset/.

9   As detailed in Chapter Two; Jonathan Kearsley, '"There It Was, China's List of Grievances": How 9News Got the Dossier at the Heart of the Latest Diplomatic Scuffle Between Canberra and Beijing', Nine News, 23 November 2020, https://www.9news.com.au/national/china-dossier-canberra-beijing-diplomatic-tensions-how-jonathan-kearsley-broke-the-story/216a985d-3289-4988-8781-e6dc479f0d74.

10 Richard Maude, 'Looking Ahead: Australia and China After the Pandemic', Asia Society, 13 May 2020, https://asiasociety.org/australia/looking-ahead-australia-and-china-after-pandemic.

11 Allan Gyngell, *Fear of Abandonment: Australia in the World Since 1942* (Melbourne: La Trobe University Press, 2017), pp. 169–71.

12 *Ibid.*, pp. 287–90.

13 Mark Harrison, 'Saying the Unsayable in Australia's Relations with China', Lowy Institute *Interpreter*, 15 December 2017, https://www.lowyinstitute.org/the-interpreter/saying-unsayable-australia-s-relations-china.

14 Thomas Wilkins, 'Averting a Sino-American Conflict: A Review of Kevin Rudd's *The Avoidable War*', Sasakawa Peace Foundation, August 2022, https://www.spf.org/iina/en/articles/thomas_06.html.

15 Harrison, 'Saying the Unsayable in Australia's Relations with China'.

16 Australian Government, Department of Foreign Affairs and Trade, 'China–Australia Free Trade Agreement', https://www.dfat.gov.au/trade/agreements/in-force/chafta/Pages/australia-china-fta.

17 Philip Dorling and Richard Baker, 'China's Fury at Defence Paper', *Sydney Morning Herald*, 10 December 2010, https://www.smh.com.au/national/chinas-fury-at-defence-paper-20101209-18rel.html.

18 'Stern Hu Release: Here's Why the Former Mining Executive Was Convicted in China', ABC News, 4 July 2018, https://www.abc.net.au/news/2018-07-04/stern-hu-explainer-why-china-jailed-the-former-mining-executive/9936578.

19 John Fitzgerald, 'Australia–China Relations and the Trump Factor', *Inside Story*, 14 October 2020, https://insidestory.org.au/australia-china-relations-and-the-trump-factor/.

20 John Garnaut, '"Fear and Greed" Drive Australia's China Policy, Tony Abbott Tells Angela Merkel', *Sydney Morning Herald*, 16 April 2015, https://www.smh.com.au/politics/federal/fear-and-greed-drive-australias-china-policy-tony-abbott-tells-angela-merkel-20150416-1mmdty.html.

21 Angus Grigg and Lisa Murray, 'Malcolm Turnbull Under Increasing Pressure to Be Firm with China', *Australian Financial Review*, 3 September 2016, https://www.afr.com/policy/economy/malcolm-turnbull-under-increasing-pressure-to-be-firm-with-china-20160831-gr5rr7.

22 Angus Grigg and Lisa Murray, 'Malcolm Turnbull Calls China a "Frenemy", Toughens Stance Towards Beijing', *Australian Financial Review*, 16 June 2017,

https://www.afr.com/policy/foreign-affairs/malcolm-turnbull-calls-china-a-frenemy-toughens-stance-towards-beijing-20170615-gwrnsp.

23 Stephen Dziedzic and Andrew Greene, 'US Official Urges Australia to Participate in South China Sea Freedom of Navigation Operations', ABC News, 27 July 2020, https://www.abc.net.au/news/2020-07-27/australia-pressured-to-participate-in-south-china-sea-operation/12496326; and David Wroe, 'US to Fly F-22 Raptors In and Out of Australia amid South China Sea tensions', *Sydney Morning Herald*, 14 December 2016, https://www.smh.com.au/politics/federal/us-to-fly-f22-raptors-in-and-out-of-australia-amid-south-china-sea-tensions-20161214-gtb2uh.html.

24 Peter Hartcher, 'Red Flag: Waking Up to China's Challenge', *Quarterly Essay*, no. 76, November 2019, p. 31.

25 John Garnaut, 'How China Interferes in Australia and How Democracies Can Push Back', *Foreign Affairs*, 9 March 2018, https://www.foreignaffairs.com/articles/china/2018-03-09/how-china-interferes-australia.

26 Christopher Knaus and Tom Phillips, 'Turnbull Says Australia Will "Stand Up" to China as Foreign Influence Row Heats Up', *Guardian*, 9 December 2017, https://www.theguardian.com/australia-news/2017/dec/09/china-says-turnbulls-remarks-have-poisoned-the-atmosphere-of-relations.

27 Australian Government, Attorney-General's Department, 'Foreign Influence Transparency Scheme', https://www.ag.gov.au/integrity/foreign-influence-transparency-scheme.

28 Saheli Roy Choudhury, 'Former Australian PM Turnbull Explains Why His Government Banned Huawei, ZTE from Selling 5G Equipment', CNBC, 28 March 2019, https://www.cnbc.com/2019/03/28/malcolm-turnbull-on-australias-decision-to-ban-chinas-huawei-and-zte.html.

29 Malcolm Turnbull, *A Bigger Picture* (Melbourne: Hardie Grant Books, 2020), p. 423.

30 Bob Carr, 'If Australia Listened to Our Hawks on China, We'd Have Been Hung Out to Dry', *Sydney Morning Herald*, 24 May 2017, https://www.smh.com.au/opinion/if-australia-listened-to-our-hawks-on-china-wed-have-been-hung-out-to-dry-20170523-gwaw1w.html.

31 Fitzgerald, 'Australia–China Relations and the Trump Factor'.

32 Gareth Evans, 'Australia and China: Getting Out of the Hole', *Pearls and Irritations*, 27 November 2020, https://johnmenadue.com/australia-and-china-getting-out-of-the-hole/.

33 Farz Edraki, 'Spy Chief Nick Warner on the Security Threats Facing Australia, from Terrorism to North Korea', ABC News, 6 April 2019, https://www.abc.net.au/news/2019-04-06/australia-spy-chief-nick-warner-biggest-threats-to-the-nation/10974214.

34 Hartcher, 'Red Flag: Waking Up to China's Challenge', p. 34.

Chapter Two

1   Malcolm Turnbull, *A Bigger Picture* (Melbourne: Hardie Grant Books, 2020), p. 423.

2   *Ibid.*, p. 428.

3   Australian Government, Department of Home Affairs, 'Countering Foreign Interference', https://www.homeaffairs.gov.au/about-us/our-portfolios/national-security/countering-foreign-interference.

4   According to Alex Joske, 'Premier Zhou Enlai, one of the PRC's founding revolutionaries and a pioneer of the CCP's United Front, advocated "using the legal to mask the illegal; deftly integrating the legal and the illegal", "nestling intelligence within the United Front" and "using the United Front to push forth intelligence"'. Joske, 'The Party Speaks for You', ASPI, 9 June 2020, https://www.aspi.org.au/report/party-speaks-you.

5   Donald Horne, *The Lucky Country: Australia in the Sixties* (Sydney: Angus and Robertson, 1964), p. 104.

6   Natasha Kassam, 'Generation Why? Younger Australians Wary of United States', Lowy Institute *Interpreter*, 24 June 2020, https://www.lowyinstitute.org/the-interpreter/generation-why-younger-australians-wary-united-states.

7   Graeme Dobell, 'An Anti-alliance Prime Minister', ASPI *Strategist*, 8 May 2014, https://www.aspistrategist.org.au/an-anti-alliance-prime-minister/.

8   '"It Would Make a Cat Laugh": Key Moments from Paul Keating's National Press Club Appearance', *Guardian*, 10 November 2021, https://www.theguardian.com/australia-news/2021/nov/10/it-would-make-a-cat-laugh-key-moments-from-paul-keatings-national-press-club-appearance; Daniel Hurst, 'Former Australian PM Paul Keating Criticises Liz Truss Over "Demented" China Comments', *Guardian*, 24 January 2022, https://www.theguardian.com/australia-news/2022/jan/24/former-australian-pm-paul-keating-criticises-liz-truss-over-demented-china-comments; and Michael Koziol, 'Paul Keating Says "Cut the Tag" with the US After Donald Trump's Shock Win', *Sydney Morning Herald*, 10 November 2016, https://www.smh.com.au/politics/federal/paul-keating-says-cut-the-tag-with-the-us-after-donald-trumps-shock-win-20161110-gsms4e.html.

9   Katharine Murphy, 'Australia Risks Adopting a Cold War Mindset with China, Warns Gareth Evans', *Guardian*, 23 August 2016, https://www.theguardian.com/business/2016/aug/23/australia-risks-adopting-a-cold-war-mindset-with-china-warns-gareth-evans; Eliza Laschon, 'Labor Says Scott Morrison's "Megaphone Diplomacy" Is Making Australia's China Relationship "Terrible"', ABC News, 29 September 2019, https://www.abc.net.au/news/2019-09-29/richard-marles-says-scott-morrison-damaging-china-relationship/11558442; and 'Address to UK Policy Exchange Virtual, Online', speech delivered by Scott Morrison, Australia's prime minister, 23 November 2020, https://parlinfo.aph.gov.au/parlInfo/search/display/display.w3p;query=Id%3A%22media%2Fpressrel%2F7656326%22;src1=sm1.

10 'China Says It Is More Democratic than America', *The Economist*, 4 December 2021, https://www.economist.com/china/2021/12/04/china-says-it-is-more-democratic-than-america.

11 'Xi Jinping Amends the Chinese Dream', *The Economist*, 10 November 2022, https://www.economist.com/china/2022/11/10/xi-jinping-amends-the-chinese-dream.

12 Louisa Lim and Julia Bergin, 'Inside China's Audacious Global Propaganda Campaign', *Guardian*, 7 December 2018, https://www.theguardian.com/news/2018/dec/07/china-plan-for-global-media-dominance-propaganda-xi-jinping.

13 'Keynote Speech at the Yushan Forum', speech delivered by Malcolm Turnbull, former Australian prime minister, 8 October 2020, https://www.malcolmturnbull.com.au/media/keynote-speech-at-the-yushan-forum.

14 Laura Silver, 'China's International Image Remains Broadly Negative as Views of the U.S. Rebound', Pew Research Center, 30 June 2021, https://www.pewresearch.org/fact-tank/2021/06/30/chinas-international-image-remains-broadly-negative-as-views-of-the-u-s-rebound/.

15 Jade Macmillan, 'Foreign Interference More of "an Existential Threat" to Australia than Terrorism: ASIO Chief', ABC News, 4 September 2019, https://www.abc.net.au/news/2019-09-04/asio-chief-foreign-interference-more-of-a-threat-than-terrorism/11479796.

16 Jichang Lulu, 'Repurposing Democracy: The European Parliament China Friendship Cluster', Sinopsis, 26 November 2019, https://sinopsis.cz/wp-content/uploads/2019/11/ep.pdf.

17 John Fitzgerald, 'Old Hu's "Gum" Attack on Australia a Clear Sign of China's Global Mindset', *Crikey*, 1 May 2020, https://www.crikey.com.au/2020/05/01/old-hus-gum-attack-on-australia-a-clear-sign-of-chinas-global-mindset/.

18 David O. Shullman, 'Protect the Party: China's Growing Influence in the Developing World', Brookings Institution, 22 January 2019, https://www.brookings.edu/articles/protect-the-party-chinas-growing-influence-in-the-developing-world/.

19 Timothy Heath, 'Beijing's Influence Operations Target Chinese Diaspora', *War on the Rocks*, 1 March 2018, https://warontherocks.com/2018/03/beijings-influence-operations-target-chinese-diaspora/.

20 Joske, 'The Party Speaks for You'.

21 Anne-Marie Brady, 'Magic Weapons: China's Political Influence Activities Under Xi Jinping', Wilson Center, 18 September 2017, https://www.wilsoncenter.org/article/magic-weapons-chinas-political-influence-activities-under-xi-jinping.

22 IISS, 'China's Political-influence Operations: Implications for Regional Security', in *Asia-Pacific Regional Security Assessment 2019*, May 2019, pp. 6–62.

23 Human Rights Watch, 'Australia: Beijing Threatening Academic Freedom', 29 June 2021, https://www.hrw.org/news/2021/06/30/australia-beijing-threatening-academic-freedom.

24 Daniel Hurst, 'Uighurs Tell Australian Inquiry of "Intimidation and Harassment" from Chinese Government', *Guardian*, 8 October 2020,

https://www.theguardian.com/
australia-news/2020/oct/09/
uighurs-to-tell-australian-inquiry-of-
intimidation-and-harassment-from-
chinese-government.

25   Luke Slattery, 'Mack Poked the
Dragon and Parents Paid Price',
Australian, 25 April 2020, https://
www.theaustralian.com.au/weekend-
australian-magazine/swimmer-
mack-hortons-family-reveals-fallout-
from-drug-protest/news-story/
a3f11ec2851c90b4171b8021c168a200.

26   Mazoe Ford, 'Australian Yang
Hengjun Formally Charged with
Espionage in China After Almost
Two Years' Detainment', ABC News,
9 October 2020, https://www.abc.
net.au/news/2020-10-10/australian-
writer-yang-hengjun-charged-with-
espionage-china/12750150.

27   Kirsty Needham, 'Australia Says
Yang Hengjun Under "Arbitrary
Detention" in China After Espionage
Verdict Postponed', Reuters, 28 May
2021, https://www.reuters.com/
world/china/australia-says-yang-
hengjun-under-arbitrary-detention-
china-after-espionage-2021-05-28/;
and Daniel McCulloch, 'Yang
Hengjun Jailing "Arbitrary
Detention"', 7News, 26 May 2021,
https://7news.com.au/politics/law-
and-order/australian-writer-to-face-
trial-in-china-c-2942061.

28   Minister for Foreign Affairs, Senator
the Hon Penny Wong, 'Detention of
Cheng Lei', 13 August 2022, https://
www.foreignminister.gov.au/
minister/penny-wong/media-release/
detention-cheng-lei.

29   Turnbull, *A Bigger Picture*, pp. 422–3.

30   Matthew Knott, 'Joe Biden's Asia
Tsar: China's Harshness to Australia
Looks "Unyielding"', *Sydney Morning*

Herald, 7 July 2021, https://www.smh.
com.au/world/north-america/joe-
biden-s-asia-tsar-china-s-harshness-
to-australia-looks-unyielding-
20210707-p587g7.html.

31   Natasha Kassam, 'Lowy Institute Poll
2021', Lowy Institute, 23 June 2021,
p. 12, https://poll.lowyinstitute.org/
files/lowyinsitutepoll-2021.pdf.

32   Jonathan Kearsley, Eryk Bagshaw
and Anthony Galloway, '"If You
Make China the Enemy, China
Will Be the Enemy": Beijing's Fresh
Threat to Australia', *Sydney Morning
Herald*, 18 November 2020, https://
www.smh.com.au/world/asia/
if-you-make-china-the-enemy-china-
will-be-the-enemy-beijing-s-fresh-
threat-to-australia-20201118-p56fqs.
html; and Richard McGregor, 'China
Sends a Message with Australian
Crackdown', *Financial Times*, 25
November 2020, https://www.ft.com/
content/9ed5f582-423d-41c4-ba23-
0441f7dee165.

33   Turnbull, *A Bigger Picture*, p. 424.

34   Primrose Riordan, 'China's Veiled
Threat to Bill Shorten on Extradition
Treaty', *Australian*, 4 December 2017,
https://www.theaustralian.com.
au/national-affairs/foreign-affairs/
chinas-veiled-threat-to-bill-shorten-
on-extradition-treaty/news-story/
ad793a4366ad2f94694e89c92d52a978.

35   James Massola, Tom McIlroy and
Fergus Hunter, 'China Extradition
Deal Collapses as Malcolm Turnbull
Pulls Plug Under Pressure from
Labor, Backbenchers', *Sydney
Morning Herald*, 28 March 2017,
https://www.smh.com.au/politics/
federal/foolishness-to-mess-with-
china-extradition-deal-deputy-prime-
minister-barnaby-joyce-20170328-
gv7ru6.html.

36 Riordan, 'China's Veiled Threat to Bill Shorten on Extradition Treaty'.

37 John Fitzgerald (ed.), 'Taking the Low Road: China's Influence in Australian States and Territories', ASPI, 15 February 2022, https://www.aspistrategist.org.au/taking-the-low-road-chinas-influence-in-australian-states-and-territories/.

38 Parliament of Australia, 'The Australian Constitution', October 2010, https://www.aph.gov.au/-/media/05_About_Parliament/52_Sen/523_PPP/2012_Australian_Constitution.pdf?la=en&hash=36CA5EE66398B6B00A93302D53FD31ABEA4EECAB.

39 Mitch Ryan, 'One Nation or 8? COVID Fuels Australian Power Shift Toward States', Nikkei Asia, 30 October 2021, https://asia.nikkei.com/Spotlight/Coronavirus/One-nation-or-8-COVID-fuels-Australian-power-shift-toward-states.

40 'Belt and Road Forum Doorstop', speech delivered by Steven Ciobo, Australia's minister for Trade, Tourism and Investment, 14 May 2017, https://www.trademinister.gov.au/minister/steven-ciobo/transcript/belt-and-road-forum-doorstop.

41 Anthony Galloway, 'The Call Never Came: Victoria's China Deal Was Done Through Premier Daniel Andrews' Office', *Sydney Morning Herald*, 23 April 2021, https://www.smh.com.au/politics/federal/the-call-never-came-victoria-s-china-deal-was-done-through-premier-daniel-andrews-office-20210422-p57lik.html.

42 *Ibid.*

43 Anthony Galloway, '"Flagrantly Reckless": Victoria Signed China Infrastructure Deal Without Consulting DFAT', *Age*, 26 May 2020, https://www.theage.com.au/politics/federal/flagrantly-reckless-victoria-signed-china-infrastructure-deal-without-consulting-dfat-20200526-p54wfn.html.

44 The federal government's BRI agreement is believed to relate to bilateral economic cooperation in third countries although, like Victoria's 2019 framework agreement, it has never been made public. Galloway, 'The Call Never Came: Victoria's China Deal Was Done Through Premier Daniel Andrews' Office'.

45 *Ibid.*

46 Noel Towell, 'Pallas Has a Pop at Federal Government Over "Vilification" of China', *Age*, 13 May 2020, https://www.theage.com.au/national/victoria/pallas-has-a-pop-at-federal-government-over-vilification-of-china-20200513-p54sj6.html.

47 Jason Scott, 'China Blasts Australia's Decision to Cancel Belt and Road Deal', Bloomberg, 21 April 2021, https://www.bloomberg.com/news/articles/2021-04-21/australia-cancels-state-s-deals-with-china-s-belt-and-road.

48 Galloway, 'The Call Never Came: Victoria's China Deal Was Done Through Premier Daniel Andrews' Office'.

49 Australian Government, Department of Foreign Affairs and Trade, 'Foreign Arrangements Scheme: Public Register', https://www.foreignarrangements.gov.au/public-register?search_api_fulltext=China&field_search_filter_select=All&field_arrangement_date_time%5Bmin%5D=&field_arrangement_date_time%5Bmax%5D=&field_decision_date_time%5Bmin%5D=&field_

decision_date_
time%5Bmax%5D=&field_minister_
decision_taxonomy=All&page=29.

50 Frank Chung, '"It's a Police Station
Honouring a Police State": Outrage as
Melbourne Cop Shop Raises Chinese
Communist Flag', news.com.au, 3
October 2019, https://www.news.
com.au/national/victoria/news/its-
a-police-station-honouring-a-police-
state-outrage-as-melbourne-cop-
shop-raises-chinese-communist-flag/
news-story/7d59fc8558a59eec0693c26
fb9dbf31c.

51 Brad Thompson, 'WA Premier
Demands Morrison End Anti-China
Barbs', *Australian Financial Review*,
15 June 2021, https://www.afr.com/
politics/wa-premier-demands-
morrison-end-anti-china-barbs-
20210615-p5816s.

52 Human Rights Watch, '"They Don't
Understand the Fear We Have": How
China's Long Reach of Repression
Undermines Academic Freedom at
Australia's Universities', June 2021,
https://www.hrw.org/sites/default/
files/media_2021/07/australia0621_
web.pdf.

53 Sherryn Groch, 'ANU Data Breach:
How Hackers Got Inside Australia's
Top University', *Canberra Times*,
2 October 2019, https://www.
canberratimes.com.au/story/6414841/
like-a-diamond-heist-how-hackers-
got-into-australias-top-uni/; and
'Press Conference – Attribution of
Malicious Cyber Activity to China's
Ministry of State Security', transcript
from press conference with Karen
Andrews, Australia's minister for
home affairs, 20 July 2021, Australian
Government, https://minister.
homeaffairs.gov.au/KarenAndrews/
Pages/press-conference-attribution-

of-malicious-cyber-activity-to-chinas-
ministry-of-state-security.aspx.

54 James Jin Kang, 'The Thousand
Talents Plan Is Part of China's Long
Quest to Become the Global Scientific
Leader', *Conversation*, 31 August
2020, https://theconversation.com/
the-thousand-talents-plan-is-part-
of-chinas-long-quest-to-become-the-
global-scientific-leader-145100.

55 Ben Packham, 'China Fears Spark
Grant Knockbacks', *Australian*,
17 February 2021, https://www.
theaustralian.com.au/higher-
education/china-fears-spark-grant-
knockbacks/news-story/0d2ae735052
da4d3ce18dfd6c24eec01.

56 Alex Joske, 'Picking Flowers,
Making Honey', ASPI, 30 October
2018, https://www.aspi.org.au/
report/picking-flowers-making-
honey; and Alex Joske, 'The
China Defence Universities
Tracker', ASPI, 25 November 2019,
https://www.aspi.org.au/report/
china-defence-universities-tracker.

57 Ben Packham, 'CSIRO Sinks China
Study Deal Over Submarine Fears',
Australian, 11 June 2021, https://www.
theaustralian.com.au/nation/defence/
csiro-sinks-china-studydeal-over-
submarine-fears/news-story/76b0b8b
66741508c3d652b1cda01e301.

58 Meia Nouwens and Helena
Legarda, 'China's Pursuit of
Advanced Dual-use Technologies',
IISS *Research Papers*, 18 December
2018, https://www.iiss.org/
blogs/research-paper/2018/12/
emerging-technology-dominance.

59 Nigel Pittaway, 'Australia, US Partner
on Air-launched Hypersonic Missile',
DefenseNews, 30 November 2020,
https://www.defensenews.com/
industry/techwatch/2020/11/30/

australia-us-partner-on-air-launched-hypersonic-missile/; and 'Hypersonic Precinct to Supercharge Research', *Australian Government Defence News*, 11 February 2022, https://news.defence.gov.au/technology/hypersonic-precinct-supercharge-research.

60 Packham, 'China Fears Spark Grant Knockbacks'.

61 *Ibid.*

62 Laura Walters, 'Universities Tweak Relationships with China to Protect Academic Freedom and Autonomy', *Stuff*, 8 August 2021, https://www.stuff.co.nz/national/education/300373849/universities-tweak-relationships-with-china-to-protect-academic-freedom-and-autonomy; and Zhuang Pinghui, 'China's Confucius Institutes Rebrand After Overseas Propaganda Rows', *South China Morning Post*, 4 July 2020, https://www.scmp.com/news/china/diplomacy/article/3091837/chinas-confucius-institutes-rebrand-after-overseas-propaganda.

63 Fergus Hunter, 'UQ Course on "Understanding China" Established with Chinese Government Funding', *Sydney Morning Herald*, 13 October 2019, https://www.smh.com.au/politics/federal/uq-course-on-understanding-china-established-with-chinese-government-funding-20191011-p52zun.html.

64 Lisa Visentin, 'China-backed Confucius Institutes Face Closure Under Veto Laws', *Sydney Morning Herald*, 10 May 2021, https://www.smh.com.au/politics/federal/china-backed-confucius-institutes-face-closure-under-veto-laws-20210423-p57lvo.html.

65 Kirsty Needham, 'Chinese Censorship Found at Australian Universities – Rights Group', Reuters, 30 June 2021, https://www.reuters.com/world/china/chinese-censorship-surveillance-found-australian-universities-rights-group-2021-06-29/.

66 Margaret Simons, 'High Price: Inside the Chinese Student Boom', *Australian Foreign Affairs*, no. 7, October 2019, pp. 28–53.

67 Australian Government, Department of Foreign Affairs and Trade, 'Trade in Services Australia 2018–19', April 2020, https://www.dfat.gov.au/sites/default/files/trade-in-services-australia-2018-19.pdf.

68 'Australian Universities and China', speech delivered by Peter Varghese, chancellor of the University of Queensland, Adelaide, 4 October 2018, https://about.uq.edu.au/chancellor/speeches-and-articles/australian-universities-and-china.

69 Joyce Y.M. Nip and Andrew Ross, 'Cultural Sensitivity or Censorship? Lecturers Are Finding It Difficult to Talk About China in Class', *Conversation*, 7 July 2021, https://theconversation.com/cultural-sensitivity-or-censorship-lecturers-are-finding-it-difficult-to-talk-about-china-in-class-164066.

70 Needham, 'Chinese Censorship Found at Australian Universities – Rights Group'.

71 Max Walden and Stephen Dziedzic, 'UNSW Under Fire for Deleting Social Media Posts Critical of China Over Hong Kong', ABC News, 3 August 2020, https://www.abc.net.au/news/2020-08-03/unsw-under-fire-for-deleting-china-social-media-posts/12517306.

72 Naaman Zhou, 'UNSW Criticised for Letter in Chinese with No

Mention of Freedom of Speech', *Guardian*, 7 August 2020, https://www.theguardian.com/australia-news/2020/aug/07/unsw-criticised-for-letter-in-chinese-with-no-mention-of-freedom-of-speech.

73 Shashank Bengali and Maria Petrakis, 'An Australian Student Denounced His University's Ties to China. Then He Became a Target', *Los Angeles Times*, 21 December 2020, https://www.latimes.com/world-nation/story/2020-12-21/student-australia-china-xi-jinping-uighurs-muslims; and Damien Cave, 'Student Activist in Australia Is Suspended After China Protests', *New York Times*, 29 May 2020, https://www.nytimes.com/2020/05/29/world/australia/drew-pavlou-china-university-queensland.html.

74 Shannon Molloy, 'The Australian Uni Student China Wanted to Silence, Whose Simple Protest Sparked a Living Hell', news.com.au, 24 June 2020, https://www.news.com.au/lifestyle/real-life/news-life/the-australian-uni-student-china-wanted-to-silence-whose-simple-protest-sparked-a-living-hell/news-story/4fcea3b66535bed6d6e08a320cd246ae.

75 John Power, 'University of Queensland Faces Heat for Naming Chinese Diplomat Xu Jie as Faculty Member', *South China Morning Post*, 26 July 2019, https://www.scmp.com/week-asia/geopolitics/article/3020168/university-queensland-faces-heat-naming-chinese-diplomat.

76 Jocelyn Garcia and Matt Dennien, 'University of Queensland Activist Suspended for Two Years', *Brisbane Times*, 30 May 2020, https://www.brisbanetimes.com.au/national/queensland/university-of-queensland-activist-suspended-for-two-years-20200529-p54xv8.html.

77 Australian Associated Press, 'Queensland Student Drew Pavlou's Suspension Reduced but Will Remain Out of University Until 2021', *Guardian*, 13 July 2020, https://www.theguardian.com/australia-news/2020/jul/13/queensland-student-drew-pavlous-suspension-reduced-but-will-remain-out-of-university-until-2021.

78 For example, Ministry of Foreign Affairs of the People's Republic of China, 'Foreign Ministry Spokesperson Zhao Lijian's Regular Press Conference on October 15, 2020', https://www.fmprc.gov.cn/mfa_eng/xwfw_665399/s2510_665401/2511_665403/202010/t20201015_693418.html; Liu Xin and Fan Lingzhi, 'Australian Agency Fabricating "Xinjiang Labor" Receives Fund from US Govt: Spokesperson', *Global Times*, 16 March 2020, https://www.globaltimes.cn/page/202003/1182778.shtml; and Joske, 'The China Defence Universities Tracker'.

79 'How China's "Sharp Power" Is Muting Criticism Abroad', *The Economist*, 14 December 2017, https://www.economist.com/briefing/2017/12/14/how-chinas-sharp-power-is-muting-criticism-abroad.

80 Turnbull, *A Bigger Picture*, p. 422.

81 Melissa Conley Tyler and Julian Dusting, 'What Should Australia Do About … Its Foreign Interference and Espionage Laws?', *China Matters Explores*, May 2021, https://chinamatters.org.au/policy-brief/policy-brief-may-2021/.

82 Ben Packham, 'Foreign Influence

Laws "Failing", Says One of the Architects of the Laws', *Australian*, 6 December 2021, https://www.theaustralian.com.au/nation/politics/foreign-influence-laws-failing-says-one-of-the-architects-of-the-laws/news-story/f3bb48f7a9a464ff9e3816674788be25.

83 Daniel Ward, 'Making Australia's Foreign Influence Laws Work', ASPI *Strategist*, 22 July 2021, https://www.aspistrategist.org.au/making-australias-foreign-influence-laws-work/.

84 Daniel Hurst, 'Liberal Senator Looking for "Heroes" Not Just "Villains" at Inquiry into Universities' Foreign Links', *Guardian*, 5 February 2021, https://www.theguardian.com/australia-news/2021/feb/06/liberal-senator-looking-for-heroes-not-just-villains-at-inquiry-into-universities-foreign-links.

85 Parliamentary Joint Committee on Intelligence and Security, 'List of Recommendations', March 2022, https://www.aph.gov.au/Parliamentary_Business/Committees/Joint/Intelligence_and_Security/NationalSecurityRisks/Report/section?id=committees%2freportjnt%2f024611%2f75668.

86 Australian Government, Department of Home Affairs, 'Australia's Counter Foreign Interference Strategy', https://www.homeaffairs.gov.au/about-us/our-portfolios/national-security/countering-foreign-interference/cfi-strategy.

87 David Walker, 'Sinophobia 101: Why Is Australia's History of Anxiety About the Rise of China Still Relevant', Asialink *Insights*, 17 May 2022, https://asialink.unimelb.edu.au/insights/sinophobia-101-why-is-australias-history-of-anxiety-about-the-rise-of-china-still-relevant; Naveen Razik, '"Race-baiting McCarthyism": Eric Abetz Slammed for Asking Chinese Australians to Denounce Communist Party During Diaspora Inquiry', SBS News, 15 October 2020, https://www.sbs.com.au/news/article/race-baiting-mccarthyism-eric-abetz-slammed-for-asking-chinese-australians-to-denounce-communist-party-during-diaspora-inquiry/n59s7ttp1; and Su-Lin Tan, 'China, Australia and the US Are Using Racism as a Political Football', *South China Morning Post*, 13 June 2020, https://www.scmp.com/week-asia/opinion/article/3088832/china-australia-and-us-are-using-racism-political-football.

88 Turnbull, *A Bigger Picture*, p. 435.

89 Nick McKenzie, Kate Wong and Charlotte Grieve, 'Beijing Controls Chinese-language Media Agencies in Australia, Says Intel Agency', *Sydney Morning Herald*, 2 December 2020, https://www.smh.com.au/politics/federal/beijing-controls-chinese-language-media-agencies-in-australia-says-intel-agency-20201202-p56k10.html.

90 National Foundation for Australia–China Relations, 'About', https://www.australiachinafoundation.org.au/about; and personal communication by Australian government official to author.

91 Laura Zhou, 'China Appoints International Affairs Expert as New Consul General in Brisbane', *South China Morning Post*, 17 June 2022, https://www.scmp.com/news/china/diplomacy/article/3181993/china-appoints-international-affairs-expert-new-consul-general.

Chapter Three

1   Geoffrey Blainey, *The Tyranny of Distance: How Distance Shaped Australia's History* (Melbourne: Sun Books, 1966), pp. 62–3.

2   Australian Government, Department of Foreign Affairs and Trade, 'Australia's Exports to China, 2001 to 2011', p. 2, https://www.dfat.gov.au/sites/default/files/australias-exports-to-china-2001-2011.pdf.

3   Clive Williams, 'Does Australia Have a "One China", "Two Chinas" or "One China, One Taiwan" Policy — or All Three?', ASPI *Strategist*, 2 August 2021, https://www.aspistrategist.org.au/does-australia-have-a-one-china-two-chinas-or-one-china-one-taiwan-policy-or-all-three/; Australian Government, Department of Foreign Affairs and Trade, 'Australia's Trade in Goods and Services 2021–22', https://www.dfat.gov.au/trade/trade-and-investment-data-information-and-publications/trade-statistics/trade-in-goods-and-services/australias-trade-goods-and-services-2021–22; and Australian Government, Department of Foreign Affairs and Trade, 'China Country Brief', https://www.dfat.gov.au/geo/china/china-country-brief.

4   John Lee, 'How China Overreached in Australia', Hudson Institute, 29 August 2021, https://www.hudson.org/research/17228-how-china-overreached-in-australia#.

5   Xu Xiujun and Lin Kaiwen, 'The Strategic Positioning and Realistic Choice of Sino-Australia[n] Relations', *Journal of Suzhou University of Science and Technology*, vol. 37, no. 5, May 2020, pp. 35–41, http://61.181.120.82:8081/kcms/detail/detail.aspx?filename=SZTD202005008&dbcode=CJFQ&dbname=CJFD2020.

6   Mark Thomson, 'Trade, Investment and Australia's National Security … or How I Learned to Stop Worrying and Love Chinese Money', ASPI *Strategic Insights*, no. 56, 18 April 2012, https://www.aspi.org.au/report/strategic-insights-56-trade-investment-and-australias-national-securityor-how-i-learned-stop?__cf_chl_jschl_tk__=pmd_Xt0yut7mSf0kaGpqORqvHc9lSl8c6fkp3BevwyhgL7Y-1634783872-0-gqNtZGzNApCjcnBszQj9.

7   Alex Turnbull, 'China Singling Out Australian Coal Is a Sign of Their Influence on Global Energy Markets', *Guardian*, 12 October 2021, https://www.theguardian.com/commentisfree/2021/oct/12/china-singling-out-australian-coal-demonstrates-their-influence-on-global-energy-markets.

8   'China Continues to Receive Largest Share of New Zealand Exports: Statistics', Xinhua, 26 July 2021, http://www.xinhuanet.com/english/asiapacific/2021-07/26/c_1310086422.htm.

9   Australian Government, Department of Foreign Affairs and Trade, 'Trade and Investment at a Glance 2021', https://www.dfat.gov.au/publications/trade-and-investment/trade-and-investment-glance-2021#exports.

10 National Bureau of Statistics of China, 'Statistical Communiqué of the People's Republic of China on the 2019 National Economic and Social Development', 28 February 2020, http://www.stats.gov.cn/

english/PressRelease/202002/t20200228_1728917.html.

11 Muyu Xu and Gavin Maguire, 'China Coal Supplies to Tighten This Winter on Import Curbs, Strong Demand', Reuters, 14 October 2020, https://www.reuters.com/article/us-china-coal-australia-graphic-idUSKBN26Z121.

12 Lee, 'How China Overreached in Australia'.

13 Clare Jim, 'Analysis: Evergrande Woes to Take Toll on China Property Sale and Drive M&A', Reuters, 24 September 2021, https://www.reuters.com/world/asia-pacific/evergrande-woes-take-toll-china-property-sale-drive-ma-2021-09-24/.

14 Allan Gyngell, *Fear of Abandonment: Australia in the World Since 1942* (Melbourne: La Trobe University Press, 2021), p. 352.

15 East Asian Bureau of Economic Research and China Centre for International Economic Exchanges, 'Partnership for Change: Australia–China Joint Economic Report', August 2016, https://press-files.anu.edu.au/downloads/press/n2068/pdf/book.pdf.

16 Mark Kenny, 'Chinese President Xi Jinping Urges Australia to Embrace "Harmonious" Partnership with Beijing', *Sydney Morning Herald*, 18 November 2014, https://www.smh.com.au/politics/federal/chinese-president-xi-jinping-urges-australia-to-embrace-harmonious-partnership-with-beijing-20141117-11ohwq.htm; and 'Full Text of Chinese President Xi Jinping's Address to Australia's Parliament', *Straits Times*, 19 November 2014, https://www.straitstimes.com/asia/australianz/full-text-of-chinese-president-xi-jinpings-address-to-australias-parliament.

17 Peter Drysdale, 'Australia's Return to Prosperity Depends on Mending China Ties', East Asia Forum, 20 May 2020, https://www.eastasiaforum.org/2020/05/20/australias-return-to-prosperity-depends-on-mending-china-ties-2/.

18 Malcolm Turnbull, *A Bigger Picture* (Melbourne: Hardie Grant Books, 2020), p. 426.

19 'Australia, China Urged to Ease Tensions', SBS News, 14 October 2021, https://www.sbs.com.au/news/australia-china-urged-to-ease-tensions/38f2f057-5834-4038-bb09-4b5bc39502a5; and Daniel Hurst, 'Labor's Joel Fitzgibbon Accuses Coalition of Starting "Economic War with China"', *Guardian*, 8 October 2020, https://www.theguardian.com/australia-news/2020/oct/08/labors-joel-fitzgibbon-accuses-coalition-of-starting-economic-war-with-china.

20 'Australia, China Urged to Ease Tensions'.

21 Jeffrey Wilson, '"NATO for Trade": A Bad Answer to a Good Question?', Hinrich Foundation, 13 July 2021, https://www.hinrichfoundation.com/research/article/sustainable/nato-for-trade/.

22 Cynthia Kim and Hyunjoo Jin, 'With China Dream Shattered Over Missile Land Deal, Lotte Faces Costly Overhaul', Reuters, 24 October 2017, https://www.reuters.com/article/us-lotte-china-analysis-idUSKBN1CT35Y.

23 Turnbull, *A Bigger Picture*, p. 430.

24 Andrew Tillett, 'China Consumer Backlash Looms Over Morrison's Coronavirus Probe', *Australian Financial Review*, 26 April 2020, https://www.afr.com/politics/federal/

china-consumer-backlash-looms-over-morrison-s-coronavirus-probe-20200423-p54mpl.

25 Graeme Dobell, 'China and Australia Face Off in Irate and Icy Pandemic Diplomacy', ASPI *Strategist*, 4 May 2020, https://www.aspistrategist.org.au/china-and-australia-face-off-in-irate-and-icy-pandemic-diplomacy/.

26 Peter Hartcher, '"Just Not Going to Happen": US Warns China Over Australian Trade Stoush', *Sydney Morning Herald*, 16 March 2021, https://www.smh.com.au/world/north-america/just-not-going-to-happen-us-warns-china-over-australian-trade-stoush-20210316-p57b4l.html; and Weizhen Tan, 'China Restricted Imports from Australia. Now Australia Is Selling Elsewhere', CNBC, 2 June 2021, https://www.cnbc.com/2021/06/03/australia-finds-new-markets-for-coal-barley-amid-china-trade-fight.html.

27 Jeffrey Wilson, 'Adapting Australia to an Era of Geoeconomic Competition', Perth USAsia Centre, January 2021, https://perthusasia.edu.au/getattachment/Our-Work/Geoeconomics-Report/PU-184-Geoecon-210526-WEB.pdf.aspx?lang=en-AU.

28 Hudson Lockett and Primrose Riordan, 'China Coal Futures Drop on Threat of State Intervention in Energy Crisis', *Financial Times*, 20 October 2021, https://www.ft.com/content/041b24fb-e8bd-44dd-b546-5a5ff9c9f564.

29 Lee, 'How China Overreached in Australia'.

30 Denny Roy, 'Xi Jinping's Top Five Foreign Policy Mistakes', Pacific Forum *PacNet*, no. 49, 22 October 2021, https://pacforum.org/publication/pacnet-49-xi-jinpings-top-five-foreign-policy-mistakes.

31 Tan, 'China Restricted Imports from Australia. Now Australia Is Selling Elsewhere'.

32 Agence France-Presse, 'Smuggling Australian Rock Lobsters into China a National Security Threat, Hong Kong Customs Chief Says', *Guardian*, 22 October 2021, https://www.theguardian.com/world/2021/oct/22/smuggling-australian-rock-lobsters-into-china-a-national-security-threat-hong-kong-customs-chief-says.

33 Jeffrey Wilson, 'Australia Shows the World What Decoupling from China Looks Like', 9 November 2021, *Foreign Policy*, https://foreignpolicy.com/2021/11/09/australia-china-decoupling-trade-sanctions-coronavirus-geopolitics/.

34 Colin Heseltine, 'We Must Restore Normality to Our China Relationship', *Australian*, 5 November 2021, https://www.theaustralian.com.au/inquirer/we-must-restore-normality-to-our-vital-relationship-with-china/news-story/682faf4ad1120642b489746a157688c0.

35 Stephen Dziedzic, 'Chinese Official Declares Beijing Has Targeted Australian Goods as Economic Punishment', ABC News, 7 July 2021, https://www.abc.net.au/news/2021-07-07/australia-china-trade-tensions-official-economic-punishment/100273964.

36 Wilson, 'Adapting Australia to an Era of Geoeconomic Competition', p. 10.

37 Terry Macalister, 'Rio's Deal with Chinalco Collapses', *Guardian*, 4 June 2009, https://www.theguardian.com/business/2009/jun/04/rio-tinto-chinalco-investment.

38 Peter Hartcher, '"Let Me Buy Rio

Tinto": China's Brazen Bid to Buy Our Companies', *Sydney Morning Herald*, 11 September 2018, https://www.smh.com.au/national/let-me-buy-rio-tinto-china-s-brazen-bid-to-buy-our-companies-20180910-p502rz.html.

39 Naaman Zhou, 'More than 80% of Australians Mistakenly Believe Chinese Investors Are Driving Up House Prices', *Guardian*, 8 July 2021, https://www.theguardian.com/australia-news/2021/jul/08/more-than-80-of-australians-mistakenly-believe-chinese-investors-are-driving-up-house-prices.

40 Dan Hu, 'China–Australia Relations Doomed', *University of Western Australia News*, 17 December 2020, https://www.uwa.edu.au/news/article/2020/december/china-australia-relations-doomed.

41 Michael Smith, 'Chinese Investment in Australia Plunges 70 Per Cent', *Australian Financial Review*, 22 April 2022, https://www.afr.com/world/asia/chinese-investment-in-australia-plunges-70-per-cent-20220421-p5af59.

42 'Chinese Company Landbridge to Operate Darwin Port Under $506m 99-year Lease Deal', ABC News, 13 October 2015, https://www.abc.net.au/news/2015-10-13/chinese-company-landbridge-wins-99-year-darwin-port-lease/6850870.

43 Geoff Wade, 'Landbridge, Darwin and the PRC', ASPI *Strategist*, 9 November 2015, https://www.aspistrategist.org.au/landbridge-darwin-and-the-prc/.

44 '"Let Us Know Next Time": How the World's Most Powerful Man Slammed Australia Over Darwin Port Sale', NT News, 19 November 2015, https://www.ntnews.com.au/business/let-us-know-next-time-how-the-worlds-most-powerful-man-slammed-australia-over-darwin-port-sale/news-story/79197882757c204eb761e5539532d5d2.

45 David Uren, 'Former Trade Minister Andrew Robb Takes Role with Chinese Company Behind Lease of Darwin Port', *Australian*, 30 October 2016, https://www.theaustralian.com.au/nation/politics/former-trade-minister-andrew-robb--takes-role-with-chinese-company-behind-lease-of-darwin-port/news-story/307aa3fa44c9188da7c28069aff18331.

46 Helen Davidson, 'Darwin Port Deal with Chinese Group Poses No Threat, Says Defence Official', *Guardian*, 15 December 2015, https://www.theguardian.com/australia-news/2015/dec/15/darwin-port-deal-with-chinese-group-poses-no-threat-says-defence-official.

47 Christopher Walsh, 'How and Why Did the Northern Territory Lease the Darwin Port to China, and at What Risk?', ABC News, 13 March 2019, https://www.abc.net.au/news/2019-03-12/why-did-northern-territory-sell-darwin-port-to-china-what-risk/10755720.

48 Jano Gibson, 'Chinese-owned Company Landbridge Rejects "Myths and Mistruths" About Darwin Port Lease', ABC News, 28 August 2022, https://www.abc.net.au/news/2022-08-29/darwin-port-nt-landbridge-rejects-chinese-influence-claims/101379670.

49 Angus Grigg and Angela Macdonald-Smith, 'China's State Grid Demands Equal Treatment in $10 Billion Ausgrid Auction', *Australian Financial Review*, 31 March 2016, https://www.afr.com/companies/energy/chinas-

state-grid-demands-equal-treatment-in-10b-ausgrid-auction-20160331-gnupy1.

50 Turnbull, *A Bigger Picture*, p. 425.

51 Peter Hartcher, 'Revealed: Why the Sale of Ausgrid to Chinese Buyers Was Vetoed', *Sydney Morning Herald*, 28 May 2018, https://www.smh.com.au/opinion/revealed-why-the-sale-of-ausgrid-to-chinese-buyers-was-vetoed-20180528-p4zhxh.html.

52 Brian Fung and Ellen Nakashima, 'Huawei Reportedly Gets the Green Light to Participate in Britain's 5G Rollout, a Would-be Setback for the U.S.', *Washington Post*, 25 April 2019, https://www.washingtonpost.com/technology/2019/04/25/huawei-gets-green-light-participate-britains-g-rollout-reversal-us/.

53 Turnbull, *A Bigger Picture*, p. 435.

54 Tim Biggs and Jennifer Duke, 'China's Huawei, ZTE Banned from 5G Network', *Sydney Morning Herald*, 23 August 2018, https://www.smh.com.au/technology/government-implies-5g-china-ban-in-new-security-advice-20180823-p4zz77.html.

55 Turnbull, *A Bigger Picture*, p. 435.

56 Samantha Hoffman and Elsa Kania, 'Huawei and the Ambiguity of China's Intelligence and Counter-espionage Laws', ASPI *Strategist*, 13 September 2018, https://www.aspistrategist.org.au/huawei-and-the-ambiguity-of-chinas-intelligence-and-counter-espionage-laws/.

57 Michael Slezak and Ariel Bogle, 'Huawei Banned from 5G Mobile Infrastructure Rollout in Australia', ABC News, 23 August 2018, https://www.abc.net.au/news/2018-08-23/huawei-banned-from-providing-5g-mobile-technology-australia/10155438.

58 Peter Hartcher, 'Huawei? No Way! Why Australia Banned the World's Biggest Telecoms Firm', *Sydney Morning Herald*, 21 May 2021, https://www.smh.com.au/national/huawei-no-way-why-australia-banned-the-world-s-biggest-telecoms-firm-20210503-p57oc9.html.

59 Maggie Lu-YueYang, 'Australia Blocks China's Huawei from Broadband Tender', Reuters, 26 March 2012, https://www.reuters.com/article/us-australia-huawei-nbn-idUSBRE82P0GA20120326.

60 Turnbull, *A Bigger Picture*, p. 434.

61 *Ibid*.

62 Hartcher, 'Huawei? No Way! Why Australia Banned the World's Biggest Telecoms Firm'.

63 Turnbull, *A Bigger Picture*, p. 434.

64 Jordan Robertson and Jamie Tarabay, 'Chinese Spies Accused of Using Huawei in Secret Australia Telecom Hack', Bloomberg, 16 December 2021, https://www.bloomberg.com/news/articles/2021-12-16/chinese-spies-accused-of-using-huawei-in-secret-australian-telecom-hack.

65 Hartcher, 'Huawei? No Way! Why Australia Banned the World's Biggest Telecoms Firm'.

66 'Huawei Faces Ban from UK 5G Network, with Experts Warning of Chinese Spying', ABC News, 5 July 2020, https://www.abc.net.au/news/2020-07-06/huawei-faces-uk-ban-with-experts-warning-of-chinese-spying/12424608.

67 Wilson, 'Adapting Australia to an Era of Geoeconomic Competition', p. 32.

68 *Ibid*.

69 Clark Packard, 'Trump's Real Trade War Is Being Waged on the WTO', *Foreign Policy*, 9 January 2020, https://

foreignpolicy.com/2020/01/09/ trumps-real-trade-war-is-being- waged-on-the-wto/.

70 Lidia Kelly, 'Australia Takes Wine Dispute with China to WTO', Reuters, 19 June 2021, https://www. reuters.com/world/asia-pacific/ australia-takes-wine-dispute-with- china-wto-2021-06-19/.

71 Stephen Dziedzic, 'Australia Attacks China's Policy of Economic Punishment at the WTO, Accuses It of Contravening Rules', ABC News, 21 October 2021, https://www.abc.net. au/news/2021-10-21/australia-wto- blasts-china-economic-punishment- retaliation/100555410.

72 Samantha Hawley and Jack Hawke, 'Scott Morrison Says G7 Leaders Back Australia's Stand Over China', ABC News, 13 June 2021, https://www.abc. net.au/news/2021-06-14/morrison- g7-leaders-back-australia-stand-on- china/100212798.

73 Wilson, 'Adapting Australia to an Era of Geoeconomic Competition', p. 32; and 'Australia Uses WTO Forum to Blast China's Trade Tactics', Radio New Zealand, 21 October 2021.

74 Wilson, 'Australia Shows the World What Decoupling from China Looks Like'.

75 Daphne Psaledakis and Simon Lewis, 'U.S. Will Not Leave Australia Alone to Face China Coercion – Blinken', Reuters, 13 May 2021, https://www.reuters.com/world/ asia-pacific/us-will-not-leave- australia-alone-face-china-coercion- blinken-2021-05-13/.

76 Sue-Lin Tan, 'US Exports to China Grow at "Expense" of Australia After Beijing's Trade Ban', South China Morning Post, 19 May 2021, https:// www.scmp.com/economy/global-

economy/article/3133952/us-exports- china-grow-expense-australia-after- beijings-trade.

77 Grace Ho, 'US Will Not Join Regional Trade Pact CPTPP, but Pursue Specific Tie-ups with Allies: US Commerce Secretary', Straits Times, 17 November 2021, https://www. straitstimes.com/singapore/politics/ us-will-not-join-asian-trade-pact- cptpp-but-pursue-specific-tie-ups- with-allies.

78 Jonas Parello-Plesner, 'An "Economic Article 5" to Counter China', Wall Street Journal, 11 February 2021, https://www.wsj.com/articles/ an-economic-article-5-to-counter- china-11613084046.

79 Will Glasgow, 'Australia Leads Widespread Criticism of China at the WTO', Australian, 21 October 2021, https://www.theaustralian.com.au/ nation/politics/australia-calls-out- chinas-bad-behaviour-at-the-wto/ news-story/2ccf3b8b68434fa07e5927d a1d07987f.

80 Wilson, 'Adapting Australia to an Era of Geoeconomic Competition', p. 19.

81 Australian Government, Department of Foreign Affairs and Trade, 'Indonesia–Australia Comprehensive Economic Partnership Agreement', https://www.dfat.gov.au/trade/ agreements/in-force/iacepa/Pages/ indonesia-australia-comprehensive- economic-partnership-agreement.

82 Minister for Trade, Tourism and Investment, the Hon Dan Tehan MP, 'Historic Trade Deal with India', 2 April 2022, https:// www.trademinister.gov.au/ minister/dan-tehan/media-release/ historic-trade-deal-india.

83 James Rogers et al., 'Breaking the China Supply Chain: How the

"Five Eyes" Can Decouple from Strategic Dependency', Henry Jackson Society, May 2020, https://henryjacksonsociety.org/wp-content/uploads/2020/05/Breaking-the-China-Chain.pdf.

84 Gareth Hutchens, 'Australia Loses Another Oil Refinery, Leaving Our

Fuel Supply Vulnerable to Regional Crises', ABC News, 11 February 2021, https://www.abc.net.au/news/2021-02-11/australia-loses-another-oil-refinery-risking-fuel-supply/13139648.

85 Wilson, 'Adapting Australia to an Era of Geoeconomic Competition', p. 26.

Chapter Four

1   Reuters, 'Chinese Troops, Frigate Join Australia's Largest Maritime Drill for First Time', *South China Morning Post*, 9 September 2018, https://www.scmp.com/news/china/diplomacy/article/2163419/chinese-troops-frigate-join-australias-largest-maritime-drill.

2   See, for example, Ben Blanchard, 'Indian, Australian Warships Arrive in China for Naval Parade', Reuters, 21 April 2019, https://www.reuters.com/article/us-china-military-anniversary-idUSKCN1RX04W.

3   Australian Government, Department of Defence, 'Exercise KOWARI Starts in North Queensland', 28 August 2019, https://news.defence.gov.au/media/media-releases/exercise-kowari-starts-north-queensland.

4   Andrew Greene, 'Second Chinese Spy Ship Approaches Australia to Monitor Military Exercises After Being "on Our Radar for Some Time"', ABC News, 17 July 2021, https://www.abc.net.au/news/2021-07-18/second-chinese-spy-ship-australia-monitor-military-exercises/100302198.

5   See, for example, a debate in the American journal *Foreign Affairs* by two American scholars who previously held government posts:

Aaron L. Friedberg, 'An Answer to Aggression: How to Push Back Against Beijing', *Foreign Affairs*, September/October 2020, https://www.foreignaffairs.com/articles/china/2020-08-11/ccp-answer-aggression; and Ryan Hass, 'China Is Not Ten Feet Tall: How Alarmism Undermines American Strategy', *Foreign Affairs*, 3 March 2021, https://www.foreignaffairs.com/articles/china/2021-03-03/china-not-ten-feet-tall.

6   IISS, *Strategic Survey 2020: The Annual Assessment of Geopolitics* (London: Routledge for the IISS, 2020), pp. 118–19.

7   Asia Maritime Transparency Initiative, Center for Strategic and International Studies, 'China Island Tracker', https://amti.csis.org/island-tracker/china/; and Minnie Chan, 'Major Development Plan for Woody Island Unveiled', *South China Morning Post*, 4 November 2012, https://www.scmp.com/news/china/article/1074996/major-development-plan-woody-island-unveiled.

8   Asia Maritime Transparency Initiative, Center for Strategic and International Studies, 'Comparing Aerial and Satellite Images of China's

Spratly Outposts', 16 February 2018, https://amti.csis.org/comparing-aerial-satellite-images-chinas-spratly-outposts/; and J. Michael Dahm, 'Beyond "Conventional Wisdom": Evaluating the PLA's South China Sea Bases in Operational Context', *War on the Rocks*, 17 March 2020, https://warontherocks.com/2020/03/beyond-conventional-wisdom-evaluating-the-plas-south-china-sea-bases-in-operational-context/.

9   Dahm, 'Beyond "Conventional Wisdom": Evaluating the PLA's South China Sea Bases in Operational Context'.

10 Erika Gehlen, 'Stop China from Winning Without Fighting', U.S. Naval Institute *Proceedings*, vol. 148/2/1/1,429, February 2022, https://www.usni.org/magazines/proceedings/2022/february/stop-china-winning-without-fighting; and Lyle J. Morris et al., 'Gaining Competitive Advantage in the Gray Zone: Response Options for Coercive Aggression Below the Threshold of Major War', RAND Corporation, 2019, https://www.rand.org/pubs/research_reports/RR2942.html.

11 United States, Office of the Secretary of Defense, 'Military and Security Developments Involving the People's Republic of China', Annual Report to Congress, 2021, https://media.defense.gov/2021/Nov/03/2002885874/-1/-1/0/2021-CMPR-FINAL.PDF.

12 Franz-Stefan Gady, 'China's Navy Deploys New H-6J Anti-ship Cruise Missile-carrying Bombers', *Diplomat*, 12 October 2018, https://thediplomat.com/2018/10/chinas-navy-deploys-new-h-6j-anti-ship-cruise-missile-carrying-bombers/; and Office of the Secretary of Defense, 'Military and Security Developments Involving the People's Republic of China'.

13 David Lague, 'China Expands Its Amphibious Forces in Challenge to U.S. Supremacy Beyond Asia', *Special Report*, Reuters, 20 July 2020, https://www.reuters.com/investigates/special-report/china-military-amphibious/.

14 David Feeney, '"The Ostrich Sticks Its Head in the Sand and Thinks Itself Safe": Australia's Need for a Grand Strategy', Strategic and Defence Studies Centre, Australian National University College of Asia and the Pacific *Centre of Gravity*, December 2018, p. 3, http://bellschool.anu.edu.au/sites/default/files/publications/attachments/2018-12/cog_46.pdf.

15 Australian Government, Department of Foreign Affairs and Trade, '2017 Foreign Policy White Paper', p. 18, https://www.dfat.gov.au/sites/default/files/2017-foreign-policy-white-paper.pdf.

16 Matthew Doran and Bill Birtles, '"It Would Be [a] Shame if a Plane Fell from the Sky": China's Warning to RAAF Over South China Sea Flights', ABC News, 16 December 2015, https://www.abc.net.au/news/2015-12-16/chinese-editorial-warns-raaf-planes-could-be-shot-down/7034664.

17 Correspondence between a senior official in Australia's Department of Defence and this book's author, August 2021.

18 Reuters, 'Australia Says Chinese Fighter Jet Intercepted Australian Surveillance Aircraft', VOA, 5 June 2022, https://www.voanews.com/a/australia-says-chinese-fighter-jet-intercepted-australian-surveillance-aircraft-/6603915.html.

19 Malcolm Turnbull, *A Bigger Picture* (Melbourne: Hardie Grant Books, 2020), pp. 421–2.

20 Stephen Kuper, 'RAN, US Navy Join Forces for South China Sea Patrol', *Defence Connect*, 24 April 2020, https://www.defenceconnect.com.au/maritime-antisub/5972-ran-us-navy-join-forces-for-south-china-sea-patrol.

21 Thomas Schelling, *Arms and Influence* (New Haven, CT: Yale University Press, 1966).

22 Euan Graham, 'Laser Incident Near Australia Paints China in a Bad Light', IISS *Analysis*, 25 February 2022, https://www.iiss.org/blogs/analysis/2022/02/laser-incident-near-australia-paints-china-in-a-bad-light.

23 Euan Graham, 'Black Swan 2020: China's NEO that Goes Geo', Lowy Institute *Interpreter*, 25 July 2016, https://www.lowyinstitute.org/the-interpreter/black-swan-2020-china-s-neo-goes-geo.

24 Jim Molan, 'War-gaming Tomorrow: "It's Possible This Will End in an All-out Invasion"', *Australian*, 11 September 2021, https://www.theaustralian.com.au/inquirer/wargaming-tomorrow-its-possible-to-envision-this-ending-in-an-allout-invasion/news-story/4229ad3877a242dfc91e7ec3c954b7cd.

25 Thomas Shugart, 'Australia and the Growing Reach of China's Military', Lowy Institute, 9 August 2021, https://www.lowyinstitute.org/publications/australia-and-growing-reach-china-s-military.

26 Daljit Singh, 'The "Indo-Pacific" Is Here to Stay', ISEAS–Yusof Ishak Institute *Fulcrum*, 22 December 2020, https://fulcrum.sg/the-indo-pacific-is-here-to-stay/.

27 Graham, 'Laser Incident Near Australia Paints China in a Bad Light'.

28 IISS, *The Military Balance 2022* (Abingdon: Routledge for the IISS, 2022), pp. 248–9, 257–8.

29 *Ibid.*, p. 251; and H.I. Sutton, 'Chinese Increasing Nuclear Submarine Shipyard Capacity', US Naval Institute News, 12 October 2020, https://news.usni.org/2020/10/12/chinese-increasing-nuclear-submarine-shipyard-capacity.

30 David Wroe, 'Chinese Naval Ships Close to Australia? "Get Used to It", Experts Warn', *Sydney Morning Herald*, 10 March 2017, https://www.smh.com.au/politics/federal/chinese-naval-ships-close-to-australia-get-used-to-it-experts-warn-20170309-guunxi.html.

31 Jérôme Henry, 'China's Military Deployments in the Gulf of Aden: Anti-piracy and Beyond', *Asie.Visions*, no. 89, Institut Français des Relations Internationales, November 2016, https://www.ifri.org/sites/default/files/atoms/files/chinas_military_deployments_in_the_gulf_of_aden_anti-piracy_and_beyond_0.pdf.

32 James Goldrick, 'Australia's Essential Need: Not Seaborne Trade but Seaborne Supply', Lowy Institute *Interpreter*, 3 September 2021, https://www.lowyinstitute.org/the-interpreter/australia-s-essential-need-not-seaborne-trade-seaborne-supply.

33 Ellen McCutchan, 'Fact Check: Does Australia Have 3 Weeks of Petrol in Reserve?', ABC News, 23 May 2018, https://www.abc.net.au/news/2018-05-23/fact-check-jim-molan-fuel-security/9687606; and United Nations, 'Agreement on an International Energy Program', 18 November 1974, p. 273, https://

treaties.un.org/doc/Publication/
UNTS/Volume%201040/volume-1040-
A-15664-English.pdf.

34 Euan Graham, 'The Lion and the
    Kangaroo: Australia's Strategic
    Partnership with Singapore', Lowy
    Institute, 16 May 2016, https://www.
    lowyinstitute.org/publications/lion-
    and-kangaroo-australia-s-strategic-
    partnership-singapore.

35 James Goldrick, 'Australia's Naval
    Presence in the South China Sea
    Is Nothing New', ASPI *Strategist*,
    5 February 2021, https://www.
    aspistrategist.org.au/australias-naval-
    presence-in-the-south-china-sea-is-
    nothing-new/.

36 Anthony Bergin and Tony Press,
    'We Can't Just Go with the Floe in
    Antarctica', ASPI, 27 April 2020,
    https://www.aspi.org.au/opinion/
    we-cant-just-go-floe-antarctica.

37 Elizabeth Buchanan, 'The (Other)
    Continent We Can't Defend',
    Lowy Institute *Interpreter*, 13
    August 2019, https://www.
    lowyinstitute.org/the-interpreter/
    other-continent-we-can-t-defend.

38 Xu Keyue, 'Japan–Australia Pact
    Shows "Willingness to Be US Pawns",
    While Risking Regional Peace', *Global
    Times*, 24 October 2022, https://www.
    globaltimes.cn/page/202210/1277785.
    shtml.

39 Euan Graham, 'The Future
    for US Marines in Darwin',
    Lowy Institute *Interpreter*, 31
    August 2017, https://www.
    lowyinstitute.org/the-interpreter/
    future-us-marines-darwin.

40 Australian Government, Department
    of Defence, 'United States Force
    Posture Initiatives', https://www.
    defence.gov.au/Initiatives/USFPI/.

41 Greg Hadley, 'Two More B-2

Bombers Arrive in Australia to Train
with RAAF', *Air & Space Forces
Magazine*, 14 July 2022, https://www.
airforcemag.com/two-more-b-2-
bombers-arrive-in-australia-to-train-
with-raaf/.

42 Jim Thomas, Zack Cooper and
    Iskander Rehman, 'Gateway
    to the Indo-Pacific: Australian
    Defense Strategy and the Future
    of the Australia–U.S. Alliance',
    Center for Strategic and Budgetary
    Assessments, 9 November 2013,
    pp. 13–21, https://csbaonline.org/
    research/publications/gateway-
    to-the-indo-pacific-australian-
    defense-strategy-and-the-future-of-t/
    publication/1.

43 C. Todd Lopez, 'U.S. Withdraws
    from Intermediate-Range Nuclear
    Forces Treaty', US Department of
    Defense, 2 August 2019, https://www.
    defense.gov/Explore/News/Article/
    Article/1924779/us-withdraws-from-
    intermediate-range-nuclear-forces-
    treaty/.

44 James Holmes, 'It's Time for a
    Massive U.S. Navy Base in Australia',
    National Interest, 17 November 2019,
    https://nationalinterest.org/blog/
    buzz/its-time-massive-us-navy-
    base-australia-97051; and Center
    for Strategic and International
    Studies, 'U.S. Force Posture Strategy
    in the Asia Pacific Region: An
    Independent Assessment', August
    2012, p. 19, https://csis-website-prod.
    s3.amazonaws.com/s3fs-public/
    legacy_files/files/publication/120814_
    FINAL_PACOM_optimized.pdf.

45 Brendan Nicholson, 'No US
    Military Bases Here, Says Smith,
    but Washington Confirms Plan
    as Part of Asia-Pacific Pivot',
    Australian, 3 August 2012, https://

www.theaustralian.com.au/
national-affairs/defence/no-us-
military-bases-here-says-smith-but-
washington-confirms-plan-as-part-
of-asia-pacific-pivot/news-story/
fe82b3962114f5a686c5c01d876c34f7.

46 US Navy, 'Senate Armed Services
Subcommittee on Readiness and
Management Support Holds
Hearing on Navy and Marine
Corps Readiness', 2 December 2020,
https://www.navy.mil/Press-Office/
Testimony/display-testimony/
Article/2433784/senate-armed-
services-subcommittee-on-readiness-
and-management-support-holds-he.

47 Ken Moriyasu, 'US Navy Chief Wants
Indian Ocean "1st Fleet," Possibly
in Singapore', Nikkei Asia, 19
November 2020, https://asia.nikkei.
com/Politics/International-relations/
Indo-Pacific/US-Navy-chief-wants-
Indian-Ocean-1st-Fleet-possibly-in-
Singapore.

48 Andrew Tillett and Philip Coorey,
'Dutton Signals More US Troops in
Australia', *Australian Financial Review*,
10 June 2021, https://www.afr.com/
politics/federal/dutton-flags-more-us-
troops-in-australia-20210610-p5800r.

49 Colin Clark, 'Aussie PM Says
"Extended" Visits for US, UK
Nuke Subs Likely at Western Port',
Breaking Defense, 15 March 2022,
https://breakingdefense.com/2022/03/
aussie-pm-says-extended-visits-for-
us-uk-nuke-subs-likely-at-western-
port/.

50 Andrew Greene, 'PM Says No
Nuclear Submarine Decision Before
Election, as New Subs Base Planned
for Australia's East Coast', ABC
News, 6 March 2022, https://www.
abc.net.au/news/2022-03-07/nuclear-
submarine-base-shortlist-brisbane-
newcastle-port-kembla/100887204.

51 US Department of State, 'Joint
Statement on Australia–U.S.
Ministerial Consultations (AUSMIN)
2021', 16 September 2021, https://
www.state.gov/joint-statement-
on-australia-u-s-ministerial-
consultations-ausmin-2021/.

52 Brendan Thomas-Noone, 'Ebbing
Opportunity: Australia and the US
National Technology and Industrial
Base', United States Studies Centre,
25 November 2019, https://www.ussc.
edu.au/analysis/australia-and-the-us-
national-technology-and-industrial-
base.

53 Julie Hare, 'Australian Universities
Have Expertise to Support AUKUS
Security Pact', *Australian Financial
Review*, 16 September 2021, https://
www.afr.com/companies/energy/
australian-universities-have-
expertise-to-support-aukus-security-
pact-20210916-p58s62.

54 John Blaxland, 'Defence Update:
In an Increasingly Dangerous
Neighbourhood, Australia Needs
a Stronger Security System',
Conversation, 1 July 2020, https://
theconversation.com/defence-update-
in-an-increasingly-dangerous-
neighbourhood-australia-needs-a-
stronger-security-system-141771.

55 For a doctrinal view from Australia's
navy, see Justin Jones (ed.), *A
Maritime School of Strategic Thought
for Australia: Perspectives*, *Sea Power
Series* 1 (Canberra: Sea Power Centre,
Australia, 2013).

56 James Goldrick, 'Australia's Essential
Need: Not Seaborne Trade but
Seaborne Supply', Lowy Institute
Interpreter, 15 June 2022, https://www.
lowyinstitute.org/the-interpreter/
australia-s-essential-need-not-

seaborne-trade-seaborne-supply.

57 Angelique Donnellan, 'Australia's Attack Class Submarine Project Faces Criticism Over Rising Costs and Milestone Delays', ABC News, 20 January 2021, https://www.abc.net.au/news/2021-01-20/australia-attack-class-submarines-project-costs-delays-criticism/13074440.

58 IISS, *The Military Balance 2021* (Abingdon: Routledge for the IISS, 2021), pp. 241–3.

59 Australian Government, Department of Defence, '2020 Defence Strategic Update', 1 July 2020, p. 3, https://www.defence.gov.au/about/strategic-planning/2020-defence-strategic-update.

60 Rod McGuirk, 'Australia Plans $190 Billion Defense Boost Over Decade', Associated Press, 1 July 2020, https://apnews.com/article/9a1fffde814f3d5d0d2c32d1758fba65; and 'Speech – Australian Strategic Policy Institute', speech delivered by Linda Reynolds, Australia's Minister for Defence, 2 July 2020, https://www.minister.defence.gov.au/minister/lreynolds/speeches/speech-australian-strategic-policy-institute.

61 Australian Government, Department of Defence, '2020 Defence Strategic Update', p. 4.

62 *Ibid.*, p. 12

63 Mallory Shelbourne, 'Davidson: China Could Try to Take Control of Taiwan in "Next Six Years"', US Naval Institute News, 9 March 2021, https://news.usni.org/2021/03/09/davidson-china-could-try-to-take-control-of-taiwan-in-next-six-years.

64 Australian Government, Department of Defence, '2020 Defence Strategic Update', p. 29.

65 *Ibid.*, p. 27.

66 Stephan Fruehling, 'Does the AUKUS Submarine Deal Compromise Australia's Sovereignty?', ASPI *Strategist*, 1 October 2021, https://www.aspistrategist.org.au/does-the-aukus-submarine-deal-compromise-australias-sovereignty/.

67 Donald Greenlees, 'ANZUS at 70: Konfrontasi and East Timor—America's Indonesian Balancing Act', ASPI *Strategist*, 23 August 2021, https://www.aspistrategist.org.au/anzus-at-70-konfrontasi-and-east-timor-americas-indonesian-balancing-act/.

68 Matthew Doran, 'Criminals Exploited Microsoft Exchange After China "Propped Open the Door"', Intelligence Agency Says', ABC News, 29 July 2021, https://www.abc.net.au/news/2021-07-29/china-microsoft-exchange-hack-criminals-weakness-propped-open/100335008.

69 Colin Packham, 'Australia Concluded China Was Behind Hack on Parliament, Political Parties – Sources', Reuters, 15 September 2019, https://www.reuters.com/article/us-australia-china-cyber-exclusive-idUSKBN1W00VF.

70 Jade Macmillan and Andrew Greene, 'Australia to Spend $270b Building Larger Military to Prepare for "Poorer, More Dangerous" World and Rise of China', ABC News, 1 July 2021, https://www.abc.net.au/news/2020-06-30/australia-unveils-10-year-defence-strategy/12408232.

71 IISS, *The Military Balance 2021*, p. 224.

72 Australian Government, Department of Defence, 'Defence Workforce to Grow Above 100,000', 10 March 2022, https://www.minister.defence.gov.au/media-releases/2022-03-10/defence-workforce-grow-above-100000.

73 Australian Government, Department of Defence, '2020 Defence Strategic Update', p. 27.

74 Kym Bergmann, 'Army to Get Long-range Missile Capability', *Australian*, 31 October 2020, https://www.theaustralian.com.au/special-reports/defence/army-to-acquire-longrange-missile-capability/news-story/25640827c9c242e6d9670b124936c271; and Fabian Hoffman, 'Australia Seeks Improved Missile Capabilities', IISS *Analysis*, 16 November 2021, https://www.iiss.org/blogs/analysis/2021/11/australia-seeks-improved-missile-capabilities.

75 William Leben, 'What's the Plan for "Sovereign" Munitions for the ADF?', ASPI *Strategist*, 3 November 2022, https://www.aspistrategist.org.au/whats-the-plan-for-sovereign-munitions-for-the-adf/.

76 John R. Hoehn, 'Precision-guided Munitions: Background and Issues for Congress', Congressional Research Service, 11 June 2021, https://sgp.fas.org/crs/weapons/R45996.pdf.

77 Natasha Turak, 'The U.S. and Europe Are Running Out of Weapons to Send to Ukraine', CNBC News, 28 September 2022, https://www.cnbc.com/2022/09/28/the-us-and-europe-are-running-out-of-weapons-to-send-to-ukraine.html.

78 Australian Government, Department of Defence, 'Australia and US Partner to Spearhead Precision Strike Missile Capability', 12 August 2021, https://www.minister.defence.gov.au/minister/peter-dutton/media-releases/australia-and-us-partner-spearhead-precision-strike-missile.

79 Peter Hunter, 'More of the Same Isn't the Answer to Australia's Security Challenges', ASPI *Strategist*, 7 August 2019, https://www.aspistrategist.org.au/more-of-the-same-isnt-the-answer-to-australias-security-challenges/.

80 Hugh White, *How to Defend Australia* (Melbourne: La Trobe University Press, 2019).

81 Australian Government, Department of Defence, '2020 Defence Strategic Update', p. 26.

82 Australian Government, Department of Defence, 'Joint Statement – Defence Strategic Review', 3 August 2022, https://www.minister.defence.gov.au/minister/rmarles/statements/joint-statement-defence-strategic-review.

83 Aaron Mehta, 'Australia Cleared to Buy $185 Million in Aegis Equipment', Defense News, 27 June 2018, https://www.defensenews.com/global/asia-pacific/2018/06/27/australia-cleared-to-buy-185-million-in-aegis-equipment/; and Marcus Hellyer, 'In for the Long Haul (Part 2): Can the Anzacs Remain Relevant?', ASPI *Strategist*, 4 April 2019, https://www.aspistrategist.org.au/in-for-the-long-haul-part-2-can-the-anzacs-remain-relevant/.

84 Marcus Hellyer, 'Delivering a Stronger Navy, Faster', ASPI, 2 November 2021, https://www.aspi.org.au/report/delivering-stronger-navy-faster.

85 Andrew Tillett, 'Navy Ships May Be Delayed', *Australian Financial Review*, 1 February 2022, https://www.afr.com/politics/federal/navy-ships-may-be-delayed-20220201-p59sye.

86 Andrew Tillett, 'Design Issues Weigh Down $45b Frigate Program', *Australian Financial Review*, 31 May 2021, https://www.afr.com/politics/federal/45-billion-frigate-problem-weighed-down-by-design-issues-20210531-p57wmv.

87 Dinakar Peri, 'India, Australia Are Guardians of the Flanks of the Indian Ocean: Australian Navy Office', *Hindu*, 2 November 2022, https://www.thehindu.com/news/national/india-australia-are-guardians-of-the-flanks-of-the-indian-ocean-australian-navy-officer/article66083029.ece.

88 Andrew Brown, 'The History of the Radford–Collins Agreement', Royal Australian Navy, https://www.navy.gov.au/history/feature-histories/history-radford-collins-agreement.

89 Nick Childs, 'US and Allies Test Aircraft Carrier Options', IISS Military Balance Blog, 15 October 2021, https://www.iiss.org/blogs/military-balance/2021/10/us-and-allies-test-aircraft-carrier-options.

90 Marcus Hellyer, 'What Exactly Is the Collins Life-of-type Extension? Part 2—A Mindset', ASPI *Strategist*, 20 November 2018, aspistrategist.org.au/what-exactly-is-the-collins-life-of-type-extension-part-2-a-mindset/; and Xavier Vavasseur, 'Australia Confirms Life-of-type Extension for Collins-class Submarines', Naval News, 19 September 2021, https://www.navalnews.com/naval-news/2021/09/australia-confirms-life-of-type-extension-for-collins-class-submarines/.

91 Mathieu Duchâtel, 'Australia and the Future of Deterrence Against China', Institut Montaigne, 22 September 2021, https://www.institutmontaigne.org/en/blog/australia-and-future-deterrence-against-china.

92 Matthew P. Funaiole, Joseph S. Bermudez, Jr and Brian Hart, 'A Glimpse of Chinese Ballistic Missile Submarines', Center for Strategic and International Studies, 4 August 2021, https://www.csis.org/analysis/glimpse-chinese-ballistic-missile-submarines.

93 Henry Boyd and Joseph Dempsey, 'Beyond JL-2: China's Development of a Successor SLBM Continues', IISS Military Balance Blog, 7 August 2017, https://www.iiss.org/blogs/military-balance/2017/08/china-successor-slbm.

94 Duchâtel, 'Australia and the Future of Deterrence Against China'.

95 According to the Defence Strategic Update, 'the Government will also prioritise the acquisition of strike weapons to increase the ADF's maritime deterrence and long-range land strike capabilities'; Australian Government, Department of Defence, '2020 Defense Strategic Update', p. 37.

96 Marcus Hellyer, 'Can Australia Get Second-hand Nuclear Submarines? The US Option', ASPI *Strategist*, 15 October 2021, https://www.aspistrategist.org.au/can-australia-get-second-hand-nuclear-submarines-the-us-option/.

97 Duchâtel, 'Australia and the Future of Deterrence Against China'.

98 US Marine Corps, 'A Concept for Stand-in Forces', December 2021, https://www.hqmc.marines.mil/Portals/142/Users/183/35/4535/211201_A%20Concept%20for%20Stand-In%20Forces.pdf?ver=EIdvoO4fwI2OaJDSB5gDDA%3d%3d.

99 Bergmann, 'Army to Get Long-range Missile Capability'.

100 Minister for Foreign Affairs, Minister for Women, Senator the Hon Marise Payne, 'Australia to Pursue Nuclear-powered Submarines Through New Trilateral Enhanced Security Partnership', 16 September 2021,

https://www.foreignminister.gov.au/minister/marise-payne/media-release/australia-pursue-nuclear-powered-submarines-through-new-trilateral-enhanced-security-partnership.

101 White, *How to Defend Australia*, p. 234.

102 Allan Gyngell, *Fear of Abandonment: Australia in the World Since 1942* (Melbourne: La Trobe University Press, 2021), p. 150; and Mark Fitzpatrick (ed.), *Preventing Nuclear Dangers in Southeast Asia and Australia* (London: IISS, 2009), p. 168.

103 Katharine Murphy, 'Essential Poll: Majority of Australians Back Aukus Submarine Pact, but Fear It Will Inflame Tensions with China', *Guardian*, 27 September 2021, https://www.theguardian.com/australia-news/2021/sep/28/essential-poll-majority-of-australians-back-aukus-submarine-pact-but-fear-it-will-inflame-tensions-with-china.

104 Australian Government, Department of Defence, '2020 Defence Strategic Update', p. 27.

105 Rod Lyon, 'Should Australia Build Its Own Nuclear Arsenal?', ASPI *Strategist*, 24 October 2019, https://www.aspistrategist.org.au/should-australia-build-its-own-nuclear-arsenal/.

106 White, *How to Defend Australia*, p. 245.

Chapter Five

1 Australian Government, Department of Foreign Affairs and Trade, '2017 Foreign Policy White Paper', p. 18, https://www.dfat.gov.au/sites/default/files/2017-foreign-policy-white-paper.pdf.

2 Ashley Townshend, 'Australia's New Regional Security Posture', *Asia-Pacific Regional Security Assessment 2021* (London: Routledge for the IISS, 2021), p. 91.

3 Rory Medcalf, *Contest for the Indo-Pacific: Why China Won't Map the Future* (Melbourne: La Trobe University Press, 2020), pp. 156–7.

4 *Ibid*.

5 Australian Government, Department of Foreign Affairs and Trade, '2017 Foreign Policy White Paper', p. 25.

6 Minister for Trade, Tourism and Investment, the Hon Dan Tehan MP, 'Joint Statement by the Hon Dan Tehan MP, Australian Minister for Trade, Tourism and Investment, and Ambassador Katherine Tai, United States Trade Representative', 29 March 2022, https://www.trademinister.gov.au/minister/dan-tehan/media-release/joint-statement-hon-dan-tehan-mp-australian-minister-trade-tourism-and-investment-and-ambassador-katherine-tai-united-states-trade-representative.

7 James Wise, 'Devaluing DFAT', Lowy Institute *Interpreter*, 16 July 2020, https://www.lowyinstitute.org/the-interpreter/devaluing-dfat.

8 Peter Jennings, 'The Many Ways in Which China Is Pushing Us Around … Without Resistance', ASPI, 8 June 2019, https://www.aspi.org.au/opinion/many-ways-which-china-pushing-us-around-without-resistance.

9 Andrew Davies and Peter Layton, 'We'll Have Six of Them and Four of Those', ASPI *Special Report*,

November 2009, http://ad-aspi.
s3.ap-southeast-2.amazonaws.com/
import/9_42_04_AM_SR25_COTS-
MOTS.pdf?VersionId=6MToZ0Yk7VB
nC0F3DapNrRe46lcghiEi.

10 Euan Graham, 'The Fix: Solving
Australia's Foreign Affairs
Challenges', *Australian Foreign Affairs*,
no. 6, July 2019, pp. 88–93, https://
www.australianforeignaffairs.com/
articles/the-fix/2019/08/the-fix/
euan-graham.

11 Rory Medcalf, 'Toward a Shared
Alliance Strategy in a Contested
Indo-Pacific: A View from Australia',
National Bureau of Asian Research,
21 May 2019, https://www.nbr.org/
publication/toward-a-shared-alliance-
strategy-in-a-contested-indo-pacific-
a-view-from-australia/.

12 Rod Lyon, 'Hard Times in Australian
Strategic Thinking', ASPI *Strategist*,
19 October 2018, https://www.
aspistrategist.org.au/hard-times-in-
australian-strategic-thinking/.

13 Medcalf, *Contest for the Indo-Pacific:
Why China Won't Map the Future*,
p. 156.

14 'The Indo Pacific and Its Strategic
Challenges: An Australian
Perspective', speech delivered by
Peter Varghese, Chancellor of the
University of Queensland, Singapore,
8 January 2019, https://about.uq.edu.
au/chancellor/speeches-and-articles/
indo-pacific-and-its-strategic-
challenges-australian-perspective.

15 Australian Government, Department
of Foreign Affairs and Trade, '2017
Foreign Policy White Paper', p. 42.

16 *Ibid*.

17 Nick Bisley, 'Indo-Pacific: The
Maritime and the Continental',
ASPI *Strategist*, 21 November 2016,
https://www.aspistrategist.org.au/
indo-pacific-maritime-continental/.

18 Euan Graham, 'The Quad Deserves
Its Second Chance', Strategic and
Defence Studies Centre, Australian
National University College of Asia
and the Pacific *Centre of Gravity
Series*, March 2018, p. 6, https://
bellschool.anu.edu.au/sites/default/
files/uploads/2018-03/cog_39_web_-_
debating_the_quad.pdf.

19 Australian Government, Department
of Foreign Affairs and Trade, '2017
Foreign Policy White Paper', p. 40.

20 *Ibid.*, p. 41.

21 Franz-Stefan Gady, 'Why Japan Lost
the Bid to Build Australia's New
Subs', *Diplomat*, 27 April 2016, https://
thediplomat.com/2016/04/why-japan-
lost-the-bid-to-build-australias-new-
subs/.

22 Ministry of Foreign Affairs of Japan,
'Japan–Australia Reciprocal Access
Agreement', 6 January 2022, https://
www.mofa.go.jp/a_o/ocn/au/
page4e_001195.html.

23 Tim Huxley, 'Australian Defence
Engagement with Southeast Asia',
Strategic and Defence Studies Centre,
Australian National University
College of Asia and the Pacific
Centre of Gravity Series, November
2012, p. 4, https://sdsc.bellschool.
anu.edu.au/sites/default/files/
publications/attachments/2020-10/
cog_2_2018_softproof_v4.pdf.

24 Andrew Davies, 'Australia's Security
and Defence Outlook', *Asia-Pacific
Regional Security Assessment 2020*
(London: Routledge for the IISS,
2020), p. 126.

25 Australian Government, Department
of Foreign Affairs and Trade, '2017
Foreign Policy White Paper', p. 42.

26 Bill Paterson, 'Time for Less Rhetoric
and More Substance from Australia–

South Korea Ministerial Talks', ASPI *Strategist*, 10 September 2021, https://www.aspistrategist.org.au/time-for-less-rhetoric-and-more-substance-from-australia-south-korea-ministerial-talks/.

27 Lesley Seebeck, 'AUKUS and Australian Grand Strategy', ASPI *Strategist*, 9 November 2021, https://www.aspistrategist.org.au/aukus-and-australian-grand-strategy/.

28 Australian Government, Department of Foreign Affairs and Trade, '2017 Foreign Policy White Paper', p. 47.

29 Reuters, '"Inconceivable" Australia Would Not Join US to Defend Taiwan', *Australian Financial Review*, 13 November 2021, https://www.afr.com/politics/federal/inconceivable-australia-would-not-join-us-to-defend-taiwan-20211113-p598mi.

30 Australian Government, Department of Foreign Affairs and Trade, 'Joint Statement Australia–U.S. Ministerial Consultations (AUSMIN) 2020', https://www.dfat.gov.au/geo/united-states-of-america/ausmin/joint-statement-ausmin-2020; and Australian Government, Department of Foreign Affairs and Trade, 'Joint Statement Australia–U.S. Ministerial Consultations (AUSMIN) 2021', https://www.dfat.gov.au/geo/united-states-of-america/ausmin/joint-statement-australia-us-ministerial-consultations-ausmin-2021.

31 Natasha Kassam and Mark Harrison, 'Stoking Fears of War Could Serve China's Goals. Australian Policy Needs Rethinking', *Guardian*, 3 May 2021, https://www.theguardian.com/commentisfree/2021/may/03/stoking-fears-of-war-could-serve-chinas-goals-australian-policy-needs-rethinking.

32 Mark Harrison, 'Keating Out of Date and Out of Touch on Taiwan', ASPI *Strategist*, 12 November 2021, https://www.aspistrategist.org.au/keating-out-of-date-and-out-of-touch-on-taiwan/.

33 'Minister for Defence – 16th IISS Asia Security Summit: The Shangri-La Dialogue', speech by Marise Payne, Australia's Minister for Defence, 3 June 2017, https://www.minister.defence.gov.au/minister/marise-payne/speeches/minister-defence-16th-iiss-asia-security-summit-shangri-la-dialogue.

34 Australian Government, Department of Foreign Affairs and Trade, '2017 Foreign Policy White Paper', pp. 41–2.

35 Australian Government, Department of Defence, '2016 Defence White Paper', https://www.defence.gov.au/about/publications/2016-defence-white-paper.

36 Australian Government, Department of Foreign Affairs and Trade, '2017 Foreign Policy White Paper', pp. 46, 118.

37 Medcalf, *Contest for the Indo-Pacific: Why China Won't Map the Future*, p. 157.

38 Liu Dan and Tang Xiaosong, 'Australia's Public Diplomacy Towards China's Neighbouring Countries: Taking Southeast Asia as an Example', *Journal of International Relations*, no. 1, 2019, https://kns.cnki.net/kcms/detail/detail.aspx?dbcode=CJFD&dbname=CJFDLAST2019&filename=GGXY201901003&uniplatform=NZKPT&v=Otslyes8i04oGfUVN8j_Uz5OAbE_URZlcGDAYDjazVcMhVJgfWtPYAcz2kw4bs2c; and Guo Liyu, 'Research on the Security and Defense Relations Between Australia and ASEAN After the Cold War',

East China Normal University, 2017, https://kns.cnki.net/kcms/detail/detail.aspx?dbcode=CMFD&dbname=CMFD201702&filename=1017081690.nh&uniplatform=NZKPT&v=dsV14bbp9shoz3WhXtZWUrL-linnw2DKskHF6xFRTEbOtTsEAxwfwYJZbBBbSUq9.

39 Australian Government, Department of Defence, '2016 Defence White Paper', p. 130.

40 Association of Southeast Asian Nations, 'Joint Statement of the ASEAN–Australia Special Summit: The Sydney Declaration', 18 March 2018, https://asean.org/wp-content/uploads/2021/08/Joint-Statement-of-the-ASEAN-Australia-Special-Summit-Sydney-Declaration-FINAL.pdf.

41 White House, 'Fact Sheet: Quad Leaders' Summit', 24 September 2021, https://www.whitehouse.gov/briefing-room/statements-releases/2021/09/24/fact-sheet-quad-leaders-summit/.

42 See, for example, White House, 'Joint Statement from Quad Leaders', 24 September 2021, https://www.whitehouse.gov/briefing-room/statements-releases/2021/09/24/joint-statement-from-quad-leaders/.

43 Yogesh Joshi, Ippeita Nishida and Nishant Rajeev, 'Institutionalising the Quad: Can It Seize the Momentum for the Future?', Institute of South Asian Studies, National University of Singapore, and Sasakawa Peace Foundation, April 2021, pp. 12–14, https://www.isas.nus.edu.sg/wp-content/uploads/2021/04/Institutionalising-the-Quad-Full.pdf.

44 Townshend, 'Australia's New Regional Security Posture', p. 108.

45 Mason Richey, 'The Right Angle of the Quadrilateral', East Asia Forum, 12 May 2021, https://www.eastasiaforum.org/2021/05/12/the-right-angle-of-the-quadrilateral/; and Kevin Rudd, 'Why the Quad Alarms China', Foreign Affairs, 6 August 2021, https://www.foreignaffairs.com/articles/united-states/2021-08-06/why-quad-alarms-china.

46 Andrew Greene, Stephen Dziedzic and James Oaten, 'Australia to Rejoin "Quad" Naval Exercises in Move Certain to Infuriate Beijing', ABC News, 19 October 2020, https://www.abc.net.au/news/2020-10-20/australia-rejoins-naval-exercise-in-move-certain-to-anger-china/12784186.

47 David Brewster, 'Australia–India: Naval Drills Show Trust, yet Political Caution Still', Lowy Institute Interpreter, 12 April 2019, https://www.lowyinstitute.org/the-interpreter/australia-india-naval-drills-show-trust-yet-political-caution-still.

48 Australian Government, Department of Foreign Affairs and Trade, '2017 Foreign Policy White Paper', p. 43.

49 Wang Guanghou, 'Analysis of Australia's ASEAN Policy', International Forum, vol. 15, no. 5, 2013, https://kns.cnki.net/kcms/detail/detail.aspx?dbcode=CJFD&dbname=CJFD2013&filename=GJLT201305004&uniplatform=NZKPT&v=K9r-c2xDSy5SoRUH5XO25dIzWk6-2fK_Bw86kT_R_XyvMEAOnBTmRlDAHYrveKB_.

50 Australian Government, Department of Foreign Affairs and Trade, 'ASEAN Key Economic Indicators', https://www.dfat.gov.au/sites/default/files/asean-cef.pdf.

51 Euan Graham, 'The Lion and the Kangaroo: Australia's Strategic Partnership with Singapore', Lowy

Institute, 12 May 2016, https://www.lowyinstitute.org/publications/lion-and-kangaroo-australia-s-strategic-partnership-singapore. Winston Churchill's original concept of the 'Malay Barrier' was in relation to a line he identified as necessary to hold, from Burma through the Malay Peninsula and Singapore via Java to northern Australia; Brian P. Farrell, *The Defence and Fall of Singapore, 1940–1942* (Singapore: Monsoon Books, 2021), p. 201.

52 James Goldrick, 'Australia Must Speak Carefully and Carry a Big Enough Stick in the South China Sea', ASPI *Strategist*, 3 August 2022, https://www.aspistrategist.org.au/australia-must-speak-carefully-and-carry-a-big-enough-stick-in-the-south-china-sea/.

53 David Feeney, '"The Ostrich Sticks Its Head in the Sand and Thinks Itself Safe": Australia's Need for a Grand Strategy', Strategic and Defence Studies Centre, Australian National University College of Asia and the Pacific *Centre of Gravity Series*, December 2018, p. 4, https://sdsc.bellschool.anu.edu.au/sites/default/files/publications/attachments/2018-12/cog_46.pdf.

54 Permanent Mission of the Commonwealth of Australia to the United Nations, Letter to the Secretary-General of the United Nations, no. 20/026, 23 July 2020, https://www.un.org/depts/los/clcs_new/submissions_files/mys_12_12_2019/2020_07_23_AUS_NV_UN_001_OLA-2020-00373.pdf.

55 Jonathan Kearsley, Eryk Bagshaw and Anthony Galloway, '"If You Make China the Enemy, China Will Be the Enemy": Beijing's Fresh Threat to Australia', *Sydney Morning Herald*, 18 November 2020, https://www.smh.com.au/world/asia/if-you-make-china-the-enemy-china-will-be-the-enemy-beijing-s-fresh-threat-to-australia-20201118-p56fqs.html; and Richard McGregor, 'China Sends a Message with Australian Crackdown', *Financial Times*, 25 November 2020, https://www.ft.com/content/9ed5f582-423d-41c4-ba23-0441f7dee165.

56 Jack Detsch, 'Washington Worries China Is Winning Over Thailand', *Foreign Policy*, 17 June 2022, https://foreignpolicy.com/2022/06/17/china-thailand-submarines-military-influence/.

57 Dominic Giannini, 'Fears Australia Caught Flat-footed in Asia', 7NEWS, 8 November 2021, https://7news.com.au/politics/defence/fears-australia-caught-flat-footed-in-asia-c-4477125.

58 Anthony Galloway, '"Step Down in Southeast Asia": DFAT Still Working on Foreign Aid Plan', *Sydney Morning Herald*, 7 October 2020, https://www.smh.com.au/politics/federal/step-down-in-southeast-asia-dfat-still-working-on-foreign-aid-plan-20201007-p562rl.html.

59 Hervé Lemahieu, 'The Case for Australia to Step Up in South-east Asia', *Australian Financial Review*, 23 October 2020, https://www.afr.com/policy/foreign-affairs/the-case-for-australia-to-step-up-in-south-east-asia-20201021-p56743.

60 For a critique of slow Australian aid to Indonesia, see Stephen Dziedzic, 'Senior Australian Diplomat Gary Quinlan Urges Australia to Increase Support to South-east Asia', ABC News, 3 September 2021, https://www.abc.net.au/news/2021-09-02/gary-quinlan-southeast-asia-aid-cuts-indonesia-covid/100425268.

61 Townshend, 'Australia's New Regional Security Posture', p. 101.

62 Australian Government, Department of Foreign Affairs and Trade, 'Investing in Our Southeast Asian Partnerships', https://www.dfat.gov.au/geo/southeast-asia/investing-our-southeast-asian-partnerships.

63 Huxley, 'Australian Defence Engagement with Southeast Asia', p. 5.

64 Singapore Ministry of Defence, 'FPDA Defence Ministers' Joint Statement on Continued Commitment to the FPDA', 27 November 2020, https://www.mindef.gov.sg/web/portal/mindef/news-and-events/latest-releases/article-detail/2020/November/27nov20_fs.

65 Clement Yong, 'Five Power Defence Arrangements Needs to Stay Nimble Amid New Threats: PM Lee', Straits Times, 21 October 2021, https://www.straitstimes.com/singapore/fpda-needs-to-stay-nimble-amid-new-threats-pm-lee.

66 Dzirhan Mahadzir, 'Malaysian [sic] and Singapore Drill with U.K., Australia and New Zealand in Bersama Gold 2021', USNI News, 8 October 2021, https://news.usni.org/2021/10/08/malaysian-and-singapore-drill-with-allis-u-k-australia-and-new-zealand-in-bersama-gold-2021; and Benjamin Felton, 'RMAF Butterworth Redevelopment', Australian Defence Magazine, 25 August 2022, https://www.australiandefence.com.au/defence/estate/rmaf-butterworth-redevelopment.

67 Paya Lebar Air Base is scheduled to close around 2030. Changi Air Base East is the most obvious candidate to replace it as a hub for foreign air-force operations from Singapore; Ministry of Defence and the Singapore Armed Forces, 'Written Reply by Minister for Defence, Dr Ng Eng Hen to Parliamentary Question on Updated Timeline for RSAF Operations to Be Moved from Paya Lebar Air Base to Tengah Air Base', 5 October 2020, https://www.mindef.gov.sg/web/portal/mindef/news-and-events/latest-releases/article-detail/2020/october/05oct20_pq1/!ut/p/z0/fY1PE8EwFMQ_i0OOmfdktM7FAdPiUCZyMcGjoZL-yZSPLzUOTm67O7v7AwUSlNWduWpvnNVl8HsVH8br2XSOI7FaR_kQk12ep9FktdiOY1iC-l8ID6LJptkVVKV9wY29OJACBYJ0J--O1IDEKEiBh6oe9gNzq2uVgDo56-nlQT6MPdOFf7z1DAv3IIaWni3X9sypC2nLsNSeWs8bKkm3FIiew_CLYfiLqe5qv0mTwRvHST4r/; and J. Vitor Tossini, 'The British Defence Singapore Support Unit – Enabling the Tilt', UK Defence Journal, 1 August 2021, https://ukdefencejournal.org.uk/the-british-defence-singapore-support-unit-enabling-the-tilt/.

68 Mike Yeo, 'RAAF's Mysterious Surveillance Missions from Singapore', Australian Defence Magazine, 12 November 2021, https://www.australiandefence.com.au/news/raaf-s-mysterious-surveillance-missions-from-singapore#:~:text=A%20RAAF%20Boeing%20P%2D8A,over%20the%20South%20China%20Sea.

69 Manuel Mogato and Tom Westbrook, 'Australia to Send Spy Planes to Help Philippines Fight Militants', Reuters, 22 June 2017, https://www.reuters.com/article/us-philippines-militants-australia-idUSKBN19D2TU.

70 Australian Government, Department of Defence, 'Deepening Relations with Brunei Darussalam', 21 October 2020, https://www.minister.defence.gov.au/minister/lreynolds/media-releases/deepening-relations-brunei-darussalam; and Euan Graham, 'What's in a Visit to Brunei?', ASPI *Strategist*, 23 October 2020, https://www.aspistrategist.org.au/whats-in-a-visit-to-brunei/.

71 Joyce Ann L. Rocamora, 'PH, Australia Finalize Defense Logistics Accord', *Philippine News Agency*, 18 August 2021, https://www.pna.gov.ph/articles/1150845.

72 Euan Graham, 'Southeast Asia's Neglected Navigational and Overflight Challenges', Lowy Institute *Interpreter*, 27 February 2017, https://www.lowyinstitute.org/the-interpreter/southeast-asia-s-neglected-navigational-and-overflight-challenges.

73 'AUKUS Raises Risk of Tensions, Regional Arms Race: Malaysian PM', Xinhua, 18 September 2021, http://www.xinhuanet.com/english/asiapacific/2021-09/18/c_1310196519.htm.

74 Euan Graham, 'Aerial Manoeuvres in the South China Sea', IISS *Analysis*, 9 June 2021, https://www.iiss.org/blogs/analysis/2021/06/aerial-manoeuvres-south-china-sea.

75 James Goldrick, 'Australia's Naval Presence in the South China Sea Is Nothing New', ASPI *Strategist*, 5 February 2021, https://www.aspistrategist.org.au/australias-naval-presence-in-the-south-china-sea-is-nothing-new/.

76 Graham, 'What's in a Visit to Brunei?'; and Minister for Foreign Affairs, Minister for Women, Senator the Hon Marise Payne, 'Joint Visit to Indonesia, India, the Republic of Korea, and the United States', 8 September 2021, https://www.foreignminister.gov.au/minister/marise-payne/media-release/joint-visit-indonesia-india-republic-korea-and-united-states.

77 'Australian Navy Ships Touring SE Asia Make Port Call in Vietnam', Radio Free Asia, 20 September 2021, https://www.rfa.org/english/news/vietnam/australia-navy-09202021153320.html.

78 Australian Government, Department of Defence, 'Indo-Pacific Endeavour – Indo-Pacific Region', https://www.defence.gov.au/operations/indo-pacific-endeavour.

79 Australian Government, Department of Defence, '2016 Defence White Paper', p. 125.

80 Republic of Indonesia, Ministry of Foreign Affairs, 'Statement on Australia's Nuclear-powered Submarines Program', 17 September 2021, https://kemlu.go.id/portal/en/read/2937/siaran_pers/statement-on-australias-nuclear-powered-submarines-program.

81 Tom Allard, Kate Lamb and Agustinus Beo Da Costa, 'China Protested Indonesian Drilling, Military Exercises', Reuters, 1 December 2021, https://www.reuters.com/world/asia-pacific/exclusive-china-protested-indonesian-drilling-military-exercises-2021-12-01/.

82 'Opening Address Q&A', IISS Manama Dialogue 2021, 19 November 2021, https://www.iiss.org/events/manama-dialogue/manama-dialogue-2021.

83 Australian Government, Department of Defence, '2016 Defence White Paper', p. 129.

84 Ben Bland and Jeevan Vasagar, 'Mystery Over Seized Singapore Army Vehicles in Hong Kong', *Financial Times*, 25 November 2016, https://www.ft.com/content/1a0fbcd0-b2e5-11e6-9c37-5787335499a0.

85 Australian Government, Department of Defence, 'Australia–Singapore Military Training Initiative', https://defence.gov.au/Initiatives/ASMTI/Home/Background.asp.

86 Training areas in northern Queensland, expanded since 2016 at Singapore's expense, are capable of hosting 14,000 Singaporean personnel and have the capacity to host two large, unilateral combined-arms exercises annually. Singapore additionally conducts basic flight training in Western Australia. A treaty on military training and development, ratified in December 2020, guarantees these arrangements for 25 years. Euan Graham, 'Australia–Singapore Comprehensive Strategic Partnership Lives Up to Its Billing', ASPI *Strategist*, 17 October 2022, https://www.aspistrategist.org.au/australia-singapore-comprehensive-strategic-partnership-lives-up-to-its-billing/.

87 Republic of the Philippines, Department of Foreign Affairs, 'Statement of Foreign Affairs Teodoro L. Locsin, Jr. on the Australia–United Kingdom–United States (AUKUS) Enhanced Trilateral Security Partnership', 19 September 2021, https://dfa.gov.ph/dfa-news/statements-and-advisoriesupdate/29484-statement-of-foreign-affairs-teodoro-l-locsin-jr-on-the-australia-united-kingdom-united-states-aukus-enhanced-trilateral-security-partnership.

88 Australian Government, Department of Defence, 'Australia Continues Support for Vietnam's Peacekeeping Commitments', 3 May 2021, https://news.defence.gov.au/media/media-releases/australia-continues-support-vietnams-peacekeeping-commitments.

89 Australian Embassy Vietnam, 'Defence Cooperation Program', https://vietnam.embassy.gov.au/hnoi/DefCoop.html.

90 Hai Hong Nguyen, 'Australia Can Count on Vietnam to Support AUKUS', ASPI *Strategist*, 27 October 2021, https://www.aspistrategist.org.au/australia-can-count-on-vietnam-to-support-aukus/.

91 Suchart Klaikaew, 'Cobra Gold Partnership', Indo-Pacific Defense Forum, 22 October 2022, https://ipdefenseforum.com/2020/10/cobra-gold-partnership/.

92 Australian Government, Department of Foreign Affairs and Trade, 'Australia and Timor-Leste Maritime Boundaries', March 2018, https://www.dfat.gov.au/sites/default/files/aus-timor-maritime-boundary-fact-sheet.pdf.

93 Australian Embassy Timor-Leste, 'Defence Co-Operation', https://timorleste.embassy.gov.au/dili/Defence.html#:~:text=In%202017%2C%20Timor%2DLeste%20accepted,commitment%20to%20regional%20maritime%20security.

94 Meaghan Tobin, 'Chinese Cash: Enough to Keep East Timor Out of Asean?', *South China Morning Post*, 3 August 2019, https://www.scmp.com/week-asia/geopolitics/article/3021219/chinese-cash-enough-keep-east-timor-out-asean.

Chapter Six

1   Seth Robson, 'Pacific Island Nation of Palau Offers to Host US Military Bases, Report Says', *Stars and Stripes*, 9 September 2020, https://www.stripes.com/theaters/asia_pacific/pacific-island-nation-of-palau-offers-to-host-us-military-bases-report-says-1.644342.

2   Allan Gyngell, *Fear of Abandonment: Australia in the World Since 1942* (Melbourne: La Trobe University Press, 2021), p. 266.

3   David Feeney, '"The Ostrich Sticks Its Head in the Sand and Thinks Itself Safe": Australia's Need for a Grand Strategy', Strategic and Defence Studies Centre, Australian National University College of Asia and the Pacific *Centre of Gravity*, December 2018, p. 9, http://bellschool.anu.edu.au/sites/default/files/publications/attachments/2018-12/cog_46.pdf.

4   Fumi Matsumoto, 'Australian Leader Embarks on Pacific Trip to Regain "Backyard"', Nikkei Asia, 17 January 2019, https://asia.nikkei.com/Politics/International-relations/Australian-leader-embarks-on-Pacific-trip-to-regain-backyard.

5   Australian Government, Department of Foreign Affairs and Trade, 'Stepping Up Australia's Engagement with Our Pacific Family', September 2019, https://www.dfat.gov.au/sites/default/files/stepping-up-australias-engagement-with-our-pacific-family.pdf.

6   'Australia – the Indispensable Power in a Congested Sea', speech delivered by Jenny Hayward-Jones to the Royal United Services Institute's 2nd International Defence and Security Dialogue, 26 February 2013, https://www.lowyinstitute.org/publications/australia-indispensable-power-congested-sea: 'External interest in the Pacific Islands region can be broadly sorted into four categories: (1) traditional powers – Australia, New Zealand, the United States, France, the European Union and Japan, (2) ascendant or resurgent states – China, India, Russia, and the Republic of Korea, (3) vote buyers and marginalised states – Cuba, Taiwan, Israel, the United Arab Emirates, Iran and Georgia, and (4) investors – Malaysia and Indonesia.'

7   Graeme Dobell, 'The Pacific "Arc of Instability"', *Correspondents Report*, ABC Radio National, 20 August 2006, https://www.abc.net.au/correspondents/content/2006/s1719019.htm.

8   Chengxin Pan, Matthew Clarke and Sophie Loy-Wilson, 'Australia's Pivot to the Pacific', Australian Institute of International Affairs, 14 November 2018, https://www.internationalaffairs.org.au/australianoutlook/australias-pivot-to-the-pacific/.

9   Thom Woodroofe, 'Australia Has Neglected Its Relationship with the Pacific – but That Can Change', *Guardian*, 25 April 2018, https://www.theguardian.com/australia-news/2018/apr/25/australia-has-neglected-its-relationship-with-the-pacific-but-that-can-change.

10 Gyngell, *Fear of Abandonment: Australia in the World Since 1942*, p. 272.

11 Cabinet External Relations and Security Committee, 'Minute of Decision: The Pacific Reset: The First Year', New Zealand Foreign Affairs and Trade, 4 December 2018, https://www.mfat.govt.nz/assets/OIA/R-R-The-Pacific-reset-The-First-Year.PDF.

12 'An Address by New Zealand Prime Minister Jacinda Ardern', speech delivered by Jacinda Ardern, New Zealand's prime minister, at the Lowy Institute, Sydney, 7 July 2022, https://www.lowyinstitute.org/publications/address-new-zealand-prime-minister-jacinda-ardern.

13 Quoted in Feeney, '"The Ostrich Sticks Its Head in the Sand and Thinks Itself Safe": Australia's Need for a Grand Strategy', p. 9. See also Andrew Tillett, 'Australia Fails to Lead in the Pacific: Labor's Richard Marles', *Australian Financial Review*, 21 November 2017, https://www.afr.com/politics/australia-fails-to-lead-in-the-pacific-labors-richard-marles-20171120-gzp0m3.

14 'Address – "Australia and the Pacific: A New Chapter"', speech delivered by Scott Morrison, Australia's prime minister, 8 November 2018, https://pmtranscripts.pmc.gov.au/release/transcript-41938.

15 Graeme Dobell, 'China Challenges Australia in the South Pacific', ASPI *Strategist*, 2 October 2018, https://www.aspistrategist.org.au/china-challenges-australia-in-the-south-pacific/.

16 Denghua Zhang and Shivani, 'Fiji's Balancing Act on Foreign Interests in the Pacific', East Asia Forum, 3 September 2021, https://www.eastasiaforum.org/2021/09/03/fijis-balancing-act-on-foreign-interests-in-the-pacific/.

17 'China to Fund Renovation of Vanuatu PM's Offices', Radio New Zealand, 16 May 2016, https://www.rnz.co.nz/international/pacific-news/304024/china-to-fund-renovation-of-vanuatu-pm's-offices.

18 Melanesian Spearhead Group, 'MSG Secretariat and People's Republic of China Discusses [sic] Possible Partnership Arrangement', 9 December 2020, https://msgsec.info/msg-secretariat-and-peoples-republic-of-china-discusses-possible-partnership-arrangement/; and 'MSG Secretariat Building Handed Over to Vanuatu Government', Radio New Zealand, 6 November 2007, https://www.rnz.co.nz/international/pacific-news/173745/msg-secretariat-building-handed-over-to-vanuatu-government.

19 Jamie Tahana, 'Beijing Tries to Whip Up Support for South China Sea Claims', Radio New Zealand, 1 June 2016, https://www.rnz.co.nz/international/pacific-news/305309/beijing-tries-to-whip-up-support-for-south-china-sea-claims.

20 Charlotte Greenfield, 'Vanuatu to Seek More Belt and Road Assistance from Beijing: PM', Reuters, 22 May 2019, https://www.reuters.com/article/us-pacific-china-vanuatu-idUSKCN1SS0R7.

21 Gordon Peake and Graeme Smith, 'Solomon Islands: Cops Bearing Gifts', Lowy Institute *Interpreter*, 25 January 2022, https://www.lowyinstitute.org/the-interpreter/solomon-islands-cops-bearing-gifts.

22 'China Supports Defence Force with K17.5 Million Gift', *National*, 7 November 2017, https://www.thenational.com.pg/china-supports-defence-force-k17-5-million-gift/.

23 'China-aided Hydrographic Survey Vessel Handed Over to Fijian Navy', Xinhua, 21 December 2018, http://www.xinhuanet.com/english/2018-12/21/c_137689720.htm.

24 'Dozens of Fraud Suspects Repatriated to China from Fiji', Reuters, 6 August 2017, https://www.reuters.com/article/uk-china-crime-idUKKBN1AM0GR.

214 | Australia's Security in China's Shadow

25 Andrew Greene, 'Chinese Police Begin Work in Solomon Islands to Maintain Law and Order, as Australian Officials Watch Closely', ABC News, 23 February 2022, https://www.abc.net.au/news/2022-02-24/chinese-police-land-in-solomon-islands-month-after-riots/100855948.

26 'Samoa PM Turns First Sod on New Police Academy', Radio New Zealand, 26 October 2022, https://www.rnz.co.nz/international/pacific-news/477396/samoa-pm-turns-first-sod-on-new-police-academy.

27 Ma Feng, 'The South Pacific and the 21st Century Maritime Silk Road', Chinese Academy of Social Sciences, 23 May 2017, https://web.archive.org/web/20210716101033/http:/www.cssn.cn/jjx/jjx_gzf/201705/t20170523_3528652.shtml.

28 US Department of Defense, 'Annual Report to Congress: Military and Security Developments Involving the People's Republic of China 2018', 2018, p. 111, https://media.defense.gov/2018/Aug/16/2001955282/-1/-1/1/2018-CHINA-MILITARY-POWER-REPORT.PDF.

29 'Xi Pledges to Join PNG for Community with Shared Future for China, Pacific Island Nations', Xinhua, 26 October 2021, http://www.xinhuanet.com/english/asiapacific/2021-10/26/c_1310269889.htm.

30 See, for example, World Bank, 'Solomon Islands Roads and Aviation Project', https://projects.worldbank.org/en/projects-operations/procurement-detail/OP00109845; Government of Samoa, 'Faleolo International Airport Upgrade', 30 November 2016, http://www.samoagovt.ws/2016/11/faleolo-international-airport-upgrade/;

Asian Development Bank, 'PNG: Civil Aviation Development Investment Program – Tranche 2 & 3', August 2020, https://www.adb.org/sites/default/files/project-documents/43141/43141-043-43141-044-emr-en_2.pdf; and International Monetary Fund, 'Vanuatu', IMF Country Report no. 15/149, June 2015, https://www.imf.org/external/pubs/ft/scr/2015/cr15149.pdf.

31 Yang Zhen and Fang Xiaozhi, 'Strategic Choices for China's Sea Power and Navy Buildup: A Maritime Security Perspective', Global Review, vol. 4, 2015, pp. 85–101, https://cnki.net/KCMS/detail/detail.aspx?filename=GJZW201504007&dbcode=CJFD&dbname=CJFD2015.

32 Feeney, '"The Ostrich Sticks Its Head in the Sand and Thinks Itself Safe": Australia's Need for a Grand Strategy', p. 9.

33 Peter Wood, with Alex Stone and Taylor A. Lee, 'China's Ground Segment: Building the Pillars of a Great Space Power', China Aerospace Institute, p. 70, https://www.airuniversity.af.edu/Portals/10/CASI/documents/Research/Space/2021-03-01%20Chinas%20Ground%20Segment.pdf?ver=z4ogY_MrxaDurwVt-R9J6w%3d%3d; and Jonas Parello-Plesner and Mathieu Duchâtel, 'China's Strong Arm: Protecting Citizens and Assets Abroad', Adelphi 451 (Abingdon: Routledge for the IISS, May 2015).

34 Some are surveyed in Denghua Zhang, 'China's Military Engagement with Pacific Island Countries', Asia & the Pacific Policy Society, 17 August 2020, https://www.policyforum.net/chinas-military-engagement-with-pacific-island-countries/.

35 Qin Sheng, 'The South Pacific Offensive of the "Indo-Pacific" Strategy: Status Quo, Motive Forces and Prospects', *Asia-Pacific Security and Maritime Affairs*, June 2019, http://www.cnki.com.cn/Article/CJFDTOTAL-YFZH201906006.htm.

36 Greg Torode and Philip Wen, 'Explainer: Possible Chinese Military Base in S. Pacific Fills Gap, Sends Strong Message to U.S. and Allies', Reuters, 10 April 2018, https://www.reuters.com/article/us-china-defence-vanuatu-base-explainer-idUSKBN1HH1B4.

37 Chen Xulong, 'The Importance and Role of Pacific Island Countries to China's National Security', China Institute of International Studies, 2 June 2015, https://www.ciis.org.cn/yjcg/xslw/202007/t20200710_1218.html.

38 H.I. Sutton, 'Satellite Images Show that Chinese Navy Is Expanding Overseas Base', *Forbes*, 10 May 2020, https://www.forbes.com/sites/hisutton/2020/05/10/satellite-images-show-chinese-navy-is-expanding-overseas-base/?sh=ca80ae368691.

39 See, for example, Michael O'Keefe, 'Response to Rumours of a Chinese Military Base in Vanuatu Speaks Volumes About Australian Foreign Policy', Conversation, 11 March 2018, https://theconversation.com/response-to-rumours-of-a-chinese-military-base-in-vanuatu-speaks-volumes-about-australian-foreign-policy-94813.

40 'Australia's Vaccine Diplomacy in Pacific Islands Wards Off Beijing, Prime Minister Says', Reuters, 13 March 2022, https://www.reuters.com/world/asia-pacific/australias-vaccine-diplomacy-pacific-islands-wards-off-beijing-pm-morrison-2022-03-13/.

41 Nick Warner, 'Australia Must End Its Pacific Stupor Before It's Too Late', Cipher Brief, 2 May 2022, https://www.thecipherbrief.com/column_article/australia-must-end-its-pacific-stupor-before-its-too-late. Nick Warner is the former director general of Australia's Office of National Intelligence.

42 Liu Zhen, 'China Confirms Signing of Solomon Islands Security Pact as US Warns of Regional Instability', *South China Morning Post*, 19 April 2022, https://www.scmp.com/news/china/diplomacy/article/3174811/china-confirms-signing-controversial-solomon-islands-security.

43 Kirsty Needham and Martin Quin Pollard, 'U.S. Concerned After China Says It Signs Security Pact with Solomon Islands', Reuters, 19 April 2022, https://www.reuters.com/world/asia-pacific/chinese-officials-travel-solomon-islands-sign-agreements-parliament-told-2022-04-19/.

44 The meaning of 'transition' here is ambiguous, but hints at a desire to project naval forces into a broader area of the Southwest Pacific; Damien Cave, 'China and Solomon Islands Draft Secret Security Pact, Raising Alarm in the Pacific', *New York Times*, 24 March 2022, https://www.nytimes.com/2022/03/24/world/asia/china-solomon-islands-security-pact.html.

45 Damien Cave, 'China Is Leasing an Entire Pacific Island. Its Residents Are Shocked', *New York Times*, 17 October 2019, https://www.nytimes.com/2019/10/16/world/australia/china-tulagi-solomon-islands-pacific.html.

46 David Wroe, 'China Eyes Vanuatu Military Base in Plan with Global Ramifications', *Sydney Morning Herald*, 9 April 2018, https://www.smh.com.au/politics/federal/china-eyes-vanuatu-military-base-in-plan-with-global-ramifications-20180409-p4z8j9.html.

47 David Wroe, 'The Great Wharf from China, Raising Eyebrows Across the Pacific', *Sydney Morning Herald*, 11 April 2018, https://www.smh.com.au/politics/federal/the-great-wharf-from-china-raising-eyebrows-across-the-pacific-20180411-p4z8yu.html.

48 Government of Vanuatu, Finance and Treasury, 'Economic Assessment for Luganville Main Wharf Renovation and Extension Project', December 2013, https://doft.gov.vu/index.php/economy/luganville-main-wharf-project.

49 Gao Wensheng, 'The Value, Risks and China's Countermeasures of the South Pacific Energy Strategy Channel', *World Regional Studies*, vol. 26, no. 6, December 2017, pp. 1–10, http://www.cnki.com.cn/Article/CJFDTOTAL-SJDJ201706001.htm.

50 Graeme Smith, 'China's Guide to Investment Cooperation in Papua New Guinea', Australian National University, Department of Pacific Affairs, *In Brief*, 2019/25, https://dpa.bellschool.anu.edu.au/sites/default/files/publications/attachments/2019-12/ib2019-25_smith.pdf.

51 Luke Kama, 'Airport Job Contract Signed', *National*, 20 December 2016, https://www.thenational.com.pg/airport-job-contract-signed/.

52 Asian Development Bank, 'Papua New Guinea: Lae Port Development Project', *Completion Report*, April 2017, https://www.adb.org/sites/default/files/project-documents/40037/40037-013-pcr-en.pdf.

53 Ben Packham, 'Move to Head Off China with Australian Base in PNG', *Australian*, 20 September 2018, https://www.theaustralian.com.au/nation/foreign-affairs/move-to-head-off-china-with-australian-base-in-png/news-story/fa4d3f407ffa73dd8240071e03ba7828.

54 Angus Livingston, 'Australia to Upgrade Papua New Guinea's Ports for $580 Million', *Sydney Morning Herald*, 21 January 2022, https://www.smh.com.au/politics/federal/australia-to-upgrade-papua-new-guinea-s-ports-for-580-million-20220121-p59q79.html.

55 Jeffrey Wall, 'China to Build $200 Million Fishery Project on Australia's Doorstep', ASPI *Strategist*, 8 December 2020, https://www.aspistrategist.org.au/china-to-build-200-million-fishery-project-on-australias-doorstep/.

56 Kristy Sexton-McGrath, 'Torres Strait Islanders' Fear Over $200m Chinese Fishery Handshake with PNG', ABC News, 16 December 2020, https://www.abc.net.au/news/2020-12-16/china-fishery-fears-for-torres-strait-islanders/12988998.

57 Primrose Riordan, 'Australia Beats China to Funding Fiji Base', *Australian*, 7 September 2018, https://www.theaustralian.com.au/nation/defence/australia-beats-china-to-funding-fiji-base/news-story/60d05ca8eb2bec629080c2c844255bbd; and Republic of Fiji Military Forces, 'Blackrock Officially Opens', https://rfmf.mil.fj/blackrock-officially-opens.

58 Rosi Doviverata, 'China Happy to Help Fiji Set Up a New Navy Base',

Fiji Sun, 6 November 2015, https://fijisun.com.fj/2015/11/06/china-happy-to-help-fiji-set-up-a-new-navy-base/.

59 Jonathan Barrett, 'Kiribati Says China-backed Pacific Airstrip Project for Civilian Use', Reuters, 13 May 2021, https://www.reuters.com/world/asia-pacific/kiribati-says-china-backed-pacific-airstrip-project-civilian-use-2021-05-13/; and Phil Mercer, 'Plan to Upgrade WWII-era Pacific Ocean Airstrip Sparks Unease', Voice of America, 10 June 2021, https://www.voanews.com/a/east-asia-pacific_plan-upgrade-wwii-era-pacific-ocean-airstrip-sparks-unease/6206844.html.

60 Barbara Dreaver, 'Fears Over China's Involvement in Kiribati's Ditching of Marine Reserve', 1News, 11 November 2021, https://www.1news.co.nz/2021/11/11/fears-over-chinas-involvement-in-kiribatis-ditching-of-marine-reserve/.

61 Wood, Stone and Lee, 'China's Ground Segment: Building the Pillars of a Great Space Power'.

62 'Fijian PM Clarifies Chinese Ship's Docking in Suva Port', Xinhua, 13 June 2018, http://www.xinhuanet.com/english/2018-06/13/c_137251825.htm.

63 Liu Zhen, 'Could Ties with Kiribati Be a Boost to China's Space Ambitions?', *South China Morning Post*, 21 September 2019, https://www.scmp.com/news/china/diplomacy/article/3029812/could-ties-kiribati-be-boost-chinas-space-ambitions.

64 Reuters, 'Samoa's Disputed Leader Promises Chinese-backed Port at $132m, a Third of Proposed Cost', *Straits Times*, 10 June 2021, https://www.straitstimes.com/asia/samoas-disputed-leader-promises-chinese-backed-port-at-a-third-of-the-cost.

65 Australian Infrastructure Financing Facility for the Pacific, 'Investments', https://www.aiffp.gov.au/investments.

66 Japan Bank for International Cooperation, 'Buyer's Credit for State-owned Submarine Cable Corporation of Palau', 14 January 2021, https://www.jbic.go.jp/en/information/press/press-2020/0114-014143.html.

67 Tom Westbrook, 'PNG Upholds Deal with Huawei to Lay Internet Cable, Derides Counter-offer', Reuters, 26 November 2018, https://www.reuters.com/article/us-papua-huawei-tech-idUSKCN1NV0DR.

68 Amy Remeikis, 'Australia Supplants China to Build Undersea Cable for Solomon Islands', *Guardian*, 13 June 2018, https://www.theguardian.com/world/2018/jun/13/australia-supplants-china-to-build-undersea-cable-for-solomon-islands.

69 Colin Packham and Paulina Duran, 'Telstra in Talks to Buy Digicel Pacific in Australian Govt-backed Bid', Reuters, 19 July 2021, https://www.reuters.com/business/media-telecom/telstra-talks-buy-digicel-pacific-with-australian-government-help-2021-07-18/; and Stephen Dziedzic, 'US, Japan Back Australia's Digicel Pacific Purchase with $150 Million in Credit Guarantees', ABC News, 16 November 2022, https://www.abc.net.au/news/2022-11-17/us-japan-back-australias-digicel-pacific-telco-purchase/101662258.

70 Joanne Wallis et al., 'Mapping Security Cooperation in the

Pacific Islands – Research Report', Department of Pacific Affairs, Coral Bell School of Asia Pacific Affairs, Australian National University College of Asia and the Pacific, 2021, p. 12, https://dpa.bellschool. anu.edu.au/experts-publications/ publications/8060/mapping-security-cooperation-pacific-islands-research-report.

71 Jenny Hayward-Jones, 'Australia's Costly Investment in Solomon Islands: The Lessons of RAMSI', Lowy Institute, 8 May 2014, https://www.lowyinstitute.org/ the-interpreter/high-price-ramsi-australia-s-lessons-solomon-islands.

72 Australian Government, Department of Defence, 'Australia-led Combined Task Force Concludes Role with RAMSI', 2 July 2013, https://news. defence.gov.au/media/media-releases/australia-led-combined-task-force-concludes-role-ramsi.

73 Max Walden, Stephen Dziedzic and Evan Wasuka, 'Here's What's Behind the Violent Protests in the Solomon Islands Capital, Honiara', ABC News, 25 November 2021, https://www.abc. net.au/news/2021-11-25/solomon-islands-protests-explainer-china-taiwan/100648086.

74 Australian Government, Department of Foreign Affairs and Trade, 'Agreement Between the Government of Australia and the Government of Solomon Islands Concerning the Basis for Deployment of Police, Armed Forces, and Other Personnel to Solomon Islands', 14 August 2017, http://www.austlii.edu.au/au/other/ dfat/treaties/ATS/2018/14.html.

75 James Batley, former Australian High Commissioner to Solomon Islands, quoted in Emily Jane Smith, 'Pacific Puzzle: How China and Australia Fit in to Solomon Islands Protests', Dateline, SBS News, 3 December 2021, https://www.sbs.com.au/news/ dateline/pacific-puzzle-how-china-and-australia-fit-in-to-solomon-islands-protests.

76 Kirsty Needham, 'Solomon Islands Government Seeks to Delay Election to Host Games', Reuters, 9 August 2022, https://www.reuters.com/ world/asia-pacific/solomon-islands-government-seeks-delay-election-host-games-2022-08-09/; and Michael Miller, 'Solomon Islands' Pro-China Leader Wins Bid to Delay Elections', Washington Post, 8 September 2022, https://www.washingtonpost.com/ world/2022/09/08/solomon-islands-elections-china-parliament/.

77 Karl Claxton, 'No Exit: Next Steps to Help Promote South Pacific Peace and Prosperity', ASPI Strategic Insights, April 2015, https://ad-aspi. s3.ap-southeast-2.amazonaws.com/ import/SI87_No_exit.pdf?Version Id=JVdJo4MOqzWFq7Odqedfeg Ugs__d1bjt.

78 'Helping Our Neighbours', speech delivered by Malcolm Turnbull, Australia's prime minister, 8 September 2016, https:// pmtranscripts.pmc.gov.au/release/ transcript-40437.

79 Australian Government, Department of Foreign Affairs and Trade, 'Office of the Pacific', https://www.dfat.gov. au/geo/pacific/office-of-the-pacific.

80 Lowy Institute, Pacific Aid Map, https://pacificaidmap.lowyinstitute. org/.

81 Australian Government, Department of Foreign Affairs and Trade, 'Stepping Up Australia's Engagement with Our Pacific Family'.

82 Shane McLeod, 'Plugging in PNG: Electricity, Partners and Politics', Lowy Institute *Interpreter*, 10 April 2019, https://www.lowyinstitute. org/the-interpreter/plugging-png-electricity-partners-and-politics.

83 'Chinese Government Aid to Pacific Region Fell by a Third Before Pandemic, Lowy Report Finds', ABC News, 28 September 2021, https://www.abc.net.au/ news/2021-09-29/pacific-lowy-institute-aid-development-china-influence/100498518.

84 Ministry of Foreign Affairs of the People's Republic of China, 'Joint Statement of China–Pacific Island Countries Foreign Ministers' Meeting', 21 October 2021, https:// www.fmprc.gov.cn/mfa_eng/ wjdt_665385/2649_665393/202110/ t20211021_9604831.html.

85 Jonathan Pryke and Alexandre Dayant, 'China's Declining Pacific Aid Presence', Lowy Institute *Interpreter*, 30 September 2021, https://www. lowyinstitute.org/the-interpreter/ china-s-declining-pacific-aid-presence.

86 Ben Doherty, 'Experts Dispel Claims of China Debt-trap Diplomacy in Pacific but Risks Remain', *Guardian*, 20 October 2019, https://www. theguardian.com/world/2019/oct/21/ chinese-loans-expose-pacific-islands-to-risk-of-unsustainable-debt-report-finds.

87 Graeme Smith, 'Ain't No Sunshine When Xi's Gone: What's Behind China's Declining Aid to the Pacific', Department of Pacific Affairs, Australian National University, *In Brief*, vol. 31, 12 November 2021, https://openresearch-repository.anu. edu.au/handle/1885/251756.

88 Pryke and Dayant, 'China's Declining Pacific Aid Presence'.

89 *Ibid.*

90 *Ibid.*

91 Jonathan Pryke, 'The Risks of China's Ambitions in the South Pacific', Brookings, 20 July 2020, https://www. brookings.edu/articles/the-risks-of-chinas-ambitions-in-the-south-pacific/.

92 Edward Cavanough, 'China and Taiwan Offered Us Huge Bribes, Say Solomon Islands MPs', *Guardian*, 7 December 2019, https://www. theguardian.com/world/2019/dec/08/ china-and-taiwan-offered-us-huge-bribes-say-solomon-islands-mps.

93 Australian Government, Department of Foreign Affairs and Trade, 'Australia, China and Papua New Guinea Pilot Cooperation on Malaria Control Project Independent Mid-term Review and Joint Management Response', https://www.dfat. gov.au/about-us/publications/ Pages/australia-china-png-pilot-cooperation-on-the-trilateral-malaria-project-independent-mtr-and-jmr.

94 Australian Government, Department of Foreign Affairs and Trade, 'Pacific Regional – Climate Change and Resilience', https://www.dfat.gov.au/ geo/pacific/development-assistance/ climate-change-and-resilience.

95 Daniel Hurst, 'Australia to Stand with Pacific Islands on Climate Crisis and "Respect" Region, Penny Wong Says', *Guardian*, 23 May 2002, https:// www.theguardian.com/australia-news/2022/may/23/australia-to-stand-with-pacific-islands-on-climate-crisis-and-respect-region-penny-wong-says.

96 Euan Graham, 'Mind the Gap: Views of Security in the Pacific', Lowy Institute *Interpreter*, 11 October 2018,

https://www.lowyinstitute.
org/the-interpreter/
mind-gap-views-security-pacific.

97 'Nauru Demands China Apologize
for "Disrespect" at Pacific Forum',
Reuters, 6 September 2018, https://
www.reuters.com/article/us-pacific-
forum-china-idUSKCN1LM0HM.

98 Pacific Islands Forum Secretariat,
'Boe Declaration on Regional
Security', September 2018, https://
www.forumsec.org/2018/09/05/
boe-declaration-on-regional-security/.

99 Kirsty Needham, 'China, Pacific
Islands Unable to Reach Consensus
on Regional Pact', Reuters, 30 May
2022, https://www.reuters.com/
world/asia-pacific/china-hosts-
pacific-islands-meeting-fiji-security-
ties-focus-2022-05-30/.

100 Ministry of Foreign Affairs of the
People's Republic of China, 'Joint
Statement of China–Pacific Island
Countries Foreign Ministers'
Meeting'.

101 Ben Packham, 'Australia Sets Up
Force for Pacific Neighbours',
Australian, 23 July 2019, https://
www.theaustralian.com.au/nation/
politics/australia-sets-up-force-for-
pacific-neighbours/news-story/
e873c7605543f18ba
653c990249edcbc; and Australian
Government, Department of Defence,
'ADF Presence', https://www.
defence.gov.au/programs-initiatives/
pacific-engagement/adf-presence.

102 Wallis et al., 'Mapping Security
Cooperation in the Pacific Islands –
Research Report', p. 5.

103 The Pacific Maritime Security
Program is funded by Australia's
Department of Defence to the
tune of A$2bn over 30 years. It
delivers capacity to Pacific island

countries and Timor-Leste in three
areas: through the provision of
patrol boats, an aerial-surveillance
programme and 'enhancements to
regional coordination'; Australian
Government, Department of
Defence, 'Pacific Maritime Security
Program', https://www.defence.
gov.au/programs-initiatives/
pacific-engagement/maritime-
capability#:~:text=The%20PMSP%20
is%20a%20comprehensive,Island%20
nations%20and%20
Timor%2DLest%C3%A9.

104 Ibid.

105 Australian Government, Department
of Defence, 'Commencement of
Aerial Surveillance – Pacific Maritime
Security Program', 28 January 2018,
https://www.minister.defence.
gov.au/minister/marise-payne/
media-releases/commencement-
aerial-surveillance-pacific-maritime-
security; and Philip Smart, 'Locals
Overlooked for Pacific Surveillance
Contract', Australian Defence Magazine,
8 February 2018, https://www.
australiandefence.com.au/business/
locals-overlooked-for-pacific-
surveillance-contract.

106 Andrew Tillett, 'Defence Facing
a Recruitment "Crisis": Marles',
Australian Financial Review, 14
November 2022, https://www.afr.
com/politics/federal/defence-facing-
a-recruitment-crisis-marles-20221114-
p5by1p.

107 Andrew Greene, 'Australian Special
Forces to Protect World Leaders at
APEC Meeting in Papua New Guinea',
ABC News, 11 September 2018,
https://www.abc.net.au/news/2018-09-
12/special-forces-to-png/10234058; and
Australian Government, Department
of Defence, 'Defence Supports PNG

Security Effort for APEC 2018', 12 October 2018, https://www.minister.defence.gov.au/minister/cpyne/media-releases/defence-supports-png-security-effort-apec-2018.

108 Agence France-Presse, 'PNG to Deploy Fighter Jets and Foreign Military as It Plans Major Security Operation for Apec Summit', *South China Morning Post*, 17 October 2018, https://www.scmp.com/news/asia/southeast-asia/article/2168888/png-deploy-fighter-jets-and-foreign-military-it-plans-major; and Australian Government, Department of Defence, 'Defence Supports PNG Security Effort for APEC 2018'.

109 Australian Government, Department of Defence, 'Australian Navy Arrives in Port Moresby for APEC 2018', 2 November 2018, https://www.minister.defence.gov.au/minister/cpyne/media-releases/australian-navy-arrives-port-moresby-apec-2018; and Boeing, 'Australia Takes New Boeing Communications System to APEC', 13 December 2018, https://www.boeing.com.au/featured-content/boeing-communications-system-to-apec.page.

110 'Australian Submarine Makes Emergency Stop in Solomon Islands', Radio New Zealand, 15 June 2019, https://www.rnz.co.nz/international/pacific-news/392083/australian-submarine-makes-emergency-stop-in-solomon-islands.

111 Australian National University, 'New College to Strengthen Pacific Security', 12 August 2019, https://www.anu.edu.au/news/all-news/new-college-to-strengthen-pacific-security.

112 Minister for Foreign Affairs, Minister for Women, Senator the Hon Marise Payne, 'Australia to Support New Pacific Fusion Centre', 5 September 2018, https://www.foreignminister.gov.au/minister/marise-payne/media-release/australia-support-new-pacific-fusion-centre; and Pacific Fusion Centre, https://www.pacificfusioncentre.org/.

113 'Australia, Vanuatu Sign Pacific Fusion Center MOU', *Daily Post*, 9 April 2022, https://www.dailypost.vu/news/australia-vanuatu-sign-pacific-fusion-center-mou/article_2736f810-83ae-5c0b-b573-e9dd3692e376.html.

114 Marian Faa, 'Australian Defence Force to Fund $175 Million Major Upgrade for Papua New Guinea's Naval Base on Manus Island', ABC News, 15 June 2021, https://www.abc.net.au/news/2021-06-15/major-naval-base-on-png-manus-island-lombrum-adf/100216040.

115 US Embassy to Papua New Guinea, Solomon Islands, and Vanuatu, 'U.S. Secretary of the Navy Visits Papua New Guinea', 1 November 2021, https://pg.usembassy.gov/u-s-secretary-of-the-navy-visits-papua-new-guinea/.

116 Tim Fish, 'Australia, U.S. Set to Expand Papua New Guinea Naval Base', USNI News, 23 November 2018, https://news.usni.org/2018/11/23/australia-u-s-set-expand-papa-new-guinea-naval-base; and Peter Jennings, 'Air Power Critical for Manus Expansion Plan', ASPI *Strategist*, 20 November 2018, https://www.aspistrategist.org.au/air-power-critical-for-manus-expansion-plan/.

117 Royal Navy, 'Patrol Ships Bid Farewell to Portsmouth as They Begin Indo-Pacific Deployment', 7 September 2021, https://www.royalnavy.mod.uk/news-and-latest-activity/news/2021/september/07/210907-spey-and-tamar-deploy.

Chapter Seven

1   Stephen Dziedzic, 'Australia and China Might Be on Speaking Terms, but on Policy and in Reality Remain Far Apart', ABC News, 14 November 2022, https://www.abc.net.au/news/2022-11-15/australia-china-dialogue-between-xi-albanese-remains-fraught-g20/101652990.

2   Brendan Nicholson, 'AUKUS Will Deliver the Potent Military Australia Needs: Marles', ASPI *Strategist*, 16 September 2022, https://www.aspistrategist.org.au/aukus-will-deliver-the-potent-military-australia-needs-marles/.

3   The defence posture review has since been upgraded to a Strategic Defence Review: Charbel Kadib, 'Marles Eyes Early Subs Delivery, Backs New "Posture Review"', Defence Connect, 20 June 2022, https://www.defenceconnect.com.au/key-enablers/10201-marles-eyes-early-subs-delivery-backs-new-posture-review. See also Australian Government, Department of Defence, 'Defence Strategic Review', https://www.defence.gov.au/about/reviews-inquiries/defence-strategic-review.

4   Hu Weijia, 'Despite Different "Values," Australia Should Ameliorate Ties with China', *Global Times*, 21 September 2022, https://www.globaltimes.cn/page/202209/1275719.shtml.

5   'Commentary: Australia Should Make Independent, Sensible Choices on China Ties', Xinhua, 26 November 2020, http://www.xinhuanet.com/english/2020-11/26/c_139545081.htm. See also Michael Shoebridge, 'Diagnosing the Problem: It's About China, and It's More Than the US–China Show', ASPI *Strategist*, 28 July 2020, https://www.aspistrategist.org.au/diagnosing-the-problem-its-about-china-and-its-more-than-the-us-china-show/.

6   Rory Medcalf, 'Arrest of Yang Hengjun Drags Australia into China's Hostage Diplomacy', *Australian Financial Review*, 25 January 2019, https://www.afr.com/opinion/arrest-of-yang-hengjun-drags-australia-into-chinas-hostage-diplomacy-20190124-h1af6x.

7   Anthony Galloway and Eryk Bagshaw, 'Victoria's Belt and Road Deal with China Torn Up', *Australian Financial Review*, 22 April 2021, https://www.smh.com.au/politics/federal/victoria-s-belt-and-road-deal-with-china-torn-up-20210421-p57l9q.html.

8   Reuters, 'Canada to Ban Huawei/ZTE 5G Equipment as China Tensions Ease', *Business Times*, 20 May 2022, https://www.businesstimes.com.sg/technology/canada-to-ban-huaweizte-5g-equipment-as-china-tensions-ease.

9   'Speech Introducing the National Security Legislation Amendment (Espionage and Foreign Interference) Bill 2017', speech delivered by Malcolm Turnbull, Australia's prime minister, 7 December 2017, https://www.malcolmturnbull.com.au/media/speech-introducing-the-national-security-legislation-amendment-espionage-an.

10 Daniel Hurst, 'Labor Denounces Peter Dutton's "Conspiracy Theory" that China Wants Coalition to Lose Election', *Guardian*, 5 May 2022,

https://www.theguardian.com/australia-news/2022/may/05/peter-dutton-says-he-very-strongly-believes-chinese-communist-party-wants-coalition-to-lose-election.

11 See, for example, Gareth Evans, 'Australia and China: Getting Out of the Hole', Pearls and Irritations, 27 November 2020, https://johnmenadue.com/australia-and-china-getting-out-of-the-hole/.

12 Justin Bassi, 'Xi–Albanese Meeting Shows Strength of Australia's Resolve', ASPI *Strategist*, 18 November 2022, https://www.aspistrategist.org.au/xi-albanese-meeting-shows-strength-of-australias-resolve/.

13 Daniel Hurst and Josh Butler, 'Richard Marles's "Full and Frank" Meeting with China Ends Australia's Diplomatic Freeze', *Guardian*, 12 June 2022, https://www.theguardian.com/australia-news/2022/jun/12/richard-marles-says-talks-with-china-possible-after-first-ministerial-contact-with-australia-in-two-years; and Phil Mercer, 'Australia Vows to Continue to Monitor South China Sea After Military Close Encounter', Voice of America, 14 June 2022, https://www.voanews.com/a/australia-vows-to-continue-to-monitor-south-china-sea-after-military-close-encounter/6617022.html.

14 'China as a Military Threat', Lowy Institute Poll 2022, https://poll.lowyinstitute.org/charts/china-as-a-military-threat/.

15 Laura Silver, Kat Devlin and Christine Huang, 'Unfavourable Views of China Reach Historic Highs in Many Countries', Pew Research Centre, 6 October 2020, https://www.pewresearch.org/global/2020/10/06/unfavorable-views-of-china-reach-historic-highs-in-many-countries/.

16 Jessica Parker, 'Lithuania–China Row: EU Escalates Trade Dispute with Beijing', BBC News, 27 January 2022, https://www.bbc.com/news/world-europe-60140561.

17 John Fitzgerald, 'A View from Australia', *National Commentaries: 'AUKUS, Australia, and China'*, Asan Forum, 27 December 2021, https://theasanforum.org/a-view-from-australia-3/.

18 Denny Roy, 'Xi Jinping's Top Five Foreign Policy Mistakes', Pacific Forum *PacNet*, no. 49, 22 October 2021, https://pacforum.org/wp-content/uploads/2021/10/PacNet49.2021.10.22.pdf.

19 Marcus Hellyer and Andrew Nicholls, 'How to Bridge the Capability Gap in Australia's Transition to Nuclear-powered Submarines', ASPI *Strategist*, 21 July 2022, https://www.aspistrategist.org.au/how-to-bridge-the-capability-gap-in-australias-transition-to-nuclear-powered-submarines/.

20 'China Biggest Security Threat, Says General Bipin Rawat', *Times of India*, 13 November 2021, https://timesofindia.indiatimes.com/india/china-biggest-security-threat-says-general-bipin-rawat/articleshow/87675595.cms.

21 'Video: India and Australia Share Concerns About China's Growing Military Power', ABC News, 22 June 2022, https://www.abc.net.au/news/2022-06-23/china-and-australia-share-concerns-about-chinas/13942226.

22 Australian Government, Department of Defence, '2020 Defence Strategic Update', 1 July 2020, pp. 25–7, https://www.defence.gov.au/strategicupdate-2020/.

INDEX

THE ADELPHI SERIES

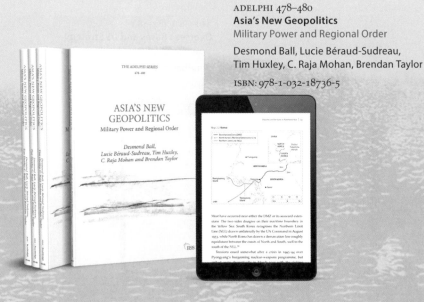

ADELPHI 478–480

Asia's New Geopolitics

Military Power and Regional Order

Desmond Ball, Lucie Béraud-Sudreau,
Tim Huxley, C. Raja Mohan, Brendan Taylor

ISBN: 978-1-032-18736-5

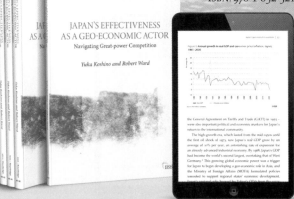

ADELPHI 481–483

**Japan's Effectiveness
as a Geo-economic Actor**

Navigating Great-power Competition

Yuka Koshino and Robert Ward

ISBN: 978-1-032-32139-4

IISS THE INTERNATIONAL INSTITUTE FOR STRATEGIC STUDIES

www.iiss.org/publications/adelphi

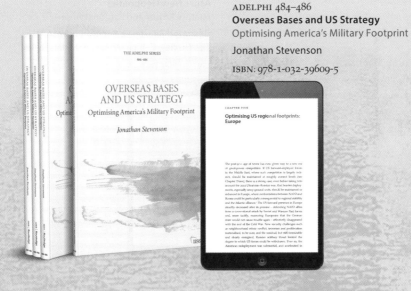

Six *Adelphi* numbers are published each year by Routledge Journals, an imprint of Taylor & Francis, 4 Park Square, Milton Park, Abingdon, Oxfordshire OX14 4RN, UK.

A subscription to the institution print edition, ISSN 1944-5571, includes free access for any number of concurrent users across a local area network to the online edition, ISSN 1944-558X. Taylor & Francis has a flexible approach to subscriptions enabling us to match individual libraries' requirements. This journal is available via a traditional institutional subscription (either print with free online access, or online-only at a discount) or as part of our libraries, subject collections or archives. For more information on our sales packages please visit www.tandfonline.com/page/librarians.

2023 Annual *Adelphi* Subscription Rates			
Institution	£973	US$1,707	€1,439
Individual	£333	US$571	€457
Online only	£827	US$1,451	€1,223

Dollar rates apply to subscribers outside Europe. Euro rates apply to all subscribers in Europe except the UK and the Republic of Ireland where the pound sterling price applies. All subscriptions are payable in advance and all rates include postage. Journals are sent by air to the USA, Canada, Mexico, India, Japan and Australasia. Subscriptions are entered on an annual basis, i.e., January to December. Payment may be made by sterling cheque, dollar cheque, international money order, National Giro, or credit card (Amex, Visa, Mastercard).

For a complete and up-to-date guide to Taylor & Francis journals and books publishing programmes, and details of advertising in our journals, visit our website: **http://www.tandfonline.com.**

Ordering information:

USA/Canada: Taylor & Francis Inc., Journals Department, 530 Walnut Street, Suite 850, Philadelphia, PA 19106, USA. **UK/Europe/Rest of World:** Routledge Journals, T&F Customer Services, T&F Informa UK Ltd., Sheepen Place, Colchester, Essex, CO3 3LP, UK.

Advertising enquiries to:

USA/Canada: The Advertising Manager, Taylor & Francis Inc., 530 Walnut Street, Suite 850, Philadelphia, PA 19106, USA. Tel: +1 (800) 354 1420. Fax: +1 (215) 207 0050. **UK/Europe/Rest of World**: The Advertising Manager, Routledge Journals, Taylor & Francis, 4 Park Square, Milton Park, Abingdon, Oxfordshire OX14 4RN, UK. Tel: +44 (0) 20 7017 6000. Fax: +44 (0) 20 7017 6336.